THE POWER
OF POSITIVE
LIVING

Norman Vincent Peale titles available in Vermilion

The Power of Positive Thinking
The Power of Positive Living
The Amazing Results of Positive Thinking
The Positive Way to Change Your Life
The Power of Positive Thinking for Young People
Stay Alive All Your Life
Courage and Confidence
You Can if You Think You Can

THE POWER OF POSITIVE LIVING

NORMAN VINCENT PEALE

Vermilion
LONDON

The Power of Positive Living

First published in Great Britain 1991 by William Heinemann Ltd
Published 1992 by Cedar. Reprinted 1992, 1993, 1994, 1995, 1996.

9 8

This edition published in the United Kingdom in 1998 by Vermilion
an imprint of Ebury Press
The Random House Group Ltd
20 Vauxhall Bridge Road,
London SW1V 2SA

Random House Australia (Pty) Limited
20 Alfred Street, Milsons Point, Sydney,
New South Wales 2061, Australia

Random House New Zealand Limited
18 Poland Road, Glenfield,
Auckland 10, New Zealand

Random House South Africa (Pty) Limited
Isle of Houghton, Corner of Boundary Road & Carse O'Gowrie,
Houghton 2198, South Africa

Random House Publishers India Private Limited
301 World Trade Tower, Hotel Intercontinental Grand Complex,
Barakhamba Lane, New Delhi 110 001, India

The Random House Group Limited Reg. No. 954009
www.randomhouse.co.uk

A CIP catalogue record for this book is available from the British Library

ISBN 9780749308216

Printed and bound in Great Britain by
CPI Antony Rowe, Chippenham, Wiltshire
Papers used by Vermilion are natural, recyclable products made from
wood grown in sustainable forests.

Dedicated to
John M. and Elizabeth P. Allen
my son-in-law and daughter
in appreciation
for their help with this book
and love always

■   ■   ■

ACKNOWLEDGMENTS

■　　　　　　　　　■　　　　　　　　　■

This book is not the work of only one person. Many people have been of great help and I want to express sincere gratitude to them.

I could never have done this book without the enthusiastic cooperation and skilled work of my secretary, Sybil Light. Her suggestions, too, have always been valuable.

To Richard H. Schneider, Senior Editor of *Guideposts* magazine, I am indebted for important research, interesting and pertinent material, and editorial assistance. I am grateful for his valuable contribution to this book.

To Eric Fellman, Rocco Murano, and Ric Cox, executives of the Foundation for Christian Living and responsible for *PLUS* magazine, I wish to express grateful thanks for their advice and counsel.

To my son-in-law, John Milton Allen, and Elizabeth Peale Allen I say thanks for their support and wise advice all the way.

My wife, Ruth Stafford Peale, gave valuable editorial review and her belief in the book sustained me all the way through. I thank her sincerely.

Pat Kossmann, former Senior Editor of Doubleday Publishers and editor for this book, used her editorial skill, wise judgment, and positive enthusiasm to bring this project to fruition.

To these and all quoted in this book I extend grateful thanks.

Norman Vincent Peale

CONTENTS

PREFACE

■   ■   ■

Most of my years have been extremely happy, but, as with all of us, some have not. And I appreciate those, too, for sorrow and struggle are great teachers. Without them I could not have appreciated the happy times as much.

But basically, I am a happy man, not dissatisfied or empty, and certainly not turned off. In fact, I'm very turned on. Sometimes I wonder if something is wrong with me. Can it be that in this day, when society's patron saint seems to be St. Vitus, I'm the one not with it?

Another thing, I love my wife, truly. Permit me a flashback. I am talking with some students in the foyer of Syracuse University Methodist Church on a balmy October day way back in A.D. 1927. Suddenly the door is flung open and a beautiful blonde stands framed against the golden autumn afternoon. My heart catches. I have never seen her before, don't know her name, but I know she is the girl for me.

It took me over two years to convince her, but now we have been married for sixty years, and despite the many stories one hears today of late-life separations and divorces, we are still in love. What's the matter with me? With her?

Because I'm so happy is one of the main reasons I'm so concerned about people who are not. I'm also bothered by the fact that unhappy folks are not running on all cylinders; consequently they are not utilizing all their creativity, and society suffers for it.

So I decided to again try doing something about it. But what can I, just one man, do about it? Make speeches? I do still make speeches, all over the world, but I admit that any speech is gone with the wind when you step off the platform.

But I could write another book. It would last longer than a speech. And I know what a book can do, having written over thirty-five of them. They are like that old poem by Longfellow:

> *I shot an arrow into the air,*
> *It fell to earth, I knew not where . . .*
> *Long, long afterward, in an oak*
> *I found the arrow, still unbroke . . .*

I believe when we discover something of great value, it is our obligation and pleasure to share it with others.

So in the pages that follow I shall simply describe what I discovered that helped me, turned my life around. And I am sure that the same wonderful thing can happen to you. I believe it will turn your life around also. If you find new meaning, enhanced fullness of life, and deeper happiness as a result of reading this book, my purpose in writing it shall be fulfilled. I hope that you may get all this and more out of it. With the power of positive living, I wish you the best in life.

CHAPTER 1

POSITIVE THINKING STILL WORKS!

O NE UNFORGETTABLE DAY I MADE A MONUMENTAL discovery. It was a discovery that can help anyone, which is why I am telling about it here. The day started out just like any other. At 9 A.M. I had a class in what was called Economics II, with Professor Ben Arneson. I shuffled into the classroom as usual and found a seat in the back row, fervently hoping I would not be noticed.

You see, I was extremely shy. If you ever were as shy and shrinking as I was, you'll understand my misery and unhappiness. With a low self-image and an equally low self-esteem, I had little self-confidence. "I can't" was my characteristic way of reacting to any challenge. I went crawling through life figuratively on my hands and knees until this day when I discovered something so momentous that it revolutionized my life.

To my deep distress, the professor called on me to explain a point in the day's lesson. I was always a hard worker, had studied diligently, and happened to be up on the subject matter. But I was also terrified of speaking in public. With shaking knees I stood to speak, shifting nervously from one foot to the other, finally slumping down, aware that I had not only handled the subject matter awkwardly but had made a spectacle of myself.

As the class came to a close, the professor made a few announcements, concluding with, "Peale, please remain after class. I want to talk with you." Shaking in my shoes I waited until all the students had left, then quavered, "You wanted to see me, Professor?"

"Yes. Come up front and sit across from my desk," said Dr. Arneson. He sat bouncing a round eraser up and down, looking at me with what I felt was a piercing gaze. The silence deepened.

"What in the world is the matter with you, Peale?" he asked. Then he continued, "You are doing good work in this class. You'll probably get an A. But when I ask you to speak, you appear horribly embarrassed, mumble sort of incoherently, and then slump red-faced into your seat. What is the matter with you, son?"

"I don't know, Professor," I mumbled miserably; "guess I've got an inferiority complex."

"Do you want to get over it and act like a man?"

I nodded. "I'd give anything to get over being the way I am. But I don't know how."

The professor's face softened. "You *can* get over it, Norman, by doing what I did to get over my inferiority feelings."

"You?" I exclaimed. "You were the same way I am?"

"That's why I noticed the same symptoms in you," the professor said.

"But how did you get over being that way?" I asked.

His answer was quietly given, but I caught the positive undertones. "I just asked God to help me; I *believed* that He would; and . . . He did."

The room was silent for a moment as the professor regarded me. "Get going, Peale," he said, "and, never forget, be a believer in God and yourself." So saying he waved me off and began gathering up his papers.

I walked along the hall and continued down the broad flight of steps on the outside of the college building. On the fourth step from the bottom I stopped. That same step is still there, as far as I know. On it I said a prayer. Even some seventy years later I remember it distinctly: "Lord, You can take a drunk and make him sober; You can change a thief into an honest person. Can't You also take a poor mixed-up guy like me and make me normal? Please help me! Amen."

As I stood on that step I experienced a strange feeling of peace. I expected a miracle to happen then and there, and a miracle did take place. But, as so often happens with a major change, it came about over a period of time.

A few days later another professor, one who supervised my major, called me into his office and handed me a book, *The Sayings of Ralph Waldo Emerson.* "Read Emerson," he said, "and you will learn the great things that can come about by right thinking." Later, another professor gave me the *Meditations* of Marcus Aurelius, who did indeed teach that life becomes what we think. I'll always thank those kindly college teachers for trying to make something of a young man who was headed for less than his best.

Oh, I was always a hard worker, and such a person achieves something due to his work habits. But I was a failure in my thoughts. And one's thoughts determine one's life, so that even diligent work cannot compensate for failure in the thinking process.

But through the help of such professors, I was fortunate to take advantage of a system of ideas that in time helped me to master my feelings of inferiority and inadequacy. The sense of release which these ideas produced was so joyful and so wonderful that I had to tell others similarly afflicted that they, too, could be set free from their misery. The basic principle of these ideas was the almost incredible power of positive thinking.

I found by the application of these principles that even I, an ordinary and average person, could do much better in life than I had been doing. The release of personal potential was so amazing that I wanted all the other so-called ordinary people to know that they could become extra-ordinary.

But beyond positive thinking I have found there is a vital principle without which the former is of little avail. It is positive *believing*. Thinking is the body of the rocket. *Believing* is the propellant which carries it to the stars. Thinking is the birth of the deed. Believing makes it happen.

For example, I read a recent *Harvard Business Review* report in which a district manager of the Metropolitan Life Insurance Company noted that insurance agents performed better in the challenging environment of outstanding agencies as opposed to lesser agencies. To prove his point, he set up his six top agents to work with his best assistant manager. He reported the following results:

"Shortly after this selection had been made, the people in the agency began referring to this select group as a 'superstaff' because of their high esprit de corps in operating so well as a unit. Their production efforts over the first twelve weeks far surpassed our most optimistic expectations . . ."

Why? It's easy to see. Salespeople knowing they are regarded as "superstaff" *believe* they are tops and fight to live up to that image. In a way, it's somewhat similar to the "self-fulfilling prophecy" theory, in which people—all people, children and grown-ups—tend to become what's expected of them.

And look what happened to a group of agents in the same office considered "average." Normally, they might have continued on producing an average number of sales. But a remarkable, dynamic assistant manager over this group *believed* that she and her agents were just as capable as the superstaff manager and his salespeople. In fact, she convinced her agents they could outsell the superstaff. Rising to the challenge, these "average" agents, *believing* they could do it, increased their sales by a greater percentage than the superstaff did. She made them fulfill her prophecy—by believing in them.

That's what believing does.

Choose what you believe. Remember, those supposedly average agents would never have increased their sales if they continued believing they were average.

Examples like this make me realize how human thinking is such a strange and complicated mixture. Some people are steady and reliable from childhood to old age. Rarely are they in conflict with themselves.

They get good grades in school, later perform well in their work, and do well, some very well indeed. Others are less organized, dissipate their abilities to where we sadly speak of them: "Too bad, he once had a lot on the ball."

Others, seeming highly organized mentally and emotionally, become disorganized and blow one opportunity after another, despite their native ability. Others, extraordinarily favored with admirable personality traits, do not seem to have a strong purpose or the capacity to make sound decisions. Ultimately they suffer a personality breakdown. You have heard of Wall Street figures going to jail, of dignitaries being denied top-level appointments due to their lack of ethical standards. The years are strewn with such wrecks, many of whom with proper self-control could have become leaders or top executives.

Why does one person succeed and another fail? Why does one individual favorably surprise and another disappoint? I think I have an answer.

As an example, let me tell you about a man I knew some years ago. I was reminded of him one night recently when I was in Columbus, Ohio, for a speaking engagement. My room on the hotel's twenty-eighth floor offered a fairly complete panorama of the city. I noticed a group of ancient stone buildings which, as a former resident of Columbus, I recognized as the old Ohio State Penitentiary.

I think often of the boys and girls of my youth in the Ohio cities and towns where I lived—Cincinnati, Columbus, Bellefontaine, Delaware—and am happy to say that practically all of them turned out well, a few superlatively well. But as I looked down at the Ohio Penitentiary, I remembered one who didn't. Gifted with a charming personality and a brain good enough to graduate from his college cum laude, he was the last person we expected to end up in jail. He had grown up in a pleasant small village, became a top officer of the local bank and a highly respected citizen. He was so engaging that people talked of him for Congress. Word had it that he would be a "shoo-in."

Then he married a beautiful, wealthy girl from Chicago. The attractive couple became leaders of the local social set. He idolized his wife and gave her everything she wanted. Apparently she thought her husband had greater financial resources than he actually possessed. And as they began to indulge in expensive trips and cruises, his generous salary was strained.

One night when he was working alone in the bank, a thought crossed his mind: He could "borrow" some cash. The bank examiner wasn't due for another month. It was a "bull" stock market just then, with buys that were bound to go up. He could make a killing, pressed the thought. Then he could restore the "borrowed" cash and have more money to use. But, being an honorable man, he rejected the thought.

In the words of Thomas Carlyle, the famed English writer, "The thought is ancestor to the deed." What a powerful truth! On another night, alone in the bank, the same thought returned. This time the mental resistance was weaker and the hand crept forward and did the deed that the thought had suggested.

The market turned sour and the bank examiner came early for his examination. The "borrowing" was discovered and the great iron gates of the Ohio State Penitentiary clanged shut on a good man who thought wrong.

Years later the banker's daughter made an appointment to see me in my New York office. "I've always suffered because of my father," she said. "I admired and loved him. So what I want to know is, was my father a weak man? A bad man? You knew him. Tell me, please."

"No, he wasn't a bad man," I replied. "Nor do I think his problem was weakness. He was an intelligent man. But he had a problem with his thinking."

I was able to console the daughter and am happy to say that after paying his debt to society, the man and his family were reunited.

What I meant by a "problem with his thinking" was he was thinking negatively. He automatically thought of his wife as a soft, perfumed, beautiful fool. If he had thought positively about her, he would have seen her for what she actually was, an intelligent, strong woman. Her actions after his incarceration proved this. Thus he would have leveled with her about the true condition of their finances, and I'm sure the two of them would have worked it out. For they really loved each other. And nothing is impossible when two people are in love.

But that is the trouble with anyone who takes the wrong way. It may seem the easiest, most expedient way. But as Jesus Christ taught us: ". . . the gate is wide and the way is easy, that leads to destruction . . ." (Matthew 7:13). Wrongdoers are often clever and sometimes they get away with their crookedness for a time. But basically they are stupid, for in the end they are caught up, as witness those recent Wall Street figures who were once considered among the shrewdest men on "the Street."

Carlyle was so right: "The thought is ancestor to the deed." That initial thought, if given residence in the mind, is the spark that ignites the action. And success or failure depends on whether that thought is positive or negative.

What follows that thought is just as important. And that is the "deliberating process," how we *handle* the problem or opportunity.

On my office desk is a replica of Rodin's great statue *The Thinker*. Whenever a problem comes up, I try to remind myself, "Now be a thinker. Think this through in a cool intellectual process. And Norman," I tell myself, "for heaven's sake, don't decide this matter emotionally."

Yes, that little statue has saved me from many a stupid action. Oh, sure, I have my unfortunate moments. Anyone who doesn't admit this is headed for trouble. For even the smartest person can do astonishingly stupid things. The safeguard is to think, always think. And most important is to pray, which I believe is thinking in its highest form. For then your thoughts are in tune with God, Who sees a lot further down the road than you do.

Let me tell you of a time when this kind of thinking made all the difference in a man's career.

His name is Lee Buck.

Probably one of the most critical days in his life began one April afternoon in 1974 when he was at his desk in the Manhattan home office of the New York Life Insurance Company.

"Mr. Buck," said his secretary, "the chairman of the board wants to see you."

Lee was excited. He had been waiting for this call a long time, for he was sure he was going to be offered the job he'd been striving for: senior vice president in charge of marketing.

It had been his goal ever since he joined the company as a sales agent twenty years previously. And he had worked hard, advancing to his present capacity as zone vice president in charge of sales in the eastern United States. In the new post he expected he would be in charge of all the firm's ten thousand insurance salesmen throughout the United States, the most important phase of New York Life's operations. He felt sure the chairman knew he was the best candidate.

The chairman's office was on the next floor up and to save time he took the stairs. On the landing he stopped and did the most important thing anyone can do. He took a moment to think and to pray. He prayed that he would be given the wisdom and peace to accept whatever happened and to make the best of it.

In a few minutes he stepped into the chairman's large, carpeted office, where heavy drapes muted the sound of Madison Avenue traffic. The gray-haired chairman shook hands, asked Lee to sit down, and then proceeded to give him shocking news.

"Lee," he said, "George is going to be senior vice president in charge of marketing. And we'll make you senior vice president over group marketing. Will you do it?"

The chairman was a bit nervous; he knew Lee Buck's reputation for being feisty.

Lee stared at him in shock. To him the group department was a real comedown, considered by many to be a stepchild in the company. This division sold group policies to companies and organizations and did only a small percentage of the business that marketing accounted for.

Lee felt a surge of disappointment and anger. But only for a moment. For, thanks, I'm certain, to that prayer on the landing, he was able to lean back in his chair and say, "Okay."

The chairman was surprised; then he and Lee talked about what could be done with the group department. Many men or women would have considered it a comedown, but Lee decided to make it an opportunity.

He remembered the advice he had been given by a veteran insurance agent when he was new in the business: "Jump at every opportunity, son," said the veteran.

"How do I recognize the opportunities?" asked Lee.

"You can't," was the answer; "you have to keep jumping."

And so Lee jumped. In studying the group division's market potential, he found new prospects that had never been contacted. He inspired his sales force, and went out making hundreds of calls himself. By the first year he doubled the previous year's volume. Within a few years his division was responsible for the largest single new premium ever written by New York Life.

Four years after he had taken over the "stepchild" division and made it one of the most important divisions of the company, he was promoted to senior vice president in charge of marketing.

What would have happened to Lee Buck if he hadn't taken that moment on the staircase to think and pray? If he had obeyed his first impulse, that instantaneous anger we all suffer when we feel we've been treated unfairly, he could have easily estranged himself from top management. But he took that moment to pray and to think, and his resultant career in the insurance business should serve as a beacon for all young men and women striving to make careers today.

All this ruminating leads up to what influenced me to write one of the most important books I have ever written, a book that was very powerful in helping others. And helping others find happiness and success in life is what I promised to do when I first decided to become a minister of the Gospel.

But writing that book came many years after that day when I was a timid, self-conscious sophomore at Ohio Wesleyan and Professor Arneson urged me to become a believer in God and myself.

After graduating from Ohio Wesleyan and Boston University, I went to work as a minister, and for short periods served in Berkeley (Rhode Island), Brooklyn, and Syracuse, and then in 1932 returned to New York City, where I have been ever since.

While I was minister of the Marble Collegiate Church on Fifth Avenue, one of my friends was Dr. John Langdale, a recognized scholar in the thirties, who had an editorial office on Fifth Avenue.

"Why don't you write a book amplifying what you teach from the pulpit?" he suggested.

I stared at him blankly. The thought of writing such a book had never occurred to me. "I'm sorry, John," I replied, "but only accredited scholars write books on religion and psychology. And I'm certainly no scholar."

But that didn't stop John Langdale. Every time we had a chance to talk, he pressed me on the subject.

Finally, I explained that I had no facility with the scientific language that such scholars used. "I've a great respect for learning," I added, "but I'm interested only in communicating to the man on the street."

I went on to tell him that I had once done some writing, yes, but it was when I worked as a newspaper reporter.

His eyes lighted up and he leaned forward. "Tell me about it, Norman."

"Well, for three years I worked on the Findlay, Ohio, *Morning Republican* (later renamed *The Courier*). Then I went to the Detroit *Journal,* where I worked under Grove Patterson."

John Langdale leaned back in his chair and smiled. "Yes, I know about him; he's one of the greats in the history of American journalism."

"Yes, he was quite a man," I said. "I'll never forget my first day on the job. When I told him of my work on the Findlay paper, he said, 'Trained by the Hemingers, were you? There are none better. You've had the best training possible.'

"Grove Patterson then proceeded to pull out a big sheet of yellow paper and with his pen put a dot in the center. 'What's that?' he asked. 'A dot,' I replied, wondering what he was driving at.

" 'No, that is a period,' he barked, 'the greatest literary device known to man. When a period is indicated, Peale, never write beyond it.' "

John Langdale, sitting across my study, laughed. "That sounds like Grove Patterson, all right. What else did he teach you?"

"Well, he taught me to use the simplest words possible, like instead of 'procure' to use the word 'get.' 'Norman,' he would say, 'to whom are you going to write? Let's say up here is a learned university professor and down there is a ditch digger. To which of them will you write?'

" 'The ditch digger,' I answered. 'The professor will understand and so will the day laborer.'

"Grove Patterson nodded. 'The Hemingers of Findlay taught you well.' "

When I finished telling all this to Dr. Langdale, I was sure he'd give up on my writing a scholarly book. Instead, he reacted most unexpectedly.

Striding across the room, he clapped me on the shoulder and said enthusiastically. "That's great, Norman. It's time someone wrote to the masses, to the average man. And you can do it. Give them simple, straightforward American English, the greatest communicating language in the world, and I'll publish what you write!"

I was surprised that a recognized scholar would talk as he did. But he got me enthused. I went to work writing, and sixty years later I'm still at it.

My first book was called *The Art of Living*, a literary kind of volume. It sold for the stupendous price of one dollar in hardcover.

My second was *You Can Win*, a motivational book. And I still believe that every person who thinks he or she can, can be a winner. Then came a bestseller, *A Guide to Confident Living*.

Then from 1950 to 1952 I tried to condense everything I had learned through the years into another book I entitled *The Power of Faith*. I showed the manuscript to an editor in New York, who read it and sniffed, "This won't even sell ten thousand copies. My advice is to cut it down, add some other material, and maybe call it *How to Live Twenty-four Hours a Day*."

That didn't interest me much, and fed up with the whole thing, I put the manuscript on a closet shelf, where it reposed for a year.

Then Ruth, my wife, found it, dusted it off, and took it to Myron L. Boardman, then vice president of a publishing house. He liked it and a few days later Ruth and I sat in his office.

"Norman, I have a suggestion for another title. It's a phrase I have found repeated again and again throughout your manuscript."

I looked at him quizzically. "I'm not sure I know what you mean, Myron."

"No," he answered, "I don't think you were actually aware of it, but you have unconsciously repeated it again and again in your book. I think it should be the title."

Ruth and I looked at each other questioningly. Then I turned to Myron. "Well, what should it be called?"

He looked at me for a long moment, then said, "*The Power of Positive Thinking.*"

That was the first time I had heard that phrase. That afternoon I reread the manuscript and, sure enough, there it was many times.

Both Myron and Ruth agreed that this new title said the same thing as my old one, *The Power of Faith*, which Myron thought would interest only a limited audience.

I agreed to the change; the book came out, and today, after thirty-eight years, it is still selling to an ever new audience. It has sold upward of twenty million copies worldwide, making it, I am told, one of the most phenomenal selling books of all time.

At first I worried about the title. Could I have read this phrase somewhere and it stuck in my subconscious? So I had it meticulously researched. But many months of study showed that *The Power of Positive Thinking* had never before been used.

In my simple faith I concluded that Almighty God, the universe's greatest expert on timing, had given it to me to pass on to the world's reading public. Why to me of all people? Couldn't He have selected a much better agent? Of course. But I have noted that often God picks the most unlikely candidate to do His will. Maybe He chooses people of only average ability with thick skins who can take criticism. For, believe me, I had plenty of that.

Seemingly every erudite person I had heard of, and many I hadn't, pounced upon it. It was ridiculed as "too simple," "mind over matter," "a tool to get rich." The more popular the book became, the more it was denounced. A noted scholarly commentator wrote a scathing review in a fashionable literary magazine. Some ministers denounced it from their pulpits. One called it "a perversion of the Christian religion." And a well-known political figure quipped, "St. Paul is appealing, but Peale is appalling."

Naturally, I winced. But it turned out that for every adverse critic, there were hundreds of thousands of ordinary men and women who wrote me that the book changed their lives for the better. Most important, many said it helped them find God.

Gradually the phrase "the power of positive thinking" pervaded the language, then the total culture of America, and finally the world. For the book had been translated into forty-eight languages.

The letters still come. Here are some samples which the writers have allowed me to use.

> *Dear Dr. Peale:*
>
> *You have helped me so very much over the past several years. I wanted to share some of the wonderful things that have happened to myself and my family . . . I thought you might enjoy learning how positive imaging has helped me personally.*
>
> *I put three goals on my bathroom mirror with an "Expect a Miracle" sticker under the goals.*

1. *I am now director of operations for region 6.*
2. *My income is now $100,000 per year.*
3. *Free of mortgage.*

I saw these goals as already having been accomplished and held that belief through thick and thin in spite of some pretty big obstacles.

By the following June, I realized goal number 1. In October of the next year I became vice president of my company. The raise in pay did put my income over goal number 2. The company bought my house from me which made it free of mortgage. (I guess I should have been a little more careful in phrasing goal number 3; maybe I wouldn't have had to move. Just as the old saying goes, you better be careful what you wish for because you'll probably get it.)

It gets even better. Our firm merged with another and as part of it I have become regional vice president for the northeastern United States for the newly merged company at even a higher rate of pay.

At the first of this year my wife and I decided to start tithing and guess what has happened? Lo and behold, we don't even miss that money. If anything we have even more than before. Tithing really does work.

I write you all of this because you genuinely helped me and my family through your tapes, The Positive Thinkers Club, Guideposts, and your books. About ten years ago I was engaged in some very bad habits which almost cost me my family. But I saw the light.

God bless you for all the many wonderful things you have done for me, my family and millions of others in the world.

Sincerely,
Jim McComas

And another from a man who almost didn't make it.

Dear Dr. Peale:
After returning from the Army, I settled down, married and went to work—to be a success, to make a lot of money, to show my in-laws how fortunate their daughter was to

have married a man of my caliber, to show my parents that it had been worth their effort to send me to Georgetown University. I was in a hurry.

Well, things didn't go well in business. I tried hard, but somehow the harder I tried, the worse they went. I wasn't used to not succeeding. I didn't know how to handle it. About this time I started to spend much of my time at four upstate towns, Batavia, Verona, Hamburg, and Canandaigua. What they had in common was, all were homes of race tracks.

In no time I was addicted to gambling. The next decade was a downward spiral, a nightmare. Over ten years I lost jobs, my bank account, sold our cars, and even our home to finance my addiction.

Finally, I drove down to the banks of the Genesee River. I sat and pondered the past—all the opportunity I had had— and the present. I was out of work, was $100,000 in debt, had no assets, and no faith in myself. I found myself asking: "Wouldn't the world be better off without me? Wouldn't everyone, including myself, be better off if I just went into the river and never came out?"

For some reason I didn't. Instead I went to a Gamblers Anonymous meeting. Founded by an alcoholic and patterned after Alcoholics Anonymous, GA, as we call it, was just beginning in upstate New York.

Gamblers Anonymous taught me how to stop gambling, something I had long tried to do by myself without success. Just as important, it taught me that though I had done things that were bad, I myself was a worthwhile person.

Then one day, I discovered, quite by "accident," the world of positive thinking. As a result, I started to believe in myself. I began to realize much to my amazement that I wasn't tied to my past; that I could become what I wanted to be. Gamblers Anonymous taught me how to stop gambling. You taught me how to start living.

Today, I am vice president and treasurer of an insurance company. I now have the physical things I once chased, a fine home, money in the bank, but more than these things, I have my self-respect. I know that I am a worthwhile person

*who always had a lot of good (and God) within him that
was just not properly directed.*

> Sincerely,
> Michael Feller

Such letters leave me humbled. The fact that I, who have never won any laurels in scholarship, should be so selected to communicate this simple message of positive living is incredible.

And the early criticism of my book is understandable. Most new concepts were discounted when first introduced. Such is the story of all scientific progress, indeed, any form of progress. First comes opposition, ridicule, and heated criticism, then gradual acceptance followed by universal usage and finally commendation. Having lived through the advent of the telephone, automobile, radio, and television, I can understand how human nature reacts to something totally new.

The speed of a twenty-five-mile-per-hour passenger train would disorient passengers, eighteenth-century experts predicted. That the newly introduced telephone would, under certain circumstances, electrocute the user, was a common fear. And not many years ago, many people were afraid of using a microwave oven because of "dangerous electronic rays."

Of course, the importance of the role thinking plays in our lives is not all that new. The Bible tells us in Proverbs 23:7, "For as he thinketh in his heart, so *is* he . . ." Centuries ago Gautama Buddha said, "Mind is everything. We become what we think." And the Roman Emperor philosopher Marcus Aurelius declared, "Our life is what our thoughts make it."

William James, turn-of-the-century professor of philosophy, psychology, and anatomy at Harvard University, said, "The greatest discovery of my generation is that human beings can alter their lives by altering their attitudes of mind."

But what has really amazed me is how today's scientific community is reporting the proven workability of positive thinking.

Dr. Christopher Peterson at the University of Michigan reports that a confirmed pessimist is twice as likely to experience minor illnesses, the flu or sore throat for instance, as an unabashed optimist.

Dr. Martin Seligman, psychologist at the University of Pennsylvania, says that optimism can pay dividends as wide-ranging as health, longevity, job success, and higher scores on achievement tests. Pessimism, he says, not only has the opposite effect, but also seems to be at play in such mental disorders as extreme shyness and depression.

"Our expectations not only affect how we see reality, but also affect the reality itself," says Dr. Edward Jones, a psychologist at Princeton University.

Out of these discoveries on positive thinking being made every day has emerged a new young science known by the tongue-twisting name of "psychoneuroimmunology." It studies how our thoughts, emotions, and beliefs govern our susceptibility to illness. It seems the scientists have as much trouble as I do in pronouncing psychoneuroimmunology so, thankfully, they refer to it as "P.N.I."

Happily, this new science also reports on the value of humor. Of course, they are finally catching up to the Bible, in which Proverbs tells us: "A merry heart doeth good like a medicine." In this regard, Dr. William Fry, a psychiatrist with Stanford University, says that laughing stimulates the production of the alertness hormones which release endorphins in the brain. Not only do these foster a sense of relaxation and well-being, but they even dull the perception of pain.

Imagine that!

And who wouldn't like to be a patient at St. Joseph's Hospital in Houston, Texas, where the nuns make a practice of telling each patient a funny story every day.

And I understand an increasing number of cancer patients are taking part in laughter therapy groups which seem to lessen the burden of their illness and, by building their P.N.I., possibly even help in their recovery.

And so I am astonished and humbled that a workable method for a better, happier life that I have been preaching and writing about for close to forty years is now an accepted, scientific principle advocated by illustrious minds of our time.

It makes all of the ninety-two years I have lived in this wonderful country eminently worthwhile.

To sum up:

► 1. A monumental event can happen any day. Be ready for it.

► 2. Beyond positive thinking is positive believing.

► 3. A thought can ruin you. But a thought can also make you.

CHAPTER 2

BE A BELIEVER = BE AN ACHIEVER

■   ■   ■

WHEN YOU BECOME A BELIEVER IN YOURSELF you are on the road that leads to where you want to go. Belief in depth is not easy, but it is vital.

Belief comes easy when it involves the commonplace. We push a switch, believing the light will turn on. We make a hotel reservation, believing our room will be waiting. We order a product through the mail, believing it will be delivered.

It's the important things with which we seem to have trouble. The dictionary tells us that the word *believe* means "To have faith or confidence;—usually with *in* or *on;* as, to *believe* in a person."

So simply accepting something is not the same dynamic thing as *believing* it. All of the early American colonists appreciated liberty. But it was those who *believed* in it who fought for it.

Yes, truly believing in something makes all the difference. As the philosopher F. W. Robertson wrote: "To believe is to be happy; to doubt is to be wretched. To believe is to be strong. Doubt cramps energy. Belief is power. Only so far as a man believes strongly, mightily, can he act cheerfully, or do anything that is worth the doing."

And most dynamic is the promise of Jesus: "All things are possible to him who believes" (Mark 9:23).

Just recently on an airliner I found myself sitting beside a young actor who had been struggling to launch a career in New York City. He was absolutely thrilled that he and his wife had just had their first child. A little girl, he told me, six weeks old. "You know," he said, "we've decided to move back to Minnesota, where we come from. I'll never be a big-time actor there, but I'll get by. There's something there, something . . ."

His voice trailed off, but I knew what he meant. Values were there. The ones he himself had grown up with. They were so important that he was willing to sacrifice a promising career so that his child could grow up with them.

Just a straw in the wind, you say? Maybe. But there are other straws. There is an upsurge of faith in this country. One leading newsmagazine says, "From the smallest hamlet to the largest city, on television and in private, belief is a growing, moving force." Why? Because people are turning once more to the stability that only values provide. They need it. Their children need it.

In education nowadays permissiveness is on the wane. Old standards are coming back. Marva Collins is one extraordinary schoolteacher in Chicago who took a handful of underprivileged children from the slums and turned them into superachievers by appealing to their pride, by insisting that they could handle any task set before them, by telling them constantly, "I will not let you fail." Today all over the land, educators are raising standards, teaching accountability to their students, demanding hard work—and getting it.

Believing is the power of positive living. It gets things done. It reverses failure into success. Believers are achievers.

Take Ron Guidry of the New York Yankees, for instance. He was one of the greatest pitchers in big-league baseball. But he had to become a believer in himself to reach this athletic pinnacle.

Guidry retired in July 1989 as one of the all-time greats, but early in his career he passed through a time of deep discouragement. His confidence was so shattered that he decided to quit.

In 1976, Guidry was sent back to the minor leagues. When he found out about the decision, he was crushed. He told his wife, Bonnie, "We're going home to Louisiana."

Guidry was serious. So they packed and headed south. But you know, it's a wonderful thing to have the right kind of wife. Mrs. Guidry didn't nag her husband or complain. Instead, she filled him with positive attitudes. As they drove south, she would simply say something like this: "You're a great man. You've got what it takes to be the best."

Finally, they were pretty far south and stopped at a gas station. "Honey," Mrs. Guidry said, "it's going to bother me to think that you will never know whether you could have made it in the big leagues."

"What is that you say?" he asked. She knew she had reached him, for as they pulled out of the gas station, he turned the car north. He went to the minor league and worked hard. By 1977, he was brought back to the major leagues. In 1978, Guidry was the unanimous choice in the American League for the Cy Young Award for the best pitcher.

Eleven years later, Guidry left behind an outstanding baseball record as the fourth winningest pitcher in Yankee history. Had his wife not tactfully, subtly imbued him with positive thinking and the attitude of a believer so that he could face his discouraging situation, he would never have known the power he really possessed. More importantly, he proved that an achiever must be a believer.

Perhaps the word "believer" should be defined. Believer in what? A would-be achiever must believe in himself or herself, have confidence in one's ability and goals. The achiever must believe in other people, for without helping hands no ladder can be climbed. One must also believe in the country which affords opportunity, and be a believer in opportunity itself. Anyone who wants to advance must believe in the organization where he or she is employed. And all belief should be undergirded by a solid trust in the help of God.

One of the greatest examples I know of how one's faith in God can give a person strength to overcome the most challenging ordeal is what happened during the hijacking of TWA Flight 874 over the Mediterranean in June 1985.

You may remember the airliner was captained by John Testrake, a veteran pilot who had been flying over thirty years. A strong believer in God, Captain Testrake faced his most critical moment during the hijacking at a refueling stop in Beirut, Lebanon. The hijackers, violent enough to have killed a passenger, Robert Stethem, were in a frenzy as they argued with the control tower about where to refuel. The tower wanted the plane in the refueling area; the terrorists feared an ambush there and demanded it be done out on the runway. Finally, the hijackers reluctantly agreed to the refueling area and Captain Testrake guided the plane with its 153 passengers and crew toward the confined area.

"With the muzzle of a pistol quivering at the back of my neck and a grenade jammed into my face, the tension mounted," he reported. "These men were Shiites, a radical segment of the Muslim religion, who believed that dying for their beliefs rewarded them with a prime place in paradise. They were close to hysteria. One unexpected move in the fueling area could trigger a bloodbath.

"I remember how I felt as we taxied in. I had a strong feeling that we'd all be dead, and my hand gripped the throttle. The time had come when I must not succumb to fear. I had to come to grips with the situation, and the only way I could do that was to reach out to faith. Long before, I had given myself to Him. If I truly believed in Him, then I must believe in Him completely. If Jesus wishes me alive, I said to myself, the hijacker will not squeeze the trigger or drop the grenade.

"My hand on the throttle remained steady. Relaxed, I edged the ship into the fueling area and cut the engines."

Captain Testrake says there was nothing new about the faith that kept him steady under such terrifying circumstances. It was part of him, just as knowing how to fly a plane was a part of him, and it was a belief that had grown stronger over the years.

After seventeen days, during which Captain Testrake's belief in God's presence never wavered, the terrorists released the passengers and the ordeal was over.

What would have happened if the captain was not a strong believer? Would he have lost his composure at that critical moment, causing the destruction of his plane and passengers? I do not like to think of what might have happened.

Whether you're caught in an airliner hijacking or something as common as a crisis in your work, your steady belief in God will make all the difference between preservation and failure.

Recently, I spoke at a convention of executives of one of the largest oil companies in the country. They had a panel of industry leaders discussing the topic: "Top Priorities of a Business Man." It proved to be a fascinating panel discussion and they agreed the priorities were in this order: 1. God. 2. One's family. 3. His company. 4. People. 5. The U.S.A. 6. Free Enterprise. 7. Life itself.

One hard-bitten businessman I discussed this list with on a later occasion disagreed with the placement of priorities 2 and 3.

"The company should come *before* family," he insisted.

"Why?" I asked him in astonishment.

"Without a job, how could a man support his family? Feed 'em? Clothe 'em? Keep 'em warm?"

I pointed out that anthropologists and sociologists, as well as theologians, generally agree that the strength of a society is the solidarity of the family. "All you have to do is read the newspapers," I said. "Most of today's troublemakers and misfits come from broken families where there is no parental authority. The family is most important to society."

Anyway, some might list the rest of these beliefs in another order, but, I feel, most people who want to be achievers would choose the above sequence. Personally, I would add another high priority and that is the service to your community and those less fortunate.

People who say they believe in nothing are in danger of becoming the pathetic misfits of this world. I have found it is most difficult for a person who habitually runs things down to ever be a successful achiever.

I've known many achievers in various fields. And I have never known one who was not also a believer in most of the items on the above-mentioned list. True, like every person, they had their moments of self-doubt, but all had a normal self-esteem and a sound and basic belief in themselves. They had well-defined goals. And so they forged on despite adversity, opposition, even hostility, to finally achieve what they set out to do.

Look at Orville Redenbacher, whose popping corn you have probably enjoyed.

He started out as a farm boy in Indiana, where he earned 4-H ribbons for growing popcorn. Later, he devoted some forty years of his life to crossbreeding over thirty thousand hybrids to create a popcorn he believed was lighter and fluffier than ordinary popcorn. (Of course, it cost a little more, too.)

But for years he could not sell it. Farmers wouldn't buy it as seed corn, because it yielded less per acre. Wholesalers turned him down, saying, "Popcorn is popcorn, Orville. Who's going to pay more for your brand than for others on the shelves?" Retailers shrugged: "There are over eighty brands of popcorn on the market. We don't have room for another, particularly one that costs more."

But Orville Redenbacher *believed* he had something customers would want, and he didn't give up. He kept trying to sell his product and eventually consulted a marketing expert who told him to put his picture and name on the jar.

Orville was surprised. "Why, I'm just a funny-looking farmer with a funny-sounding name." But he also had sense enough to believe the expert, and so he followed his advice. It did the trick, catching people's fancy. Today, Orville Redenbacher's Gourmet Popping Corn is the world's largest-selling popcorn. Orville's self-confidence that he had a superior product carried him through.

But sometimes a person finds self-esteem difficult to come by. I remember a brilliant executive who, at a crisis in his career, nearly blew the opportunity of a lifetime. I was at a convention at an Atlantic Coast beach resort to speak at the morning session. The meeting was held in a commodious ballroom on the ground floor looking out on the ocean. Facing the audience, I could see the foaming white breakers and wide expanse of the blue sea through the huge picture windows.

It was a warm and sultry day. To compound the discomfort, the air conditioning was not working satisfactorily. Everyone removed jackets and ties, and I, the speaker, was no exception. All the time I was speaking I kept thinking I'd shorten the talk and get out there into that beautiful surf.

Proceeding to do so at the earliest opportunity, I was diving into waves and disporting myself in the cooling waters when I came up alongside another man.

We greeted each other, and then he asked, not recognizing me, "Were you in the convention meeting this morning?"

"Yes," I said, "I was there and wasn't it hot?"

"Did you hear that speech by Peale?" he asked.

"Yes, I heard it," I replied.

"Well, what did you think of it?" he asked.

That put me in a quandary. I didn't really think that I should appraise my own speech, so I turned the question back to him. "What did *you* think of it?"

He started to tell me and, thinking it might be better to absent myself during his expression of opinion, I plunged into a big wave which providentially came along at that moment. I came up just as he was finishing telling what he thought of my speech. And I never did know his opinion.

Then, thinking it would be better to admit my identity, I said, "My friend, I must level with you. I am Peale." Whereupon *he* plunged into a wave.

We both laughed about the incident and sat on the beach to sun ourselves. Then this obviously successful man began to talk. He introduced himself, saying that he was executive vice president of his company. I recognized it as a well-known national business organization. He asked me to call him "Buzz," his nickname. He told me he had read a couple of my books and then, after a rather lengthy pause, said, "I'd like to ask your opinion about a personal matter. It represents a crisis for me that has to be faced right now."

Encouraged to proceed, he said, "Our company chairman told me yesterday that they are prepared to make me president and CEO, and he was authorized to feel me out on the subject."

"Congratulations," I said.

"It isn't all that simple," he continued. Then he told me that upon receiving the offer he "equivocated," explaining he'd have to think it over and talk with his wife about it.

"Why didn't you accept?" I asked. He dug his foot in the sand, picked up a few pebbles, and one by one threw them into the sea. Finally he said quietly, "I guess I just don't believe enough in myself to handle it."

"Self-depreciation," I mused aloud; "that's astonishing. If your board thinks you can do it, why don't you think so, too?"

"That's the problem," he answered hesitantly. "It goes back to when I was a kid. Low self-esteem made me miserable then and I guess it hangs on even now. You see, I was quite overweight as a boy and didn't do very well in school. I wasn't in athletics or extra activities. I was shy, a loner. But I got a job after college and became a hard worker. I was really committed to the job and worked my head off. I suppose this is why I got ahead.

"But yesterday, when our chairman told me they wanted me to head the company, the old icy fingers of self-doubt grabbed me as they had when I was a young boy, telling me I couldn't be the leader that job requires."

I sat listening to his story as the surf boomed dully before us. Then I told him I understood perfectly, that I had been through the exact same experience.

"You?" he exclaimed. "I can't believe it!"

"Exactly the same," I reiterated.

"Well, how did you get rid of your lack of self-esteem?"

"I never did. I got on top of it."

We both lapsed into silence, thinking about the complexities of human nature and the strong hold childhood self-doubt has on us. Finally in a low voice he asked, "How did you get on top of this weakness?"

"I became a believer," I replied, "a totally committed believer." Then I hesitantly added, "I still have my moments, once in a while."

We sat there on the sand, each of us lost in thought, two grown-up former teenagers who had dragged their youthful low self-esteem along with them into adulthood. The only difference was that one had become a believer, which had helped him to live above self-doubt.

Buzz sat hunched up, knees clasped close to the chest, while he stared out to sea. I sensed he was thinking deeply. He was a top-notch executive, whether or not he realized that fact. Years of excellence at work had made him so, and I understood why his company had tapped him for the top spot of leadership. Yet here he sat doubting himself. And now he might make the mistake of his life. What could I say to this man to help him in the career crisis he was facing? How do you convince a person he's as good as he is? Just *telling* won't work, I've learned that the hard way.

Suddenly I saw that his self-deprecating description of himself as overweight no longer applied. Actually, he was a well-proportioned man with excellent physical development, but he still saw himself as that insecure fatty. "Buzz," I commented, "you must be over six feet tall. You slouch some and don't reveal your true stature. How tall are you, anyway?"

Surprised at this apparent irrelevancy, he told me that when he straightened up he was six foot four. "Terrific," I declared. "What a man! Do me a favor, won't you? Stand up now to your full height." Embarrassed, he complied.

"Boy," I said, "you *are somebody*. And you have a brain to go along with that marvelous physique. You remind me of one of the best friends I ever had, a man named Rob Rowbottom up in Rhode Island. One day I was putting myself down like you, and he said something that I've never forgotten: *'Never build a case against yourself.'*

"You've done me the honor of consulting me, a so-called mind and spirit doctor," I continued, "so I'm going to give you a prescription. Several times every day look in the mirror. Look yourself straight in the eye and say, 'Listen, you—you *are* somebody, so start being what you are supposed to be!' And then stand up to your full height: stand tall, walk tall, think tall, talk tall, and believe tall. Now go and take that job."

I'm happy to say he accepted the new post and was a great credit to his company.

Buzz wasn't the only self-disbeliever I've met. Perhaps you are one, too. If you are, apply the same prescription that Buzz used. It worked for him. It worked for me. And it will work for you, *if* you work it, starting now.

I call this the power of optimism. Recent studies by psychologists, including Richard Lazarus and Shelley Taylor of the University of California, and Jonathan Brown at Southern Methodist University, point out that sunny optimism, or in their words "positive illusions" (in which people remember their strong points and successes more than their weaknesses and failures), promotes a sense of well-being, happiness, and the capacity for good productive work. Those who think in the opposite direction, it seems, often tend toward mental problems such as depression.

Sunny optimism, according to these scientists as reported in the New York *Times*, "seems to create self-fulfilling prophecies that propel those who hold them to do better. Several studies have found that people with a positive sense of themselves will work harder and longer, and that, in turn, their perseverance allows them to do better."

Well, I thought, I said the same thing thirty-five years ago; in fact, the writer of Proverbs said it many thousands of years ago in 23:7 when he wrote: "For as he thinketh in his heart, so *is* he . . ."

However, I must emphasize that in the above "sunny optimism" prescription I gave my businessman friend Buzz, the key word is *believe*. Indeed, the basic principle of success is to be a believer. Believe in what you do, believe in yourself as able to do what you do. Believe in people, like them, and be of service to them. Don't *use* them. Sure, not everyone is on the up-and-up. But believe in people nevertheless. The more you believe in people and expect the best from them, the more they will be unconsciously motivated to live up to your belief. They will love you for what you made them be. And if you happen to be a salesman, they will buy from you because they like you and trust you.

But whatever type of work you are in, this belief in the worth of people is vital to your success. You'll also find that you will not become a success entirely on your own. The successful person has plenty of people giving him a hand along the way.

Well, then the question arises: Just how does one become a believer, especially if that person is skeptical of life?

And another question: Doesn't the word believer usually have a religious connotation?

Those are two good questions and I'm glad to answer both. Let's take the second one first, the one about the religious connotation.

You may be aware that the author of this book is a minister. As such, I believe in God and in the Christian religion and have always based my life on this faith. Sadly, too many people do not take their faith seriously. They believe in an aircraft every time they fly. They believe in a breakfast food every time they eat it. They trust in the builder or manufacturer whenever they cross a bridge or take an elevator. But they really do not believe in the power of God to sustain and guide them. I am frank to say that I believe in God and, as a Christian, in Jesus Christ to give me strength and guidance so that I can do my job much better than my natural abilities would permit. I have had so many personal experiences of receiving God's guidance in the solving of problems, whether they be personal or professional, that I have not the slightest doubt of His presence and nearness.

I sincerely respect people of other religious faiths, and I am willing to listen to the person who tells me he has no religious faith at all. But I am sorry for him. This book is designed for everyone. It is written to help any person anywhere realize his or her hopes, dreams, and goals. But I must say that in my opinion faith is a powerful asset in becoming a believer in depth.

Let us now go to the first question: How do you become a believer, an achiever? First, you must *unlearn* being a nonbeliever, and that can be a long procedure. For example, when a longtime negative thinker decides to become a positive thinker, that person may have to unlearn old negative habits of thought that have been years in forming. It can be tough, but, thank God, not at all impossible.

The best way, I've found, to eliminate negative thought is to instantly supplant it with a positive thought. This isn't easy to do, either, but it can be done. A research team from Trinity University in San Antonio, Texas, and the University of Texas has studied people's ability, or inability, to suppress a thought. They found that preoccupation with a thought could be lessened by choosing another subject as a "distractor" and concentrating on that instead.

For example, a friend of mine had an unfortunate habit of allowing his temper to get the better of him while driving. If someone cut him off, he'd erupt like Mount Vesuvius. It got so his wife and family dreaded traveling with him.

"I finally realized I was going to have to change my ways," he told me. "Seemed my blood pressure would escalate thirty points every time I got into traffic. So I trained myself to react differently. When a driver cut me off, I'd quickly assume he didn't realize he did it. It was hard to do at first, but the more I did, the easier it became. And you know something? I realized I had been cutting off other drivers, too, without being aware of it. Sometimes you just don't look before you change lanes."

My friend's blood pressure is fine now. Yes, replacing those negative habits may seem awfully difficult, but do it with the get-it-done twins: patience and perseverance.

The second step is to *say* to yourself, even though you may not believe it at first, "I am going to be successful." As you firmly repeat your strong intention again and again, it will be implanted in your subconscious mind which, in turn, will actually assist you to become what you *will* to be. But this step requires firmness, a no-kid-yourself attitude.

A third step is constant reiteration, constant assertion, constant affirmation of the believing attitude. This will help eliminate the negative effect of the constant unbelieving attitude which you have practiced for so long.

Attitudes are formed over a long period of time, and you now have to commit yourself to developing a totally different mind-set. You might undertake saying aloud at least twenty-five times a day, "I believe God loves me, God wants the best for me, God will guide me—I believe." This will drive the new dynamic idea into your nonbelieving consciousness. In doing this daily you might also articulate that wise passage from Mark 9:24: "I believe; help thou mine unbelief."

Fourth step: Have the guts to take a risk. Practice believing in the impossible until impossibilities start becoming possibilities, then actualities. Remember, that is the way achievers achieve the unachievable.

Every time I think of achieving I remember a story I have frequently told, but it teaches an important lesson that can't be repeated too often.

Bob was a salesman. He lived in Brooklyn, and was doing an average job. He was a genial, good-natured man but was lacking in the motivational drive that propels one to extra success. He was a sort of easygoing fellow, perhaps a bit too easygoing. But he didn't know he was in for a change.

As a very young preacher, I was starting a new church in a fast-growing residential section of Brooklyn when Bob and his family began attending services. He was asked to usher and proved so good at it, making people feel at home in his folksy, friendly style, that presently we made him head usher. It wasn't all that much of a job, as the small auditorium seated only about 250, but it was packed full every Sunday. Bob got to listening to the messages of positive faith, and he went for it; when I say "went for it," I mean that. He really got motivated. He became a believer. Not only did he believe implicitly in God, he developed both a spiritual and an intellectual acceptance of the truth of Christianity and started putting his faith to work in his everyday life. He was especially intrigued by the Biblical promise ". . . if you have faith as a grain of mustard seed . . . nothing shall be impossible unto you" (Matthew 17:20).

"Is that actually true, Norman?" he asked, and when assured of the validity of the statement, he believed, he really believed. It turned his life around, changing him from an indifferent salesman, an average producer, to an enterprising, enthusiastic representative. Some people now called easygoing Bob "a ball of fire." And I was soon to find out the validity of *that* statement.

Easter was coming up. It was early that year, in late March. Bob stopped to see me. "We've got a problem, old son," he said. Why he called me that, I never knew. But I didn't mind. "We'll never get the crowds in this little church on Easter," he continued. "Why, we're packed every Sunday, even in the rain." I pointed out that we could have two services, but he objected, "That wouldn't do. That would mean we can take care of only five hundred people."

We parted, not having solved the problem, and I was willing to let it go at that. Although the neighborhood was growing, we didn't know all the newcomers, and it being New York City, we assumed many to be of the Catholic and Jewish faith, and therefore we could not count on many of them coming to a Protestant Easter service.

Things went along until a few weeks before Easter, when Bob telephoned me. "Hang on to your chair, old son," he began; "I've got some news that may rock you. I signed a contract for a theater auditorium for Easter morning."

"You've what?!" I exclaimed, horrified. "Who gave you authority to do a fool thing like that?"

"The best authority in the world," he said calmly. "I took it up with Him and He said: 'Go ahead, boy, you can fill it. And I'll help you.'"

Not realizing who the "Him" he was referring to was, I countered with no little concern in my voice: "I happen to be the top authority in this organization, Bob, and I did *not* say to splurge like this!"

But he persisted that there *was* someone over me. "Who's that?" I sputtered.

"His name is God," said Bob calmly.

"But, Bob, do you know the seating capacity of that theater?"

"Sure," he said, "it's 2,500 individual seats, and we'll put a human being in every one of them."

I was still fuming and reminded him that Easter was very early, in March, and it could rain or snow or sleet. I made it sound bad.

But it didn't faze him at all. "Whatever the weather, come rain, sleet, snow, or high winds, even hurricanes, we know God will fill that big auditorium," he said. "Have some faith, be a believer, old son. Be seeing you." And he hung up.

I sat back, sighed, and said, "Guess I'll have to practice what I preach." And, believe me, to do that sometimes requires a lot of extra faith, extra believing.

The reason I tell this story is that this incident proved to be one of the most significant learning experiences of my life. In it I discovered a principle that I have tried always to employ, and when I have, things have gone well. When I have neglected it, things haven't been so good.

What happened on Easter? I awakened Easter morning out of a restless sleep and looked at the clock. It was ten minutes after five. Then realization struck me: the theater, with its vast auditorium. That dumb Bob got me into this fix. I leaped from bed, ran to the window, and what do you know? It was raining and not a gentle rain. It was pouring down steadily, rain bouncing in the street down below. Well, out of some source I had enough positive attitude to say, "Anyway, thank God that downpour isn't snow."

Then the phone rang. A familiar voice cheerily said, "Happy Easter, old son." You guessed it, the caller was Bob, who, out of his newly acquired believing spirit, declared, "We're going to have a great day, one we'll always remember." He was so right, for I'm remembering it now as I write, and it happened in 1926, almost sixty-five years ago.

In my raincoat and under an umbrella later that morning, I sloshed through puddles to the theater two blocks up Flatbush Avenue. To my astonishment, the huge parking lot was full of cars. "People must have left them overnight," I ruminated. Then I found myself in a crowd of people streaming into the theater. They were people I did not know, all bent on getting in out of the rain. I couldn't believe my eyes: The place was nearly full and the crowd was surging in. I went backstage. Peeking through the curtains, I could see that both balconies were filling up.

Then Bob strode up to me. There were tears in his eyes and a choke in his voice. For once he had no words. He just wrung my hands, then hugged me. Finally, looking up to the ceiling, he managed to say, "Thank You, God. You're wonderful." Then to me, "How do you like it, old son?" And he couldn't help adding, "O ye of little faith."

I, too, was moved. "I didn't need any faith, Bob, old boy," I said, my voice catching. "You had enough for all of us."

"Go out there and start," he ordered. "Have them sing 'Onward Christian Soldiers, Marching as to War.' "

"But, Bob, that isn't an Easter hymn," I objected.

"So what?" he said. "We're in a battle against unbelief. Let's get 'em roused up and really going. And then get 'em to sing 'Faith of Our Fathers, Living Still.' I'm excited."

Again he choked up, and so did I. We started slapping each other on the shoulder as together we went onstage. An usher came up and whispered in his ear. He leaned toward me and said, "Jack just told me we've turned hundreds away, the place is packed. Couldn't squeeze another person in here with a shoehorn." He left the stage, adding characteristically, "I'm not surprised."

But I was. I was astonished. This total experience added immeasurably to my education as a positive thinker and a positive believer, and perhaps as a positive achiever as well. For what little I've been able to accomplish in my life has been due to knowing such great believers as Bob and his theater demonstration of positive belief.

So we end this chapter with the thesis with which it began: that an achiever is a believer.

To sum up:

▶ 1. Believe in people—don't use them.

▶ 2. Replace negative attitudes with constant affirmation and optimism.

▶ 3. Have faith that what you need will be given you.

▶ 4. Get rid of low self-esteem—*believe in yourself*.

CHAPTER 3

KNOCK THE *T* OFF *CAN'T*

■   ■   ■

TOGETHER WITH MY DISCOVERY OF THE POSITIVE
thinking principle was the abandonment of the "I can't do it" reaction. For a long time I thought that only I had the miserable "I can't" feeling when facing a problem or challenge. Later, I realized that many others have to struggle with this same lack of self-confidence. The "I can't" syndrome has probably stopped more people from living full, happy lives than any of the major diseases.

"I can't stop smoking." "I can't get out of debt." "I can't make it in my job." How many times have men and women come to me pleading these excuses. And in most cases, it wasn't the smoking, the debt, the job that was the problem. It was their "I can't" attitude.

Once you overcome the crippling "I can't" block in your life, there's really no limit to what you can accomplish.

And there's a simple, effective way to do it.

When I was growing up in Cincinnati on Spencer Avenue, I was an active American kid with a lot of friends. But I was shy and bashful and often crippled by that "I can't" feeling. In a ball game when I'd get up to bat, I'd think, "I can't," and, sure enough, I'd strike out. Lined up with other boys at the start of a fifty-yard dash, I'd look at those strong, husky fellows poised next to me and quake, "I can't." And I didn't.

Everyone in my family was a public speaker, and I longed to be one. But the thought of getting up before people was frightening. I can still remember a little impish girl sitting in the front row at a school assembly giggling as I tried to make a short talk. In a loud stage whisper, she said, "Just look at his knees shake!"

Today, I think my knees would still shake if it weren't for George Reeves. On the table in my office are seven photos that mean much to me: my wife, Ruth; my mother and father; brothers Bob and Leonard; Myron Boardman; and George Reeves. Myron was my publisher when I wrote *The Power of Positive Thinking.* George Reeves was my fifth-grade teacher in the old Williams Avenue School in Cincinnati.

He was a strict disciplinarian, as many teachers were in those days. Once he gave me a paddling, which was the custom at the time. Years later I wrote about it in a syndicated newspaper column. As a result, some forty readers wrote me boasting that they, too, got a licking from George Reeves. (I've related this story in speeches all over the country, and many people have said, "Put it in your next book." And so I'm doing just that.)

Mr. Reeves, despite his stern view on deportment, was rather whimsical, with a way of saying and doing things one never forgets. One day in class he shouted, "Silence!" And when he demanded silence, believe me, he got silence.

I can still hear his footsteps as he stepped up to the chalkboard and the screech of chalk as he wrote in bold letters the word *CAN'T.*

Dusting the chalk from his fingers, he turned and asked, "What shall I do now?"

We all knew what he wanted, so we chanted, "Knock the *T* off the *CAN'T.*" And with a sweeping gesture he would erase the apostrophe and the *T,* leaving the word *CAN* standing out clear and distinct. I can see it as plainly now as on that long ago day.

After this unforgettable object lesson, Mr. Reeves said in his strong voice, "Let that be a lesson to you and never forget it. You *can,* if you think you can." He looked around the room at each one of us and added, "So always think that you can."

This was one of my earliest lessons in the power of positive thinking.

An effective way to counteract the "I can't" feeling when facing a challenge is to instantly replace it with an "I *can*" thought pattern. That will fire you with the confidence to win.

Of course, this takes practice. In eliminating any defeatist attitude you must develop a technique that works and you must *patiently* work the technique until it becomes second nature.

As you know from my experience with my professor at Ohio Wesleyan University, I didn't develop self-confidence right away. It took patient practice. But I did work at my "I can't" problem long enough to overcome it. Even so, it still bobs up just when I'm about to stand up to speak or sit down to write a book. My technique then is to visualize that big word *CAN* written on that blackboard years ago, and again hear George Reeves's strong voice sound across the years: "You *can* if you think you can. So *think* that you *can.*"

When I'm being introduced to a large crowd and I suddenly feel those butterflies in my stomach (even at age ninety-two they're still there), I often remind myself, "You *can* do it; you've done it before." Then, murmuring a prayer to God for help, I go onstage and do my best. And, as my mother used to say, "When you do your best, angels can do no better."

Of course, you'll want to develop your own technique for combating the "I can't" feeling, one that's natural to you. Even if it may seem fanciful, anything that helps you remember "I can" should be used, by all means.

Many people murmur a prayer to themselves. I know one big-league baseball player who, when his place in the batting order is coming up, fingers a cross carried in his pocket. And you have probably seen batters cross themselves as they go to the plate. It is one way of reminding themselves that God is with them.

While on the speaking circuit, I have often noticed a brilliant lecturer, who invariably receives a standing ovation, take a card from his shirt pocket and glance at it just before going onstage. I was curious as to what was on that card. One day I happened to be traveling with him on a long flight, so I asked him about it.

"Oh, it always pulls me up and over the heebie-jeebies," he said. "Bet you have your own way of doing it." He produced the card, which read, "I am with you always."

I reached in my shirt pocket and gave him my card. It read: "You *can* if you think you can. So *think* that you *can!*"

"Hmmm," smiled my friend, "a couple of scared kids who still need self-confidence."

Every time a Federal Express package is delivered to my office, I think of Mr. Reeves, who knocked the *T* off of *CAN'T.* You've probably seen the Federal Express Company's familiar red, white, and purple trucks everywhere. This enterprise has created a whole new concept in overnight air delivery now offered by many other good firms worldwide.

But did you know that at one time the brilliant idea behind Federal Express was about to die before it flew because some people couldn't knock the *t* off of *can't?*

The idea first started with Frederick Smith, who was born in Mississippi in 1944. Despite having a wealthy father, Fred Smith had a rough childhood. His father died when he was four and little Fred suffered from a bone disease that kept him from running and playing. But the boy loved airplanes, and later when he went to Yale University, he researched a paper for an economics course in which he proposed overnight air delivery of packages to almost every town in America.

His professor looked at the paper, shook his head, muttered something about "can't," and gave Fred a low grade on it. After graduating from Yale, Fred flew over two hundred combat missions in Vietnam before returning to the business world in 1970. He asked experts to study the idea he had proposed at Yale. They were obviously "I *can*" thinkers, for their advice was: "Go."

In 1972, Fred Smith, then age twenty-eight, launched what has been called "one of the boldest gambles the business world has ever seen." He chose Memphis, Tennessee, as the hub of his operations since it is located near the center of the United States. His plan called for his Federal Express planes to fly into Memphis every night with packages picked up in one hundred cities. His Memphis center would then sort the packages to be flown the same night to their destinations, where trucks would rush them to the recipients.

It took a lot of money to buy the planes and trucks, and hire all the people to do this. But Fred, being a positive-minded fellow, was a good salesman and lined up investors in what one financial expert called "the greatest sales feat of all time."

But the first day Fred put his plan into action, April 17, 1973, it looked like his old Yale professor was dead right. His fleet of twenty-five converted passenger jets handled only eighteen packages. Worse, the oil crisis made fuel prices soar. Things got so rough for the fledgling company that its pilots sometimes had to buy aircraft fuel with their personal gasoline credit cards.

In two years Federal Express lost $24 million. Many business experts predicted failure. "It can't work," they insisted, pointing out what they called the impracticality of the system, especially in view of climbing fuel prices. A package sent from Los Angeles to Seattle had to be flown way out of its way to the Memphis distributing hub before it went back to Seattle.

"But it *can* work," Fred Smith insisted and turned to now wary investors for more money. He finally got it by agreeing to a very high interest. He stuck to his guarantee of next-day delivery, and when companies saw the value of his service, he started making a profit. Today, it's an $8 billion corporation with over eighty-five thousand employees delivering over 1.5 million items around the world every day. All because Fred Smith said "Can!" when others argued "Can't."

Unfortunately, too many young men and women today would have accepted that Yale professor's dismal verdict and given up. For, as I have too often found, many educational authorities today are deeply concerned about the worsening problem among schoolchildren of low self-esteem and negative attitudes.

Researchers seem to agree that at birth children possess a normal self-esteem and self-confidence. The child instinctively knows that everything he or she wants can be obtained by crying or cooing. The child is a natural-born positive thinker, an "I *can*" individual.

But by the time children are through the fourth grade, studies show that some 80 to 85 percent of them have lost self-esteem, developed real self-doubts, and become "I can'ts." This happens through negative households, negative attitudes in the teaching process, negative attitudes of the world. To return the child to normal, healthy, positive mental attitudes takes a tough and difficult unlearning process, but it can be done.

The trouble is that low self-esteem and lack of self-confidence in childhood can plague one into adulthood, especially when facing career crises. Remember the man in the earlier chapter who almost missed a once-in-a-lifetime opportunity because he lacked the confidence to accept a top executive post? I hear the same pathetic story over and over again from people who confess this weakness to me.

Once, on a speaking date I had to attend a party hosted by local bigwigs who had underwritten the meeting's considerable expense. They wanted to meet socially the four speakers addressing the meeting. So I and the other three lecturers showed up and were dutifully shaking hands. One man was very loud and assertive. His name was Bob; he seemed quite intoxicated, and for some reason fastened himself onto me.

"Here's that wise man who knows all the answers, Mishter Positive Thinking himself," he shouted, draping an arm around my shoulder. Others tried to lead him away with no success.

Finally, I said, "Old friend, put your ear up by my mouth. I want to say something for your ears only."

"Thash great," he slurred, "a secret, jush between us fellas."

Holding him steady, I spoke clearly into his ear. "OK, Bob, cut the act. What are you trying to cover up?"

The alcoholic flush in his cheeks faded to gray. Suddenly, he seemed quite sober. "Uh, what did you say?" he stuttered.

"You heard me," I replied. "Want to level with me?"

He stood indecisively for a moment, then became subdued and said quietly, "Yes, Norman, I do want to talk with you." I normally do not put myself at the mercy of a drunk. But now I was convinced he was stone sober. The party was breaking up, so we got in a cab and headed for my hotel. On our way he said, "You saw that I wasn't really as drunk as it appeared, but I've got to tell you I was out to get completely soused."

"Why?" I asked.

"To forget."

"Bob," I said, "I figured the kind of act you were putting on was a cover-up of something. What's bugging you?"

He told how he had worked up to an executive post with a large department store chain. "But I got to tell you," he confessed, "I think the brass have an inflated opinion of my abilities."

"Don't kid me, Bob," I countered, "I'm sure they know you're capable."

"Well, the problem is," he continued, "our chain's biggest store is in trouble, and management has asked me to straighten it out and make it profitable again."

He looked out the cab window a long moment, then turned back to me. "I just can't do it, Norman. I just can't do it." He was close to sobs.

"Once in a high school football game the coach sent me in to save the situation and I blew it. It's happened again and again. I can handle a normal situation fairly well, but when it comes to a crisis like that football game or a store going under, I know I'll blow it.

"I'm a well-concealed flop, a cluck in a clutch," he said, tears showing in his eyes. "Frankly, Norman, I'm scared. And I'm not going to reveal my true self by taking on that store."

"Bob," I said, taking his arm. "I'm going to level with you. What you are right now is a big phony." He looked at me with a startled expression. "Yes, you've been lying to yourself ever since your school days, saying, 'I can't, I can't,' when all the time you have been demonstrating to your firm's management that you have superior know-how, excellent judgment and experience.

"I have a feeling you're letting that stupid football game color your whole attitude," I continued. "You do well in life, but when a crisis comes along, that old memory becomes a stumbling block.

"So don't sit there and lie to me about being a cluck in the clutch because I'm not falling for it." And sitting there in the cab in front of my hotel, I told him about George Reeves knocking the *t* off the *can't*.

"Have you any faith, Bob," I asked, "any religion, or are you just a pagan allowing some demonic little thing like that ruin your life?"

"For your information," he growled, "I'm a pretty lousy Methodist, but one brought up by God-believing parents."

"OK, then start being a good Methodist," I said. "Give God a break. He made you and He made you top-notch. He helped you become the success you are today; He'll certainly help you build up that store. So take that assignment and wow them."

And Bob did just that. Within a year he had made that store one of the most profitable units in his chain.

"With God's help, I quit dwelling on those times I blew it," he told me later, "and started concentrating on the successes in my business career, the departments I expanded, the people I had helped up the ladder. And you know something, Norman, all those good things in my memory mounted up like a tidal wave that swept those 'blew its' right out of my life."

You see, I understood Bob because he and I were so much alike, fellow sufferers from inferiority feelings. Through my faith I conquered it, and I knew he could do the same.

Too many of us let some little negative incident from the past control our whole lives. I know a man with an excellent baritone voice who doesn't use it. He won't sing in his church's choir and has turned down an offer from his local barbershop quartet singing group.

Why? When he was a high-school junior, he was one of the lead singers in his class's operetta. In the middle of a solo, his voice faltered a bit. The audience hardly noticed it, but he did. He felt so chagrined that he never sang again.

"I just don't sing" is his excuse when pressed. He has let an insignificant incident of the past ruin what could be a rich, ongoing experience. But I know how these blocks are: insidious little seeds that haunt the brain unless one does as Bob did, and with God's help, wash them out with positive memories, knocking the *t* off that *can't*.

I've found that people like Bob and others who think they "can't" require a bit of what a Florida friend calls "propping up." Last time while I was calling on this elderly but vigorous lady, her phone rang. I couldn't help overhearing her conversation. "Now, honey, don't you worry," she said. "I'll come over this evening and prop you up."

After replacing the receiver, she said in the picturesque speech of rural Florida, "That poor woman. She has all the money in the world but thinks she's having a terrible time. Says she can't do this, can't do that. She sure does take an awful lot of propping up."

"You say that woman you're going to prop up is wealthy?" I asked.

"Honey"—she calls everyone "honey"—"honey, she isn't really rich. Oh, she's got a lot of expensive real estate and scads in the bank. But you got to have something inside you to be really rich.

But when I get through with her, she'll learn not to say 'I can't' all the time."

"And what are you going to do?" I asked.

"Why, honey, I'm just going to read to her from the Book where it says, 'I can do all things through Christ Who gives me the strength' [Philippians 4:13]. When she gets *that* in her mind, she'll *stay* propped up."

When I said good-bye to this practical philosopher of the Florida back country, I was really propped up myself. I like to remember her because it points up a workable technique for licking the "I can't" thought pattern. Overcome those negative thoughts and bad memories with the assurance you *can* do all good things through God, Who strengthens you.

Think of yourself as needing propping up mentally, which is accomplished by replacing your defeatist ideas and bad memories with a totally different pattern of thought. It's called positive thinking and it works wonders when you work at it.

My first book on positive thinking, as I mentioned earlier, created mixed feelings. Among its defenders, many said perhaps the book was ahead of its time, that the idea of one thinking positive thoughts, thus turning failure into successful living was new.

Now many years later, psychologists, research scientists, and other scholars have come out with books on the workability and benefits of the positive thinking principles.

Norman Cousins has written several books on the subject, beginning with his well-known *Anatomy of an Illness;* Dr. Redford Williams, a Duke University physician, has published *The Trusting Heart;* surgeon Bernie Siegel's *Love, Medicine and Miracles* has been a bestseller; and biologist Joan Borysenko has written *Minding the Body, Mending the Mind.* These are only a few of the many current books on the subject.

Positive thinking is also now practiced in top athletes' locker rooms. "Coaches, athletes and sports psychologists are convinced that the difference between winning and losing for top-level athletes is largely a mental difference," reports the New York *Times.*

Robert Kriegel, a coauthor of *Inner Skiing* and *The C-Zone,* reported in the New York *Times* that whether a person is involved in a sport or in a business project, improved performance comes from eliminating the fear of failure by recalling successes and remembering the feelings that accompanied them, then visualizing a perfect performance and previewing victory.

"Creating a mental picture," he said, "helps people build confidence and relax."

Again, I cannot repeat too often those words of Marcus Aurelius: "Our life is what our thoughts make of it"; of Gautama Buddha: "Mind is everything. We become what we think"; and of Professor William James, the father of American psychological science, who said: "The greatest discovery of my generation is that human beings can alter their lives by altering their attitudes of mind."

Of course, to these I must add that when we make our minds amenable to God's will, we can accomplish miracles.

Sadly, the tremendous potential of our minds is untouched. I often discussed this with the late governor of New Jersey Charles Edison, who was the son of the famous inventor Thomas A. Edison. Charles and I were good friends; he liked to talk about his father, for whom he had an unbounded admiration. He told me his father often said: "The principal use of the body is to carry the brain around; and the brain is what we are."

So true. For in our brain we think, consider, evaluate. Through it we have contact with the deep thinkers of history, the great poets and artists. In it we remember, dream, pray, and have contact with God. So often we relate these functions to the heart, which is actually only a muscle pumping life-giving blood. But the brain is the seat of our mind, and it is our mind that distinguishes us human beings as created in the image of God.

And it is our mind that can cripple us or energize us. The reason why "I can't" is so prevalent today is that it's usually the easiest way to duck a challenge. Take the inside joke some engineers in General Electric's lamp division used to play on new employees years ago. They would assign the new guy the job of developing a way of frosting light bulbs on the inside. Now, all the veterans knew this was impossible. But they got a kick out of the new fellow laboring for days on the dead-end project until he caught on. But one young man by the name of Marvin Pipkin never did catch on. And what do you know? He not only discovered a technique for frosting bulbs on the inside but, in so doing, developed a new kind of etching acid which made the bulb even stronger. You see, no one told him it couldn't be done.

Another young man who didn't let the "I can't" stop him was a Colorado skier by the name of Peter Seibert, who, during World War II Army service, nearly lost a knee to a mortar blast. His doctors said he'd never ski again. Now Peter had been a champion skier. He was also a champion thinker, for a voice deep within him kept telling him, "You *can* ski again." When he got back on his feet, he got back on his skis, and fell again and again. "I told you so!" mocked the world. But Peter kept thinking, "I can. I can." And he did. For after a few years he went on to win the famous Roche Cup race.

Then he got the idea of developing a new ski resort in a mountain location he had come to love. But when he sought loans to build it, he was ridiculed. "You can't do that, Seibert," was the common answer. "The location you've chosen is right on the road to the already popular ski resort Aspen!"

But Peter Seibert knew not to listen to the "can'ts." And so he persisted, forging on to build the now famous resort known as Vail.

Both Seibert and Pipkin achieved success by going against habitual thought patterns in their fields. And as long as God allows me to live, I will continue to emphasize the undisputed fact that by changing one's own habitual thought pattern, one can thereby change his or her life. For as has been so aptly stated: "What you are to be, you are now becoming."

Consider the case of the anonymous telephone call I received one day in my New York office. It was from a woman, and after she tearfully verified I was on the line, she continued sobbing. After a couple of minutes I asked, "Where are you calling from?"

"Oklahoma City," she choked.

"Well," I commented, "you've already been on the line for two minutes and all you've done so far is to sob. Pretty expensive sobbing, if you ask me. Now tell me, what can I do for you?"

"Oh, Dr. Peale, I've read you for years. You're my only hope. You see I've just found my husband is seeing another woman. I never dreamed he'd do that. Whatever will I do?"

"Tell me about the other woman. Do you know who she is?"

"I certainly do. She's younger than I, and I must admit, she's very attractive."

"How old are you?"

"Forty-two."

"Are you a good-looking person?"

"I'm forty-two," she repeated, "as I told you."

"So what?" I said. "Forty-two is not old, and a lady shouldn't lose her good looks at that early age."

"Well, I don't want to boast," she continued, "but when we were married the newspaper called me an 'Oklahoma beauty.' "

"Have you allowed yourself to get a bit dowdy?" I suggested. "And perhaps, you think you've outgrown romance?"

There was a long silence, then a low: "Well, maybe."

"Now listen, madam, I'm no 'Dear Abby,' but you've got to drop all negative thoughts; I mean right now, and start thinking positively. Be a she-bear, the most ferocious of the species when her cub is threatened. Another, younger she-bear, and therefore not as experienced as you, is trying to take your cub. Stand up and fight. Go downtown and get a new hairdo, buy some beautiful newest-style clothes, charge them to your husband. Think glamour and romance. When he comes home to dinner, have a terrific meal ready with candlelight and all the trimmings. Do some real positive thinking. Practice positive imaging and visualize your old wonderful relationship stronger than ever."

"It all makes sense, Dr. Peale," she murmured, "but I can't. I'm afraid I'm too late for all that."

"Listen," I said, "how long has your family lived in Oklahoma?"

Surprised at this apparently irrelevant question, she replied, "Oh, my grandfather came here from Indiana about a hundred years ago."

"Was he in the famous homesteaders' 'land run' into Oklahoma Territory?"

"Yes," she brightened, "and I've been told he was a strong, courageous pioneer."

"Too bad," I sighed. "My sympathy goes to a great family gone to seed. Who would think a strong grandfather like that could produce a sniveling granddaughter sobbing, 'I can't'? It's pathetic how a fine family can deteriorate."

This apparently got to her, and her voice suddenly became firm: "I can handle this, Dr. Peale. Thank you very much." And click went the phone.

I stood holding the buzzing phone to my ear, wondering if I had spoken out of turn.

About a year later I happened to be in Oklahoma City on a speaking engagement and the phone rang in my hotel room. "This is the she-bear speaking," said a feminine voice.

"She-bear?" I repeated, puzzled.

Then she identified herself.

"How's it going?" I asked.

"Wonderfully," she replied. "That affair I called you about? It's over, nipped in the bud. All is well. You were right. I did those things you suggested, added some positive imaging, and," she added loyally, "my husband is the best man in the world."

I have never seen the lady to this day and never did learn her name. She was only a hurt and frightened human voice when she first called. But to attain what she did, she had to have persistence, imagination, a strong belief, and a continuous positive attitude. It was true; she was made of the same strong stuff her grandfather was, and she came through gloriously.

The defeatist "I can't" feeling almost always will yield to positive thinking. The very few times I've known it not to succeed happened when the person involved did not have enough faith and perseverance.

Unfortunately, an individual may have an excellent education, training, high ability, a capacity for work, all the qualities that lead to success, and still retain self-doubt which, if unrelieved in a crisis, can ruin everything else.

The "can't live with it" feeling can result in a person's death. But the "I can" feeling, if brought to the rescue, results in a joy-filled life. So it goes, people drop the "I can't," adopt the "I can," and all sorts of wonderful things happen to them.

In my career of trying to be of help to people of all races and religions, or of no religion at all, I have experienced many rewards. But one of the most memorable occurred one afternoon in New York City on a Madison Avenue bus.

A well-dressed black man riding with his young son spoke to me, calling me by name. He arose to offer me a seat, as the bus was packed. I tried to refuse and thanked him for his courtesy.

"But I will have to insist that you accept my seat because you are responsible for the success I have had in life and I've always wanted to do something for you in return," he said. "This is all too little."

Reluctantly, I sat down, then asked, "But what did I ever do for you, my friend?"

As the bus progressed up Madison Avenue, its passengers began to thin out and the man sat down next to me and told me the following story.

"A number of years ago I heard you speak at our high school. Afterwards, I told you I liked your talk on positive thinking, but I didn't think I'd ever amount to much.

" 'Why not?' you asked. 'You ought to know,' I answered, but you were obviously still puzzled, for you complimented me on my appearance and personality and other assets.

"Finally, I said: 'But I'm black.' You said, 'So was Ralph Bunche, the Under Secretary General of the UN, who used to be a janitor. So is Bill Cosby. So is Jesse Jackson.' You went on to mention other black people who had made successes when it was even tougher for black people to get ahead. Then you told me a story.

"It was about a small black boy at a county fair. A man was blowing up helium-filled balloons and letting them rise up into the sky to the delight of a crowd of children. The balloons were in all colors. 'Do you suppose that black one will go as high as those others?' asked a little boy hesitatingly.

"The man had a good deal of kindly understanding. 'Watch,' he said, 'and I'll show you.' Then he blew up the black balloon and let it go and it soared just as high as the others. 'You see,' said the man, putting a hand on the boy's shoulder, 'it isn't the color that determined how high they go; it's the stuff inside that sends them up.' "

My fellow passenger who was telling me all this was quiet for a moment as he looked at his young son sitting next to him. Then he turned back to me.

"After you told me that story, you added: 'If you will get self-doubt out of your mind, and rid yourself of that inferiority complex you are nursing, if you believe that Jesus Christ will help you, if you will give *all* of yourself to whatever you do, you will get along all right.'

"Well, I decided I had nothing to lose following your advice, and so, believing that God *would* help me, I forgot my doubts, threw myself completely into my lessons and every other good thing that came along. A year later I was elected an officer of my high-school class, where the enrollment was 90 percent white! With that encouragement I worked even harder, got a college scholarship thanks to good grades, graduated with honors, and now have a good job with a top corporation.

"You inspired me, Dr. Peale, and I am glad to have my little boy meet you. I expect him to surpass his father." I gladly shook hands with the little fellow; then it was my stop and I got off the bus, grateful for having had the opportunity of meeting another man who conquered his "can'ts."

And to prove the "I *can!*" philosophy works for anyone, regardless of race or color, let me tell you about someone you have probably seen on television a number of times without realizing that her own life story has more drama than most TV scripts.

She is Marla Gibbs, who played a feisty maid on the popular *The Jeffersons* and more recently played a starring role as the mother who holds things together in the television series *227.*

I came to know Marla Gibbs through her story in *Guideposts* magazine. And I believe it illustrates what anyone can accomplish if they step out in faith.

Back in 1972, Marla was anything but successful. She hoped to be an actress but says back then she couldn't even hold her life together or afford a home of her own. Her life was one long series of "I can'ts."

"Back then I had about as much self-confidence as a chicken in a fox's den," she laughs. "I was recovering from surgery and had been off work for six months from my job as a United Airlines reservations agent."

Worse, Marla Gibbs, a single mother with three growing youngsters, had no place to live. Her children were staying with their father while Marla recuperated in an aunt's apartment where, lying in bed, she says she "stared hopelessly at the wall. I didn't know what to do or where to turn.

"Then one Sunday morning I idly flipped on the television, and there were actor Robert Young and his wife talking about their faith. They told how they turned to God for guidance in everything. They also talked of their church which taught that God wants only the best for us, and that if we pray, believing, He hears and will answer."

When Marla was able, she went to that church and heard the preacher say that with God we can focus our thoughts on the good, thus drawing good to us, and the strength to change our lives as quickly as we change our minds.

Marla also learned about something else very important: stepping out in faith. "As the preacher said," she explains, "we can't see down that road, but the Lord can. And if we confidently take that first step He places before us, He'll show us the next and the next, until we reach our goal."

But when Marla faced that first step, it was scary. After she returned to work part-time with the airline, she looked for a desperately needed apartment. But the ones she saw were either too expensive or unfit for her daughter, Angela, and sons, Jordan and Dorian.

"Then a little voice within me spoke," says Marla, "and I recognized it as God speaking through His Holy Spirit: *You don't want an apartment, Marla. You need a house.*

Before Marla's newfound faith, she would have said, "I can't," and forgotten the thought. She didn't even have a down payment for a house. But Marla got to thinking. She remembered she had a little bit of money available, and then there was the United Airlines credit union.

It wasn't much, but Marla decided to take that first step.

"With shaking knees, I headed to a real-estate office," she relates. "Strange, though—as I did, new confidence was building within me. And when the realtor asked what kind of house I had in mind, I found myself boldly describing one with enough bedrooms for the children and a garden to raise vegetables to help with the food bills."

But after Marla had seen several houses, her confidence was shaken. The few she found were snapped up before she could even make an offer.

"I remembered the minister saying, 'When one door closes, a better one opens.' Well, I wasn't going to just sit staring at the closed ones. So I trudged on. Even if my shoes wore out, I decided, my faith wouldn't."

One of those steps of faith brought Marla to another realtor.

While she waited in her office she leafed through some photographs of homes for sale. Suddenly, one was like electricity in her hands. It showed two small houses on one lot. The price seemed to be within her range.

The realtor took her right out to see them. They seemed perfect, with enough room for her children. But what really surprised her was that the lot had a big garden in which she could raise all the vegetables her family needed. It also had a basketball hoop for her boys. She scraped up three thousand dollars for a down payment and applied for a mortgage with the Federal Housing Administration. She put her need into her church's prayer box and then waited. But after some weeks the realtor, downcast, gave her the bad news. "They turned you down, Marla—didn't think you could handle it."

Now most people would have given up, saying, "I tried, but I can't." But not Marla. She appealed in a letter to the FHA.

"I don't think Martin Luther King, Jr., worked any harder on his 'mountaintop' speech," she says. "I went on for three pages telling how I could raise my children in those houses, how the basketball hoop would let me keep an eye on the boys, how the garden would help our budget. Don't worry about me losing the place, I emphasized; I would fight like a tiger to keep it."

Several days later Marla's loan application came back *approved.*

But more than getting her a house, Marla's new self-confidence started getting her small parts in television productions. She found herself freer to interpret her roles, she was more natural, more herself. And then she was called to play a temporary bit part as a maid in the first episode of *The Jeffersons,* which was about a wealthy black family. In the show she met the Jefferson family and asked if they honestly and truly lived in such a luxurious high-rise apartment. Mrs. Jefferson answered, "Yes, indeed."

"How come we overcame," Marla quipped, "and no one told me?"

That line brought down the house and soon she became a regular on the show.

Today, Marla Gibbs says, "I believe that when God puts us on this earth, He gives us a good dose of self-confidence to make it through life. Trouble is, we drift away from Him and lose it. Best way I know to get it back is to step out in faith with Him. It can be scary at first. But I know that each time I take that step, God takes two big ones for me."

Yes, Marla Gibbs was almost a homeless woman with a family to care for. Yet she changed a negative thought pattern and stepped beyond the "I can't" attitude by opening herself to a power flow of extraordinary proportions. It put her in the "can do" class.

I know of a woman whose self-belief was so related to an absolute faith it enabled her to overcome the greatest difficulties. She had a total objective of helping people, especially those in pain. And her belief that she could heal had some remarkable results.

I am indebted to my longtime friend Arthur Gordon, the well-known writer, for this moving human story about a little boy in New York City who had infantile paralysis at the age of three. This was before the Salk vaccine and the polio left him with little spindly legs so that he could not walk. His family was very poor and times were hard, so they took him to a New York hospital and never came back for him. A social-service agency took charge of the little fellow, and he finally ended up in a small farming community in south Georgia. There, under the soft sun of Georgia among the live oaks, he fell into the hands of a wonderful woman whom everyone lovingly called Maum Jean. She was a saint. She loved everything, especially little hurt things. Because she was a midwife, no woman in the community would think of having a baby without Maum Jean present. She compounded remedies of herbs and roots, and everything that Maum Jean touched got well.

Then she found this little boy from New York. She knew very little about atrophy, but she did know that unused muscles would wither. So every night she massaged his shriveled legs until he cried with pain. And she would say, "I'm sorry, honey, but I have to do it to make you well. And don't you worry. I keep talkin' to Jesus, and He will tell me when you can walk. 'Cause, get it in your mind, you're a goin' to walk, honey, you're a goin' to walk."

She did not know all that much about hydrotherapy, but she did know that running water would help such shriveled limbs. So she had her big, husky grandsons take the boy down and put him in the water. And between massage and the running water and telling him to believe that he was going to walk, there came a day when he was twelve years old. She put him up against an old live oak tree and backed off a few feet, saying, "Now, honey, this is the day Jesus has told me you're goin' to walk. I want you to walk over to me and I'll hold out my arms and I'll catch you when you get here."

"I can't do it, Maum Jean, I can't do it!" he cried. "You know that I can't do it! My legs won't work!"

Her voice, which had been tender, now became firm. "Listen to me, boy! We're believers, aren't we? And I've been told that this is the day. Now, you walk to me, boy!"

Hesitantly, he put one foot forward, and then another and another, and then another, and fell into her arms weeping. And she was weeping, too. "What did I tell you, boy? You don't need those crutches anymore!"

Well, by and by, the crutches were gone altogether, and he grew into a man. Then one day there came to him a message from one of Maum Jean's grandsons. It said simply, "Maum Jean's dyin'. She wants you." He went back to the little community, went down a sandy road, white in the moonlight, and to her bedside. She put her soft hand on his head. "Boy, remember what I told you. Just believe, always believe."

And, actually, that is the truth in a nutshell.

▶ We become what we think.

▶ Be self-confident, have faith, and persevere.

▶ When we make our minds amendable to God's will we can accomplish miracles.

▶ To cancel the "I just can't" feeling, affirm the fact "I can, with God's help, I

    can."

And then go on and *do* it.

CHAPTER 4

DO YOU HAVE WHAT IT TAKES
TO BE HAPPY?

■ ■ ■

THE TYPE OF BELIEVING WE HAVE BEEN DISCUSS-
ing is important in finding true happiness—something I think we
all want for our lives.

He sat across the desk from me, a stocky sort of bulldog fellow
about age forty. "Is happiness possible, Dr. Peale?" he asked. "I'm
not happy and I want to be. I've heard you have a lot of know-how
on this problem. So please give it to me straight and simple: one,
two, three. I don't go for a lot of conversation or psychology or
philosophizing, or any of that stuff."

"Neither do I," I replied. "I'll give you what I know about it, one,
two, three. But first, we must determine whether you have what it
takes to be happy." As I looked at him, I remembered my secretary
telling of a man calling repeatedly for an appointment who
wouldn't take no for an answer. She said, "I've explained that your
busy schedule leaves little time for personal appointments. But
this man is persistent, and I mean persistent."

I couldn't help smiling, for it so happened that I was in the
middle of writing a piece for a sales magazine on how persistence
is a basic quality of success. "Guess I'll have to respond to my own
teaching," I told her. "Tell this persistent fellow that I'll see him."
And now there he was, an obviously successful man wanting it

businesslike: one, two, three. I liked that and was also beginning to like him.

My approach of asking if he had what it takes to be happy rather startled him, but he quickly recovered. "OK, test me, if that's part of the process."

"Well," I replied, "I'm no oracle on this subject. I only know I'm happy myself and can tell you how I got that way. But first, I must tell you something very important: I've never found happiness by reaching for happiness itself. I have a list of what I call the components of happiness. Would you like to write them down?"

Taking up a pen and pad, he said, "OK, shoot."

Here is the list, which I call the "Happiness Mix":

1. Spiritual experience

He held up his hand. "What's *that* mean?"

"Just write it down," I answered. "You said 'no conversation,' and besides, I'm running this show." He smiled at that and I knew we understood each other.

2. Deep inner peace
3. Serenity
4. Joy
5. Excitement
6. Struggle
7. Good digestion
8. Health
9. Someone to love
10. Someone to love you
11. Enough money for expenses

"There they are," I concluded, "that's my list. You might go to someone else and get a different lineup. But on the basis of this list how do you rate yourself; do you have what it takes to be happy?"

He sat studying the list. "I can check off numbers 11, 10, 9. I've got them. For 8 and 7 I rate only fairly; 6, I've got. But for 5, 4, 3, and 2 guess I draw blanks; and as far as number 1, I don't even know what you're talking about. So my score is only about 50 percent."

"But you've got two other qualities which actually should be in that list: curiosity and desire." I explained that people who have curiosity and intensity of desire usually gain their objectives.

Then my visitor, who I felt was really interested in happiness, admitted that my list was "pretty good," but he went back to number 1: spiritual experience. That obviously puzzled him.

"Come, tell me what you mean by that," he insisted.

"Sounds like you've never been inside a church," I commented.

"Oh, I've been turned off from all that stuff since—" he hesitated —"guess it was about in the late sixties. From what I can remember, your phrase 'spiritual experience' smacks of finding God and all that religious jargon."

"You're on target, all right; but it's a lot more than jargon," I said. "Actually, it refers to the highest form of human experience in which the mind is flooded with power, peace, serenity, and what the Bible calls 'joy unspeakable.' And then comes a sense of victory over anything that previously has gotten the individual down." I could tell he was interested so I continued. "You might be interested in how Jesus described His mission in this world: 'I am come that you might have life and that you might have it more abundantly' " (John 10:10).

I picked up the version of the Bible called *Good News for Modern Man* and read aloud John 10:10, the verse quoted above. It read, "I have come that you might have life and have it in all its fullness."

"Does that mean happiness?" he asked.

"Look," I said, "happiness will never come if it's a goal in itself; happiness is a by-product of a commitment to worthy causes. In my case, I have had proven to me that true commitment to Christ inevitably brings happiness."

The youngish unhappy man sat thoughtfully drumming his fingers. Then rather softly he said, "You mean Jesus is the one who can make me happy."

"That's about the size of it," I replied. "If you ever wish to pursue this further, and I can help, let me know. But you don't need me. Read Matthew, Mark, Luke, and John. Then just talk to Jesus yourself and tell Him you want to live His lifestyle. If you do this with real commitment, you will receive the power to live that way

and with it will come joy. That is what I call a spiritual experience."

I could see he was reaching for this, but I never believe in pushing it, feeling it is better to let it work out naturally.

Finally my visitor posed a question. "But if I go for Jesus and
adopt His lifestyle, I'll have to cut out the rotten things I do." A
long silence ensued. "But it could just be that the rottenness is
what makes me feel so rotten and unhappy."

Obviously, he was persuading himself, so I kept still. Actually, I
was a bit awed, for the thought came that perhaps God Himself
had taken over the interview and was conducting it without argument or religious terminology. I was impressed by His skillful
method. He just let this intelligent man find his own way to the
good life, the life of joy and fullness of meaning. He was getting
turned on to vibrant life before my eyes.

The man stood up, walked around the desk. I thought he was
coming around to shake my hand in good-bye. But instead he put
his hand on my shoulder and I saw tears in his eyes.

"At last I've met a man, a real believer, who has the guts to tell a
turned-off guy the score, the real score. You see, I knew the answer
was in faith, but did not want to admit it; and I sure would have
been disappointed if you hadn't directed me back to believing, like
you did."

Perhaps you wonder what happened to this man? The sequel is
that he found his answer and with it the happiness which satisfied
his emptiness. And he found it with gusto. His reactivated faith
reactivated him. All the time while he was turned off, he subconsciously was in search of belief without realizing it. And possibly
thousands of unhappy people today are in a similar predicament.
They, too, can find the happiness and meaning which can revolu-
tionize their lives in the same way as he did.

Some of you may be thinking, "Well, that's all very well for those
people you write about. But I'm just an ordinary Joe (or Susie)
with a load of problems and difficulties that make it impossible to
be happy." To that I simply say, the choice is *yours*.

Many people would like to choose joy. But, sadly, they actually
deny themselves mental peace and happiness by failing to deal

with a regret or sense of guilt over something that may have happened years ago.

They carry this cause of unhappiness like a burr in the mind, hoping it may go away. But such thoughts do not just go away. They must be exorcised.

Some years ago a high-level Canadian government official came to see me in my office in New York. Dignified and reserved, with scientific training, he was in charge of complex technical matters for his country. He told me that as a reader of my books he had come because of a problem that perpetually and severely plagued him. He thought his unhappiness might stem from a long-held regret.

It seemed he idolized his wife, a strong-minded and very competent woman, a leader both socially and in service agencies in their city. "She was the gentlest, kindest person I ever knew and was always looking out for me," he said. "But I was quite busy in government affairs and admittedly tense because I was trying to do well and advance. But," he added, "as a result I became very irritable and caustic."

He said that he controlled these feelings at his office, but at night he "let fly at my wife" and was "downright mean to her." He would apologize each time, and she was always forgiving.

"It was like that old song," he sighed, " 'You Always Hurt the One You Love.' "

One day his wife suffered a sudden heart attack and within twenty-four hours died. "I was devastated," he said. "I depended so on her and did not know how I could carry on."

And then it happened to him, something I've seen happen in others with a strong conscience. A thought grew in him, a thought which has the power to take away all peace, all happiness. When he came to see me it had been seven years since his wife's death. But the thought which began as a tenuous idea now rode him unmercifully, eroding all peace of mind, all happiness in his work, and threatened to ruin his career.

"And just what was this vagrant thought that has grown so big and dominating that you feel it can actually destroy you?" I asked.

He was silent for a lengthy period, obviously struggling with himself. "You must excuse my discourtesy in not answering you right away. I have never mentioned this to anyone. But I will to you, for I feel you can help me and," he added, "you are, in a sense, a stranger and therefore somewhat anonymous."

"Yes, and by training entirely confidential," I interrupted. (I have never before related this curious and pathetic incident, but now this friend is deceased.)

He said, "I was literally a devil of unkindness to my wife, and a few days after she died, suddenly every mean thing I ever did and said to her passed through my memory. Now the regret has grown so great that I've got to find peace of mind or destroy myself."

"Are you a religious believer?" I asked.

"Yes, we were both faithful Catholics. She was an angel, a saint, and the most perfect Christian I have ever known. We both went to Mass regularly."

"Why haven't you gone to confession about this?" I asked.

He avoided the question, and I took it as indicating he did not wish to discuss the matter.

He wept. "When she was near death," he said brokenly, "she said, 'I will love you for all eternity and will work for you in Heaven.' "

Suddenly I felt moved to ask him, "Would you like to make your wife happy in Heaven?"

"Oh, if I could do that I would be the happiest man in Canada."

"Well, by moping around flagellating yourself it could be that you are disturbing her enjoyment of Heaven. Why not think of *her* happiness rather than your misery. Conceive of your wife as completely understanding your deep love for her and your contrite attitude. Realize that she forgives you totally. If you do that, and mean it, I believe you will be released from your mental agony and find complete peace. Happiness and serenity will be yours here on Earth as she has found peace and happiness in Heaven."

This reasoning appealed to his logical mind and he said, "That makes sense. I will do it, and do it now." This proved to be the mental treatment he needed.

He used to communicate with me by telephone. I could sense a new verve in his attitude. Actually, this man became an enthusiastic believer. He said he felt that the relation between mortal human beings and those on the "other side" could be more natural and normal than he had imagined. "Of course, I miss my wife, but your logic convinced me that we are not really separated but working together; and I feel good about that."

Reliving this experience set me to thinking of the many happy people I've known. Some have found happiness the hard way. Take, for instance, the following incident.

Once, the President of a Central American country and his charming wife came to my office. He was in New York for medical tests. During that time his wife, who spoke fluent English, telephoned and said it was important to the President and herself that they see me. I couldn't imagine why the President of a great country wanted such an interview, but my life has been filled with many seemingly strange experiences, so I hoped for God's guidance in whatever problem there might be.

When this fine man sat in my office, he went directly to his problem. "I am a believer," he said, "but I've done things in my life of which I'm ashamed. But I've always asked forgiveness and I think our blessed Lord has been merciful to me. At present I'm in New York for a physical problem, but my real illness is of the soul." This statement was given in less than fluent English, but it was clear.

He continued, "I am an Army man who finally became a general. As you know, in our country we have had insurrections and revolutions. As a commander, I have given orders that resulted in the taking of lives. I have never personally killed another human being, but I have given orders to others which resulted in killings. And I am troubled about my eternal soul. Will God forgive me for this evil? I ask Him, 'God have mercy upon me.' Will He?" He looked at me piteously.

"Were your orders given in your country's interest, Mr. President, as in the line of duty?"

"I truly believe so, but still I can see those young men." He pounded his fist in his hand. "War is hellish. No righteous man should have anything to do with it."

"Mr. President," I said, "my heart goes out to you. Let us talk to that Man Who was acquainted with sorrows and grief, Who always has mercy for any troubled soul. Let us ask Him to forgive you for anything for which you had responsibility."

I will never forget this strong man saying, "Blessed Lord, look upon your unfaithful servant who, with all his faults, loves You. I'm so deeply sorry. I will try to be faithful to You always if only You will put Your hand upon me."

Suddenly he reacted strangely. He stood up, clicked his heels together in military fashion, and saluted. He did not salute me, but someone unseen whose very real presence was in that room. He found cleansing of mind, and with it came peace. He lived on for several years a kindly and, I feel, a happy man. It seems that he had what it took to find happiness.

There is another impediment to happiness which can be a real danger to our health. And that is hostility, or an unforgiving attitude. According to medical science, the hostility we bottle up in ourselves when we refuse to forgive can cause grave physical problems. Says Dr. Redford Williams, an internist and behavioral medicine researcher at Duke University Medical Center, "Hostility predicts the risk not just of heart disease, but mortality due to all causes."

Dr. Williams and his fellow researchers were able to study different groups of people through a major part of their lives and learn how varying degrees of hostility affected their physical health.

One study started with individuals when they were medical students and followed them through the next twenty-five years. The researchers found that those with a high degree of hostility were about five times more likely to suffer a heart attack, angina, or to die from heart disease than those with a low degree of hostility. In a similar thirty-year study which began with people when they were law students, it was found that those with a high degree of hostility were over four times more likely to have died from heart disease or other ills than those students who were less hostile.

"Believers last longer," he said.

It's true; anger, resentment, a nonforgiving nature can wreak havoc on a person physically and spiritually. I know of one woman who felt she had every right to hate. Let me tell you what happened to her.

Hasula Hanna was a hard-working widow who lived in Denver, Colorado. Her main joy in life was her thirty-five-year-old daughter, Pat, who was all she had in the world. Pat had worked in another city for a while, then returned to Denver to attend Bible college. She wanted to become a missionary. While studying she worked at a part-time job, and lived with her mother.

One evening Pat did not come home from work. Hasula became worried. It wasn't like her daughter not to call. Finally, she turned the gas off under their supper she had been cooking and began making phone calls to her friends and, in growing desperation, to local hospitals and the police. No one had any reports on her daughter.

The next morning a police officer came to take a detailed description of Pat, her car and clothing. In the meantime Mrs. Hanna asked her church congregation to pray for her daughter. Later that day her pastor came to her door with some other men. Their eyes were full of pain and Hasula knew what they had to tell her.

"You have found Pat, haven't you?"

"Yes, Mrs. Hanna, we have found her," they said.

Her body had been found at the side of a road, where it had been evidently thrown from a car. She had been raped and stabbed.

Mrs. Hanna fainted.

At the funeral she walked through the formalities like a robot, responding mechanically to the endless line of mourners from her daughter's Bible college, office, and church.

Then, days later, alone in her desolate house she began to dwell on her daughter's unknown killer. Cold hate welled within her, hate which grew more with each passing day. Even in church her mind dwelled on vengeance.

Each time she picked up her daughter's unfinished Bible homework from her desk, she cried out, wondering how could God allow this to happen to someone who was going to work for Him.

Mrs. Hanna went back to her office job. Consumed with a passion to see her daughter's killer brought to justice, she studied the newspapers and kept in touch with the police.

Finally he was caught trying to kill another woman. For the sake of identification I will call him Carlton Moore. As Mrs. Hanna stared at the face of her daughter's murderer in the *Denver Post*, she took a letter opener and drew it across the face, slashing it to ribbons.

It turned out that Carlton Moore had been raised in a troubled home with an alcoholic father and disturbed mother. He had a high I.Q., but because of neglect and abuse as a child, he had been in and out of trouble many times. He had been on parole only two months when he killed Mrs. Hanna's daughter.

At the trial Mrs. Hanna sat in the courtroom. When Carlton Moore was given a life sentence she was outraged. Why should he live when her daughter had died?

As time passed she became more bitter, keeping more and more to herself. Caustic and sharp-tongued, she hardly noticed that her fellow workers began avoiding her. A small business venture in which she had invested turned sour. She turned more inward and began rejecting invitations to dinner and social affairs.

Two years later, at age sixty-two, the only thing alive in her was the hate burning within.

Then one Sunday in her church school class, a member of the local Gideons invited those in her group to send Bibles anywhere as a memorial for loved ones.

As he talked, she says that she began hearing a soft gentle voice whispering to her in her mind.

"My life, too, had a brutal ending. Yet My Father did not turn away from His lost children."

She knew it was Jesus speaking to her.

"Set yourself free by forgiving," she seemed to hear. *"Set yourself free from your prison of hate."*

"But how can I forgive my daughter's killer and mean it, with this bitterness in my heart?" she asked.

And the answer came: *"Have you forgotten my promise? If you forgive men their trespasses, your heavenly Father also will forgive you"* (Matthew 6:14).

Shaken, Mrs. Hanna asked the Gideon representative to send several Bibles to the state penitentiary and to have one delivered personally.

"Take it to a convict named Carlton Moore and tell him, 'Because Jesus forgives her, Mrs. Hanna forgives you.' "

Mrs. Hanna said it was as if someone else was talking, not her. But as soon as the words left her mouth, she felt as if she had stepped out of an iron shell, loosening her from what was binding her.

Mrs. Hanna commented: "The old Carlton Moore died, and so did the old, embittered Hasula Hanna—when I found the miraculous power of forgiveness." Forgiveness, selflessness, compassion, all spell new life.

Happy people are often unassuming people. I met a shining example of such a well-balanced human being at a recent dinner.

"What business are you in?" I asked the man sitting next to me at the head table.

"I work in a steel mill," he said.

"Where do you work?" I asked. (He seemed well dressed for a man who worked in a steel mill.)

"Oh, I work around the office," he explained. "I help the managers when I can."

"What is your exact position in the company?"

"I am the president," he quietly told me.

When he got up to speak, he told the audience: "I am in the steel business and have done fairly well. But I didn't do it by myself. I had the help of Bill Jones, who works at the gate, and Sam Smith, who sweeps the place out, and all of the people who work at my company. I love these people. They are my friends, and we work together all along the way."

Another way to be happy, albeit it takes extra special strength, is to stand for a high value, for high standards, even if doing so is terribly difficult. But this produces a happiness of rare, exquisite quality.

I knew a young commercial artist in New York named Frank. He was an excellent illustrator with all kinds of talent and had a super sort of mind. I liked him and thought he had unlimited potential.

He was what is called a "yuppie" (young urban professional) on his way up. He had sort of an amused, slightly contemptuous attitude toward what he called "churchgoers." But my being a minister didn't seem to bother him. We were friends.

Perhaps since I was also a magazine publisher, he regarded me as being more of a fellow communications man. Anyway, we often talked and during one of our visits Frank confessed to not being very happy. "Oh, I've done all right financially," he said, "but I still haven't found what I'm really looking for. And to tell you the truth, I don't really know what it is." He leaned back with a sigh. "I suppose you can lay it to my generation, Dr. Peale. We're all a mixed-up bunch of odd ones, I guess."

I never pushed my young friend in any direction, just gently let him know where he could find some answers, that religion had been around a long time, that great artists had believed, that there were truths that had lasted. And it wasn't long before he started going to church.

Frankly, I wasn't so much surprised by that as much as I was by Frank's reaction to it. And, again, it proves people are unpredictable: The way they talk does not always reflect their real down-deep feelings. For despite Frank's attitude about "churchgoers," he was impressed by what he called "religion that made sense." He became quite taken up with what became actually a newfound faith. "I'm beginning to find some answers," he said one day as we talked. He was a thinker and became enthralled with what he called "the rationality of faith." He developed into one of the most committed present-day disciples I have ever seen. With the same enthusiasm he gave to his work, he became an avid student of the Gospels. "This Jesus," he said with his usual frankness, "was really something, nobody like Him. I go for Him and His principles one hundred percent. He makes sense."

Still, Frank did not turn his newfound faith into happiness until—

It seems that many of Frank's cleverly done illustrations were subtly sexy. The going rate for this kind of work was very good. As a result, Frank was making excellent money.

But now with his new faith, an ethical thought began bothering him, especially when he turned in one of his off-color drawings. Not long after his spiritual change, his supervisor, Fred, said, "Frank, we've landed a terrific account and I'm selecting you to handle the art for it. The illustrations have to be really erotic, Frank, so make them sizzle. You know how to do it."

That night Frank phoned me and asked how one decides what is right and wrong. "Some of my friends say there's nothing wrong with this kind of stuff, that the old way of looking at things is outdated."

"Hogwash," I replied.

"I hear you," he said, "but I want to know if there is any guideline *I* can go by. I sure want to stick to my Christian commitment."

I suggested that he might test decisions by asking, "What would Jesus do?"

"Well, that's one way," he said, "but is there any other way to really *know* what's right and what's wrong?"

"Sure," I said. And I gave him the "feel good about yourself" test. "Frank, if you don't feel good about yourself doing something, then it's wrong. But, if you have a good feeling doing the thing, then you can believe it's right."

This seemed to satisfy Frank as reasonable.

A few days later Frank's supervisor assigned him the new job.

"Now give these illustrations all you've got, Frank. You know how to titillate the viewer. Pour it on!"

He left Frank sitting at his drawing board thinking. No matter how he approached it, Frank knew deep in his mind how he would feel about himself if he executed this assignment.

To his surprise, he found himself rising from his drawing board and going to his supervisor's office.

"Fred, I can't do it," he said. He explained about his commitment to God's way and how he knew that, for him, doing this would be wrong.

His boss stared up at him. "But you've done this kind of work before."

Frank explained how his new loyalty to Jesus Christ had given him a new ethical standard which allowed him to do only those jobs he felt were right.

His supervisor sighed and said, "Frank, I understand and admire your honesty so I'll assign this job to someone else. But I'm sure you understand, son, that with our limited staff we'll have to let you go. I'm sorry."

With that Frank put on his coat, went home, and explained to his wife, Janet, that he had been fired.

"Honey," she said, hugging him, "I'm proud of you. Sometimes this is what being a Christian means. Let's have faith that God will take care of us and guide us." As days passed into weeks it became hard going for Frank and Janet. But they tightened their belts and prayed with an ever deepening faith.

One day a man from an employment agency telephoned Frank.

"There is a big job calling for a top-flight illustrator to do some high-quality work," he said, "and you've been strongly recommended for it."

Frank got the job and later found out that the person who had recommended him was the supervisor who had discharged him. He stopped in at his old office to see him. "Thanks, Fred," he said, "that was mighty decent of you. Why?"

"Because I like you, Frank, and you do excellent work. Besides . . ." he hesitated, ". . . you're quite a man, son. You have guts. Good luck, Frank."

Later Frank told me: "I really felt great about myself." Then he added, "You know something strange; during the time when it was very tough going, I was really happy and so was Janet."

The businessman, the Canadian government official, the Central American President, the widow whose daughter was killed, and the commercial artist all discovered the "Happiness Mix":

*Spiritual Experience   *Inner Peace   *Serenity   *Joy

*Excitement   *Struggle

But, above all, they had Faith and Love.

CHAPTER 5

THINGS MAY LOOK BAD . . . BUT!

■   ■   ■

SOMETIMES IT'S THE QUIET, SELF-EFFACING PER-
son who makes a lasting impression on you. That's the way it was
with Fred Brown. I knew him for over fifty years. He never talked
much, but when he did, he usually said something worth thinking
about. That was because he was a thinker, a man who carefully
considered matters before saying anything. When an idea or
thought emerged from his mind, you could be sure it was never
half-baked. For Fred had a way of going over it from every angle.
He had an unusual gift for seeing the possibilities in any situation,
no matter how dark it appeared.

The first time I really became aware of Fred's ability was at a
dinner party. All of us around the table were discussing a community project in which we were involved. It was having some rough
going. The conversation went from bad to worse, as each one of us
dwelled on the many difficulties. Finally, a gloomy apprehension
of ultimate failure seemed to possess the party, and we fell silent.

Then Fred Brown coughed. This was always an indication that
he was about to say something. After a couple more tentative
coughs he said only five words, the longest one having but six
letters. In a low voice Fred said, "Things *may* look bad . . . but!"

That was the extent of his comment. Nor did he expand upon it
or try to explain. But the effect upon all of us was interesting.

Finally, breaking the silence, one of the women said: "Well, maybe if we contacted someone at the B——— Corporation, we might get some help."

"That's a good idea," spoke up a man across the table. "If B——— does something, I'm sure I can get some help from the J——— group."

"I know a man who has a real talent for what we're trying to do," said another diner. "I never thought of asking him for assistance until now."

One by one, we began looking at the project in a positive light and by evening's end it was amazing what new ideas evolved. In the end, the project was headed toward a resounding success.

All Fred Brown did at that dinner table was gently inject a powerful alternative into a negative conversation. As a result, it turned a dismal discussion into an enthusiastic exploration of possibilities.

To me it was an incident of enormous impact. For I saw the immense positive power in the common three-letter word *but*. It says that the situation, bleak as it may appear, is not all that bad. There is hope. There are possibilities.

It is an affirmation of the positive over the despair of the negative. And thus have the greatest successes been born out of impending failure.

Probably one of the greatest proponents of the "things may look bad . . . but" philosophy is the much-loved film actor Jimmy Stewart. He told one of our editors at *Guideposts*, the magazine my wife Ruth and I publish, how the film *It's a Wonderful Life* came into being. Appearing everywhere on television at Christmas, this is a great film with a Godly message. Of all the movies Jimmy Stewart has made, he says this one is his favorite.

But it has an odd history and some strange things happened in the filming of it.

When World War II was over in 1945, Jimmy came home a general from three years of service in the Air Force to face an uncertain future. He had been away from the film business, his MGM contract had run out, and he didn't know how to get started again.

"I was just a little bit scared," he admits.

Things did look bad . . . but one day the great film director

Frank Capra talked to him about a movie he had in mind. Frank seemed a little embarrassed about what he was going to say.

"The story starts in heaven, Jimmy," he said, hesitantly, "and it's sort of the Lord telling somebody to go down to earth because there's a fellow who's in trouble, and this heavenly being goes to a small town, and . . ."

Jimmy says that Frank Capra swallowed and took a deep breath and went on. "Well, what it boils down to is this fella who thinks he's a failure in life jumps off a bridge. The Lord sends down an angel named Clarence, who hasn't earned his wings yet, and Clarence jumps into the water to save the guy. But the angel can't swim, so the guy has to save him, and then . . ."

Then Frank Capra, realizing it all sounded off the wall, stopped and wiped his brow in embarrassment. "This doesn't tell very well, does it?"

Yes, things may have looked bad . . . but—

Jimmy says he jumped up and said, "Frank, if you want to do a picture about a guy who jumps off a bridge and an angel named Clarence who hasn't won his wings yet coming down to save him, well, I'm your man!"

Production of *It's a Wonderful Life* began. And Jimmy Stewart says, "Even from the beginning there was a certain something special about the film."

It told the story of an ordinary kind of fellow named George Bailey, who feels he never amounted to much in life. He had dreams of becoming a famous architect, of traveling the world, but instead feels trapped in a humdrum job in a small town. Faced with a crisis on Christmas Eve in which he feels he has failed everyone, George Bailey breaks under the strain and leaps off a bridge into a river. That's when his guardian angel, Clarence, comes down to show him what his community would be like without him; the angel takes him back through his life to show how our ordinary everyday efforts are truly big achievements. Clarence shows George how his job has benefited many families, how his little kindnesses and thoughtful acts have changed the lives of others, and how the ripples of George's love will spread through the world, helping make it a better place.

In the making of the film, Jimmy Stewart says that things happened to him that never happened in any other picture he has made. For instance, in one scene George Bailey, faced with unjust criminal charges, ends up broken and in despair, sitting in a little roadside restaurant. He doesn't know that almost everyone in town is praying for him.

In this scene, representing George Bailey's deepest despair, Frank Capra was filming a long shot of Jimmy slumped in his chair. In the scene Jimmy raised his eyes and, following the script, pleaded, "God . . . God . . . dear Father in heaven, I'm not a praying man, but if You're up there and You can hear me, show me the way. I'm at the end of my rope. Show me the way, God . . ."

Jimmy Stewart told our editor, "As I said those words, I felt the loneliness, the hopelessness of people who had nowhere to turn, and my eyes filled with tears. I broke down sobbing. This was not planned at all, but the power of that prayer, the realization that our Father in heaven is there to help the hopeless, had reduced me to tears."

Though this was not called for in the script, Frank Capra loved the reality of it, and desperately wanted a close-up of Jimmy's face instead of the long shot he had taken. But he knew that it would be about impossible to repeat. Things looked bad . . . but—

"But Frank got his close-up anyway," says Jimmy Stewart. "The following week he worked long hours in the film laboratory, again and again enlarging the frames of that scene so that eventually it would appear as a close-up on the screen. I believe nothing like this had ever been done before. It involved thousands of individual enlargements with extra time and money. But he felt it was worth it."

Finally, after nine months filming and editing, the movie premiered in December 1946. However, the critics had mixed reactions. Some liked it, others felt it too Pollyannaish. By the end of 1947 the film was put on the shelf.

Things may have looked bad . . . but the film refused to die. People who loved it told others. And when television stations began to show it, millions of Americans who never saw it fell in love with it. Now, over forty years after it was made, *It's a Wonderful Life* has been called "an American cultural phenomenon."

"Well, maybe so," drawls Jimmy Stewart, "but it seems to me there is nothing phenomenal about the movie itself. It's simply about an ordinary man who discovers that living each ordinary day honorably, with faith in God and a selfless concern for others, can make for a truly wonderful life."

So you can understand how every time I see this film come up on my television set at Christmastime, I also think of my old friend Fred Brown. As I said, I had the privilege of knowing Fred for fifty years after that memorable dinner party when I first heard him make that statement. And when things were bad and threatening to get worse I would listen for Fred's little series of coughs. And then would come that powerful affirmation of the positive alternative and we would tighten our belts and try, try again. And always, things worked out for the better.

It was uncanny how Fred would show up with those little coughs of his at just the right time.

During the first of several bottoms of the Great Depression after the crash of 1929, Fred and I heard a noted economist on business affairs make a public statement that this country would never again enjoy prosperity.

That was an awful thing to hear when most of us were barely hanging on by our fingernails.

Walking up Fifth Avenue with Fred Brown, I gloomily asked him: "What did you think of that prognostication, Fred?"

You guessed it. After a couple of coughs he said, "Things may look bad . . . but." This time, however, he didn't stop there. He added a few words, eight of them to be exact, quite a speech for him. "God and the United States are still here."

Well, Fred Brown is now in Heaven, I'm sure, for on Earth he made it very tough for the Devil, who surely must qualify as negative thinker No. 1. I, for one, believe Fred's power-producing concept needs wider currency today. Indeed, if we Americans would refuse to be appalled by any difficulty and simply say, "Things may look bad . . . but," then we would ride our troubles instead of being ridden by them.

Fortunately, I have had the opportunity to suggest this key to success to not a few young men and women, and some older folks also.

A few have stared at me sardonically, but many have put it to work. Like the taxi driver who took me to Kennedy Airport one morning. He gave me a running account of his troubles, ranging from money problems to the rats in his apartment building.

Finally, breaking in on his negative tirade, I said, "Things may look bad . . . but."

Apparently it had an impact, for he half turned around. "Meaning just what?" he asked, puzzled but interested.

"Meaning that you have neglected to mention your assets and possibilities."

"What assets? What possibilities?"

"Well, I see several. Your clear eyes, your sturdy physique, your good brain, to name a few obvious ones."

At Kennedy I bade him good-bye, grabbed my bags, and never expected to see him again.

Several years later I hailed a cab in Manhattan and the driver proved talkative. It seemed that the governor had started a program to eliminate rats from tenement buildings in New York City.

"I could tell him just how to do that," said the cabbie.

"How?" I asked.

"Put crushed glass in all the holes like I did," he said. Then he went on to tell how after he got rid of the rats in his little apartment he and his wife one spring got to looking at a Sunday paper supplement on flower growing.

"Someone had given me the idea that I could better myself," he said, "so on my days off the wife and I drove around in Queens and what d'you know, we went all out and rented a house. It wasn't much, but I saved that newspaper supplement and we planted flowers. It dressed the place up and my wife really made it a showplace."

He went on to say how this affected their neighbors. Seems the wives prodded their husbands to plant gardens and fix up their homes and the whole neighborhood improved.

I commented, "You put into operation a principle I believe in. 'Things may look bad . . . but.' "

"Hey!" he exclaimed, and turned around to face me. Luckily we were stopped at a red light. "You know, some guy was in my cab once and gave me that same idea."

Yes, I was that guy. We had a great talk. I was so excited at meeting this man again that after we shook hands on reaching my destination and he pulled away, I realized I had not asked his name and address. I was left to hope that I'd find him again and check his development.

Difficulties and problems can be handled if you become tougher than they are. My friend George Cullum, the contractor who laid all the piping under the Dallas-Fort Worth airport, said they encountered unsuspected layers of stone.

"What did you do about it?" I asked. George replied, "Oh, we became tougher than the stone, and that was that."

The ceiling of the Sistine Chapel in Rome was painted by Michelangelo. This required his lying flat on his back. But that posed a problem, for Michelangelo had a "bad back" and if he lay long on it he suffered excruciating pain. Moreover, he had some kind of nasal obstruction which cut off much air supply when he lay on his back. So what? He lay on his back all day, every day, for twenty months. And he painted one of the greatest masterpieces of all time. He became tougher than the pain.

There is a very great truth that *to every disadvantage there may be and usually is a corresponding advantage.* Consider the old truism that behind the darkest clouds the sun is shining. In the toughest situations there is always some value that is inherently good. But if you should not find such value after persistent search for it, the positive thinker, by looking for the good, for the advantage, for the sunshine, will do better with the difficulty than the negative thinker who sees only the bad. What you deeply think and visualize has a strong tendency to produce itself in fact. So always think positively, believingly, expectantly, hopefully.

I received a letter not long ago from a man named Walter Harter. As a young man Walter lived in a small Pennsylvania town. It was during a recession period.

Now Walter was a real positive thinker. He believed that if you have faith nothing is impossible, even finding a job during a recession.

He went to the local telephone office and asked for a New York City yellow pages directory. He opened it up and scanned through. In looking through the advertisements he found a drugstore chain with 393 stores in the New York area. He started writing letters to each store manager asking for a job. Not one reply came back to his 393 letters.

So he decided to go to New York. The first store manager he visited was a sympathetic man who explained that all applications were sent to the personnel office located on Park Avenue.

When Walter arrived at the personnel office it was filled with people looking for jobs. He went to the desk and announced, "My name is Walter Harter. I'm from Pennsylvania . . ." He got no further. "Come this way," the secretary said with a smile. Inside the office a man was sitting behind an immense desk. When he was informed of Walter's identity his face lit up.

"They're all there," he said, pointing to a stack of letters, "all three hundred and ninety-three of them. I knew that someday you would walk through that door."

He started work that afternoon and in time became a store manager and later an executive. He succeeded because he was a positive thinker and practiced perseverance.

Things may look bad, but . . . but . . .

The power in that little five-word phrase is the conjunction *but*. For it is our doorway from a dismal negative to a bright positive. Bob Dylan, the well-known folk singer, had an interesting way of saying the same thing: "He who's not busy being born is busy dying."

The wonderful thing about it is we have that choice. We can smolder on the dark side, or flourish on the bright side.

There's an interesting study of what happened to two hundred Chicago executives, half of whom, it appeared, stayed on the shady side of the street while the other half stepped over to the sunny side.

They worked for the Illinois Bell Telephone Company, a division of AT&T at the time, the parent company that was divesting itself of its affiliates. A psychologist, Suzanne Kobasa, then on the faculty of the University of Chicago, studied these two hundred executives who were going through this difficult time in their lives. She came up with an interesting finding, as reported in the *New York Times*. Half of the two hundred became ill from the unusual hardships suffered during the three-and-one-half-year period of change, but the other hundred remained well. Dr. Kobasa believes that the executives who stayed well had "personality hardness, a clear sense of who they were, and looked at life's inevitable tensions as challenges rather than as threats." These were the people, I'm sure, who looked at the difficulties and said to themselves, "Things may look bad . . . but."

I have a friend who works for a Madison Avenue advertising firm. He has told me that his work often creates a great deal of tension. Under pressure the people in his office sometimes lose their composure and begin criticizing each other. I asked him how he handles these criticisms. He told me:

"When I was younger, criticism would really get me down. I would take every cross word as a personal affront. Sometimes I would join in by returning criticism for criticism. At other times I just got plain angry.

"Then I heard a preacher quote a phrase from Scripture, 'And it came to pass.' It occurred to me that this is what happens with criticism, in fact, with every difficult situation. Criticism would come, not to stay, but to pass. It would soon be over and all but forgotten. That phrase has become so important in my business dealings that I have had it printed and mounted on my office wall. It reminds me to keep my poise in the face of criticism."

I don't believe there is a hopeless situation for which there isn't a hopeful alternative.

I knew a young man from Ohio who, in looking at the alternatives, drastically changed his life. He was the son of an old friend. Raised in a small village, he had done well in college and later in business, so much so that he moved on to Columbus and Cleveland. On weekends he would return home, attend his local Baptist church with his folks. This young man had a genius for making money and continued to move up in his field until he eventually ended up on New York's Wall Street. He acquired a lot of market savvy, and was soon enjoying a sizable income. With all that, he never failed to remember his home church.

Then he married the daughter of a big investment firm executive. She was a lass who liked the fast lane, aspired to the jet set, and tooled around the city in a red Jaguar. The wedding was a sizable affair in a large New York church where one attendant calculated there was nearly a billion dollars represented in the

main-aisle pews on an Easter Sunday. The pastor, for all his cultivated sophistication, was still a believing Christian, and he faithfully tried to counsel the young couple.

"Unless the Lord build the house, they labor in vain who build
it," he told the two. The young man was impressed and said he
understood what that meant in a marriage. His fiancée was polite
but later told him, "Oh, the Rev had to get that stuff off. It's his
job."

After their marriage the country boy continued to do well. Every
so often he would send a donation to that Baptist church back
home and the members put up a bronze plaque in his honor.

However, his wife's continual striving to make it in the city's
social milieus began to get under his skin. One night as they arrived home from a party at 3 A.M. they had a knock-down, drag-
out fight.

"Get out of my sight, you back-country Amen-shouting Baptist!"
she screamed. "You're nothing but a nobody who'll never be somebody." As least, that is the way her husband later quoted it when
he came to see me.

"Norman," he said, "I thought when I made it big everything
would be wonderful.' Instead, it's not. It's sickening."

He sat slumped next to my desk staring at his shoes. Then he
confessed that despite his wife's attitude, "I just can't help it. I love
that girl. I just know there's an angel inside her. I guess she's fighting that angel."

"Pretty sharp insight," I said, adding, "maybe that could be said
of all of us. We are either fighting or ignoring the better angels of
our nature."

Then I gave him Fred Brown's success principle: "Things may
look bad . . . but."

"Hmmm," he mused, "you mean look for alternatives?"

"Sure," I answered, "they are there."

"But what can I do?" he demanded. "Give me some ideas."

I sent up a quick prayer for the right thing to say to this poten-
tially great man who was having his greatness messed up. Then I
gave him the following formula:

1. *Stop thinking only of yourself as a priority.*
2. *Drop that "making it big" goal as your great objective.*

3. *Think positively of your wife and visualize or image her as the really wonderful person she will be.*
4. *Never fight with her again, no matter the provocation.*
5. *Pray for her morning and night.*
6. *Treat her normally, but add a touch of respect and courtesy. But be careful how you do this; be sincere. Today's woman can usually see through a phony.*
7. *Get her to join with you in some form of human ministry, such as working with the homeless, the helpless.*
8. *When you feel she is ready, and she will be if you follow the previous rules faithfully, ask her to pray with you aloud. There is nothing more uplifting than to hear the other praying, rather than screaming.*
9. *Get in the habit of going to church together if she's willing. In that event, get a seat anywhere except near that "billion-dollar aisle."*
10. *Try to get an understanding of each other. This will happen in reading the Gospels and finding God together. Then you'll really have it made.*

After I listed these points, I half expected him to dismiss them as well-meaning but impractical. Instead, he listened quietly. "Please write those out. What did you call it, a 'prescription'?" he said. "I'll have copies made."

I did and he put the list in his inside coat pocket. "Over my heart," he said. "I mean it, Norman, I'll do it. So help me, God, I will."

Well, I saw the payoff some time later. I was driving from the city to my farm, and on a country road near a popular old American restaurant, there were the two of them walking hand-in-hand through a golden October afternoon. They were so engrossed in each other that I passed them by without honking, not wanting to interrupt their closeness.

Obviously, the husband had seriously decided to pursue the alternatives to a desperately failing marriage. As a result, both he and his wife became happy people by that simple expedient of "getting out of themselves" and letting their "angels" emerge instead.

It is my belief that in every man and woman there is a better, stronger, more attractive person than may appear. And when we are wise enough to let that super-being dominate, we will no longer be running on "empty." On the contrary, we will be more full of life than ever before.

"That's all pie in the sky," some may argue. "Easy to say, but impossible to do."

Then let me tell you about a prominent industrialist I met in my Manhattan office. I found his name on my daily appointment book one morning. I had never met this man personally and was surprised he wished to see me. I didn't even suspect he had heard of me. Nor did I know he was a candidate for the "Things may look bad . . . but" philosophy. But after he sat down, I could sense that he was not happy.

He got right down to business. He said he was reared on a farm and his family were what he called "old-fashioned conservatives."

"Presbyterians of the old school," he explained, "who believe in the teaching of predestination."

It was clear he loved and respected his parents, for he said, "They were the salt of the earth, strong of character and warm in their affections. I've never gotten away from their teachings," he said. "Indeed, I never wanted to."

Then he paused, looked out of my office window for a moment, and said somewhat sadly, "But I'm not the man my father was. Both he and Mom are in heaven now."

A look of abject sadness crossed his face and I could really see the deep unhappiness in this man. But I was still wondering why he had come to see me.

He turned back to me. "I know you're not a Presbyterian, but what I know about you has convinced me you can give me some sound advice."

"Well," I responded, "within the limited extent of my knowledge, I always try to advise on the basis of common sense and sound Christianity, and I regard the two as one and the same."

He nodded, then said, "Would you then say that all I was born for was to be a businessman all my life and dabble in the stock market on the side?"

Having delivered this surprising and unexpected question, he leaned back as if to say, "There it is. I've got it off my chest at last."

He grinned ruefully. "You're in a tough business, Dr. Peale, having to deal with guys like me."

"Not at all," I replied. "I'm in what might be called the people business and that's pretty exciting. People have built into them immense possibilities of success, happiness, and creativity. That's why it's a special privilege to talk with you, for you seem to be a young man of exceptional ability who's made a great success of your life."

"That's where you're wrong," he countered. "Even as a student radical in the sixties, I never had it all together. For inside I was still an old-fashioned Presbyterian at the time and didn't have the heart for it."

He went on to tell of a "fortuitous career" in which just about everything turned out well, in that now he was a top executive and was also doing very well in the stock market.

"But my basic problem, Dr. Peale," he said, "is I'm just not happy with this so-called success."

I looked at him knowingly. "You mean despite it all you feel empty?"

He sat silent, obviously reflecting, then said, "Guess you've hit the jackpot. I've made it on the outside but feel nothing on the inside. Now, Dad was a good farmer. He had it on the outside *and* the inside. He was a happy man."

I could tell this man idolized his father. "Just what did your dad have on the inside that made him so happy?" I asked.

He sat silently considering; I liked the way he examined a question before giving an answer. That was probably why he was such a success.

"Guess it was his strong character," he mused. "He always seemed to be in control. The adversities of the weather or fluctuating farm prices never threw him."

"Quite a man," I observed.

"He was, for sure," he agreed. And then, as happens when someone relaxes and lets the truth hit home, he came up with his own answer to his problem.

"I can see it now, of course. He was what he was because of his strong belief. He had a real faith which he lived every day. It all adds up." His voice and face brightened as he continued. "I guess I'd better get my own faith back in order."

"You said it better than I could," I replied. "Remember, the Lord God will guide you if you ask Him. And He will guide you correctly if you have faith and trust Him. But, don't forget, He trusts us by giving us free choice. We can go to Heaven or Hell as we choose."

"Yes," he said, "in this rat race of trying to make it, I've let my faith slide out of the picture. The difference was during the good times as well as the bad, Dad held on to his faith.

"Thanks, Dr. Peale," he said, getting up to leave. "You've given me what I came for."

"No," I said, "you found the answer yourself. No wonder you've made it big in business and in the market. You can muster the facts, and then act on them."

At the door he turned. "You know, I like you."

"Thanks," I replied. "I like you, too, and more important, God likes you. And," I added, "your parents are proud of you."

He stopped. "Are?" he queried in surprise.

"Yes, *are,*" I repeated.

He thought for a moment. "That's right," he smiled. "I believe it, too."

We can learn some valuable lessons from these examples if we, too, remember these

basic principles:

▶ Don't ever despair. Many successes have been born from seeming failure.

▶ Always see your assets and possibilities.

▶ Remember the power of that three-letter word: B-U-T.

CHAPTER 6

GET *OUT* OF YOURSELF!

■   ■   ■

THE ONE PERSON WHO MOST BLOCKS YOU FROM A full, happy, and successful life is *you.* Yes, you yourself!

He is therefore wise who makes himself an asset. We can be our own worst enemy or best friend. We can be a source of trouble or a cure for trouble. So if you feel empty, as many do, start by getting free from yourself as a first step to vibrant living.

Start by getting *out* of yourself.

The method may be as simple as helping the next person you encounter. Suppose, for example, you are reading this on an airliner, and the person across the aisle is talking too loudly. He seems to be a wise guy who thinks he knows it all. The more he talks, the more he grates on you. By the time you're halfway through the flight you find yourself disliking this man immensely, even though you don't know him.

I once had such an experience. This fellow had a rasping, strident voice that carried above all other sounds, and he talked incessantly to the man next to him. Finally, his seatmate left, I suspect to find an empty seat somewhere else on the plane. Noticing this, I got up to stretch my legs, but actually I wanted to look at this bird whose constant talk got on my nerves. I was disliking him more and more each moment. As I walked down the aisle, he stopped me with a remark: "Hey, you look sort of familiar."

Uh-oh, I thought to myself, now you've really done it. "Oh, we all see people whom we think we know," I replied, a bit nettled. As I hastened to pass, he took my sleeve. "But I *know* I know you," he persisted. "Oh, I remember now. I saw your picture on a book I've read. You're Dr. Peale. Please sit down a minute."

I admitted my identity and reluctantly sat down in the seat emptied by the man who was sitting somewhere else on the plane. Then my nemesis surprised me. Instead of continuing his nonstop chatter, he turned to me and said in a low voice: "The Lord must have sent you to me."

"Why do you think that?" I replied, nonplussed.

He did not answer but stared out the window.

I repeated the question. When he turned to face me, tears were in his eyes. In a broken, husky voice he related a tragic family problem in his hometown, to which he was traveling. My heart went out to him, and I was able not only to be of some comfort, but to give him some strengthening words. After our plane landed and we got up to leave, he took my hand and said: "Thanks, Dr. Peale, for being so thoughtful, for giving me the courage to go on."

Afterward, I realized that his loud, incessant talk was a cover-up for his true feelings, a form of whistling in the dark.

There was another experience which taught me to be careful about judging others, to remember that every person carries his or her own sorrow. Yes, you'll find life will never be empty if you get out of yourself by taking advantage of the many opportunities to help others in their struggles.

Martha was a secretary for a large insurance company. One day her boss returned from a business trip. His first stop, upon entering the office, was at Martha's desk.

"Martha, I thought I asked you to put the Holden file in my briefcase before I left," he shouted. "Do you know how embarrassing it was not to have it when I met with them yesterday?"

Her face reddened. She was aware that everyone in the office was staring at her. "I'm sorry, Mr. Jones, I was sure I put the right folder in your case."

Without another word, Mr. Jones stormed into his office.

Martha sat there trying to fight off the hurt and humiliation. As she felt her anger grow she suddenly shook her head and took a deep breath. With tremendous effort she changed the focus of her thinking from her wounded pride to Mr. Jones and his problems. His family life was in a sad state of affairs and his son was very sick.

When it was time to face her boss again, she could do so with total composure. A few days later, Mr. Jones apologized. The folder had turned up in his briefcase behind some papers.

When a young man came for counseling saying he felt empty and unhappy, I suggested he look for ways to help other people.

He smiled wryly and shook his head. "I'm not a minister, Dr. Peale, I'm just a computer programmer. What do I know about helping others?"

"More than you realize," I countered. "As a human being you have a natural compassion if you just let it out when you're with someone who's troubled. And if you do, it will make you happier. In fact, it's your business to do so, especially if you feel empty and unhappy. For your own sake, I guarantee that your sad feelings will lessen and finally disappear when you think less about yourself and more about people around you."

Ronald Reagan always struck me as a happy man who was popular despite controversial presidential decisions he needed to make. People of both parties liked him personally, for he genuinely cared about people. Even though burdened with decisions and duties of his office, he never ceased thinking of others.

Here's just one example. In our New York City apartment one May 31, my birthday, the phone rang. I picked it up to hear that familiar husky voice saying, just like any caller: "Norman, this is Ronald Reagan. I'm calling to say happy birthday and God bless you."

I was awed that the President, perhaps the busiest man in the world, not only thought of me but took the trouble to telephone. I decided that this concern for people was one explanation of his happy spirit.

Ronald Reagan was always doing kindly and thoughtful things. Senator Bob Dole told me, "Once President Reagan called and said, 'Is there anything I can do for you?' 'Yes,' I said, 'you can call my mother back in Russell, Kansas. She is sick in the hospital and would love to hear from you.'" Senator Dole reported, "He was on the phone to her within the hour."

Truly great people live extraordinary lives because, I believe, for the most part they have an ingrained habit of always thinking of other people and showing them kindnesses. Once I was in the White House Oval Office with Harry Truman, another popular President. I was there with a committee about something. As we were leaving, President Truman took each of us by the hand and asked in that homey Missouri twang, "Can I do anything for you personally?" I screwed up my courage, pulled a piece of notepaper from a memo pad I had, and said, "Mr. President, I have a little daughter. Her name is Margaret. She is a great admirer of yours and would be honored all her life if you would autograph this piece of paper." He took the paper and looked at it speculatively, his glasses reflecting the light. It was ordinary lined paper of the cheapest kind.

"Now, Dr. Peale," he said with a grin, "you really don't expect the President of the United States to sign his name on such a cheap piece of paper." He held us all in the Oval Office, ignoring impatient and distinguished callers waiting in an anteroom, while he pulled open several drawers of his desk, mumbling, "Where are those extra special White House cards?" I was embarrassed to put him to such trouble, but all my committee associates remarked later upon his concern and kindness. Finally he located the cards and inscribed one, "To Margaret Peale from her friend Harry Truman."

I thanked the President. "Oh," he smiled, "I'd do anything for a little girl or boy." Then, as a proud father, he added, "I have a daughter named Margaret." I don't believe anyone ever considered Harry Truman and Ronald Reagan as empty or unhappy. They each had the ability to forget themselves and think of other people in a considerate and kindly way.

The surest cure for an empty feeling, then, is to think and act to cultivate a genuine concern for everyone, especially those who have it rough. I realize this sounds simple, like Sunday School stuff. But let's not be so stupid as to pass it by because it's simple. Apply the acid test: *it works*. So what if it is simple? What you want is something that will for sure stop that empty "What's the use?" feeling. And this concern for others, call it love if you will, will put meaning and happiness where that big void is now.

I remember the day I went to the Thursday luncheon of our

Rotary Club of New York and happened to sit by a man who introduced himself as a Rotarian from out of town. We chatted as people will, but I began to sense that this fellow, whose name was Joe,
was troubled. It wasn't anything that he said, but if you are open
to human feelings, sorrow and anxiety communicate themselves.

Finally, I gently mentioned I could tell something was troubling
him, and added, "Can I do anything to help?"

Joe sighed heavily, looked down at his plate for a moment, then
back up at me. "How did you know I'm facing big trouble?"

"Oh, I just sensed it," I replied.

"Well," he said, trying to back off the subject, "I think I can
handle it. But it's good of you to offer."

Now I have found that a lot of people do this when you try to
help them. Feeling somewhat embarrassed, they don't want to
trouble you and so politely give you an "out."

But if you're serious about helping them, you don't take that
"out," for which they and you are usually grateful.

"See that fellow over there," I said, pointing to a man sitting
across the room. "I want you to meet him; he's a brilliant fellow
and you'll appreciate knowing him."

The man I pointed to was a baby boomer who had come up fast
in his business. George had a beautiful home in Westchester, drove
(or rather his chauffeur drove) a Rolls-Royce. And he was still in
his forties. We had known each other for a few years, and he was
always frank and open with me, I guess because I seemed to be
able to help him and also never gossiped. So about six months ago
when I congratulated George on scoring a business coup, he shook
his head. "Norman, it isn't worth a damn, not with the way things
are going at home. I got so tied up in business that not only did I
neglect my wife and children but I've become mean as the devil.
Now Joan is talking about separating." He took a deep breath. "I
had the idea if I could make big bucks I and the family would be
in clover, but I'm miserable. There is nothing inside of me." He
looked at me piteously. "I need help."

We had a number of counseling sessions in which he began
learning how to get his priorities in order, like putting God first in
his life, then his family, his business, and others, too. At the time
of this Rotary luncheon George was still straightening up his life,
but I knew he'd make it.

So after the luncheon I brought these two men together, first quietly saying on the side to George, "This man needs help, and maybe helping him will do something for you, too."

George looked surprised. "How come you figured *I* can help him?"

"I *know* you can," I said.

He shrugged, then turned to my luncheon partner, who was waiting to meet him a few steps away.

The two men took to each other at once. I've always noticed people with problems respond to each other. This is one of the secrets of Alcoholics Anonymous. Bill Wilson, who cofounded it, once said to me, "It takes one drunk to help another."

Joe leveled with George and told him he had come to New York because his son, Sam, was in jail for car theft. He was also mixed up in other antisocial activities. (This was during the youth rebellion of the sixties and the son was in it up to his neck.)

George became interested in meeting the boy and went with Joe to the jail. He sort of liked the young man and saw possibilities in him. He made application to the court and got Sam paroled to him and another Rotary member.

He devoted himself enthusiastically to the boy's rehabilitation. This took a lot of George's time, but he told me he was actually enjoying the effort. Of course, he was getting out of himself by helping Joe's son. Through it all George found himself straightening out even more, becoming more thoughtful of his family, and his marriage improved. He also found great spiritual help in his Catholic church, which he had forgotten about in his fast-lane life.

In helping to reorganize a young man, George found himself becoming reorganized and focused. He again found meaning in life, with resulting contentment and satisfaction.

And the mixed-up boy? Well, I'm writing this account soon after the Christmas season, and one of the cards I received was from him. Sam, the hostile rebel and car thief, is now a successful and well-loved Lutheran minister. How about that for God's work—a Catholic producing a Lutheran minister and remaking himself in the process.

A model named Sue Miller, at age thirty-seven, discovered that she had breast cancer, and underwent a mastectomy. For several years after her surgery, she lived like a hermit. She felt too depressed to venture beyond the walls of her home.

Finally, one day Sue was talked into planning a fashion show. The clothes—including nightgowns and swimsuits—would be modeled by women whose breasts had been surgically removed. During the fashion show, Sue writes, "I noticed a healing force at work. Those of us who were models were feeling the heady stirrings of self-confidence. The audience was beginning to realize, with a sense of wonderment, that breast cancer isn't the end of a good, happy life."

The show was so successful that Sue expanded it, took it on the road, and turned it into a gala annual event called "A Day of Caring." More important, as Sue regained her self-confidence and self-respect, she reached out to others more and more. She helped set up a program of individual guidance and support for every woman who enters a local hospital facing breast surgery, and she is pursuing a health-related degree in college so she can be even more helpful.

Because at the low point in her life—when she was physically and mentally devastated—she got outside of herself and became involved in solving the problems of others, Sue Miller found more meaning in life than she had ever known before. "You may not think you have the inner resources to cope," Sue writes, "but you do."

Carol Sasaki, a victim of sexual abuse, ran away from home at age thirteen. At eighteen, she suffered a mental breakdown after being brutally raped; and in her early twenties, Carol found herself alone, pregnant, penniless, and scared.

After the birth of her son, she became a welfare mother, but never stopped dreaming about a better life for herself and her child. She knew that a way to break free from poverty was to earn a college degree, thus making it possible to get a good job.

Carol first had to obtain her high-school equivalency diploma. The next step was college. She talked the welfare agency into paying part of her tuition, and with a student loan and a college grant, she graduated. Then with low-rent housing, low-cost day care, and part-time jobs she escaped from the welfare cycle. "For the first time," she said, "I felt in control."

Realizing that if *she* could come this far, so could other welfare mothers, Carol decided to teach welfare recipients what she had learned.

Now, Carol is thirty-three, and over twenty thousand people are part of her HOME (Helping Ourselves Means Education) network, an organization dedicated to helping the poor take the first step toward financial independence.

Isn't it amazing how a person, no matter how burdened, can create and release dynamic forces that turn back defeat? Carol Sasaki's rebound capacity, and her ability to *fight* every adversity, brought her through crises. She refused to accept defeat. And now, Carol's ability to overcome for herself has led her to showing others that they, too, can reach their goal.

Another person like this was one of the most unforgettable characters I've known. He continually lived outside of himself. He was the late Hugh M. Tilroe, a dean on the faculty of Syracuse University. He was a big man physically and big as well in his compassion for others. He was so eminently masculine in a sizable way that to say he was full of love seems too soft to go with his impressive personality. But he was that, even so. He was a powerful speaker, so much so that an effort was made to get him to run for Congress, but he opted to remain as a teacher of youth.

He was laid low, finally, with a stroke. I went to see him and found him lying in bed, his gigantic form broken and his speech twisted some. He managed to tell me that he was supposed to give a high school commencement talk in a Pennsylvania town. "I cannot go," he said pathetically. "I cannot hunt anymore"—and he was a great hunter—"can't fish anymore, can't speak anymore." Then recovering himself he said, "I'll lick this, I'll lick this, God help me." Then he asked me to take his place and speak at the commencement. At first I demurred, "No one can take Hugh Tilroe's place."

He half rose from his bed and put a faltering hand on mine. "Norman, you go and tell those young people that they have it in them to lick anything in life, and tell them I said so." Blinking back tears, I told him I would. Then I went out in Walnut Park, across from Professor Tilroe's house, and wept that this strong man had been felled like a big tree. And, as giant fallen trees do, he left a big empty place in the sky.

When I think of Professor Tilroe, I think of what he did for a rural preacher in a deep crisis many years before. The preacher had married a beautiful young woman whom he idolized. He saw her as perfection itself. But she had a weak streak, a fatal flaw. Others were aware of it, but to her husband she was always pure and chaste. He often told her he wasn't good enough for her, that she was sent to him by God Himself.

Then one evening he came home to find her gone. Finally he saw the note. "Dearest, I have gone away with [she named a man of unsavory reputation whom some knew she had been seeing]. You are the best man in the world, a saint. You are goodness itself. As for me, I wanted to be good but there's a devil in me. I can't stand your goodness and I must leave you. Try to forgive me. In my own poor way I love you. Helen."

The man fell into a chair, dazed and broken, head in hands. Then he rose and paced the floor desperately. He saw the telephone. With icy fingers he looked up a number in his address book and called. The strong voice of Professor Tilroe answered. The man tried to speak but broke into sobbing. Tilroe waited, saying, "I'm here." Then the preacher sobbed out his story.

Tilroe was businesslike. "Just stay there," he said. "I'm on my way. I'm coming, do you understand?" He was over fifty miles away in upstate New York; it was winter and the roads were not easy.

Two hours later Tilroe arrived and said, "Pack a bag. We're leaving." Putting the man beside him, he drove through heavy rain all the way back over the roads he had come. The minister told me that Tilroe patted him a couple of times on the knee with his big hand but said nothing, just drove, the only sound being the swish of the windshield wipers.

Finally they pulled up at Professor Tilroe's hunting and fishing lodge on Lake Onondaga. Tilroe picked up the bag, and the man followed him into the cabin. The Professor said, "Get washed up. I'll fix something to eat." Finally they sat down to bacon and eggs, toast and coffee. The minister didn't feel like eating and said so. "You eat that like a good boy," said Tilroe. And he did.

Then the big teacher picked up a well-worn Bible and read a few

verses. "Time for bed, boy," he said. The man meekly obeyed and
got into bed. Tilroe, standing by the bed, said a prayer: "Dear Lord
God, You love this poor, broken-hearted fellow. Heavenly Father
comfort him please. Amen."

"Now go to sleep, boy," he said, "I'll sit up and watch over you."
Several times during the night the grieving man waked from a
fitful sleep to see Tilroe sitting by the fire with a blanket over his
shoulders against the upstate cold. "As I saw that big, tough-look-
ing man with a big, loving heart, I understood what God is like,"
said the minister as he told me his story. And after a time he did
find healing, thanks to a man who lived for others.

Now, I put it to you. Do you for one minute imagine that Hugh
Tilroe was ever empty and disgusted with life? He was a big positive believer all his years, for he had the secret; he lived outside of
himself. He was a genuine man-sized friend of his fellow human
beings.

So a generation or two of Americans, many of whom have made
it big, are wondering how come it isn't all they expected. They've
got cash and all it can buy, but are not happy, in fact, are empty.
They complain there's something wrong somewhere and want to
find what it is. Most important and happily so, they want to know
what they can do about it.

To all who are searching for that confident feeling or for fullness of life, I say that one thing you can do is have a session with
yourself. Ask yourself some tough questions. Are you feeling sorry
for yourself? Blaming others for the situation you're in? If so,
you'll sink deeper and deeper into your own pit of despair. Get *out*
of yourself. Comfort someone who is suffering.

Too often in our workaday world we go about our business with
our attention fixed on ourselves, concerned about little things like
the supermarket shopping list, the departmental report we have to
make, the car that needs to be fixed.

In the office, at our club, we too often pass by people as if they
weren't there.

Here's a very simple experiment I'd like you to try for just one
day. Smile pleasantly at everyone you meet. Give a brief "Hello," if
called for. I guarantee that by the end of the day, you'll not only
feel a lot better, but you will have enhanced your reputation ten-
fold. I personally know one man who is the most popular person

in his office, not because he is so creative, or a producer, or a dispenser of favors. No, he's an ordinary middle-management kind of guy, but he makes it a sincere habit to smile and greet everyone he meets.

Did you know that the very physical act of smiling actually makes you feel better? And, by the same token, frowning puts you in a bad mood? As far back as the nineteenth century, psychologists, including the noted William James, claimed this. They were ridiculed for it by some of their colleagues.

Well, today scientific evidence indicates that William James and his fellow believers were right. The evidence shows that a person's facial expression *does* influence his mood. One of the modern psychologists supporting this theory is Dr. Robert Zajonc of the University of Michigan. And he's not alone in this thinking. Psychologists at Clark University in Worcester, Massachusetts, report from extensive research it is true: Smile and feel good, frown and feel glum.

Dr. Paul Ekman of the University of California Medical School explained in the journal *Science* that when people portray various emotions, their bodies produce matching physiological patterns such as changes in heart and breathing rates. The doctors talked about how frowns tighten facial muscles, with resulting reactions on the brain. Well, frankly, I can't begin to understand all the scientific terms. But I do understand that when you *act* happy, you'll *feel* happy. And vice versa.

In other words, when you're feeling glum, get *out* of yourself. I met a New York City bus driver who proved this for me. Now, big-city bus drivers are usually not the most cheerful people in the world. I suppose if I had to wrangle a behemoth around city streets like they do I wouldn't be too happy about it either. But one rainy, dismal morning as I stepped onto a Third Avenue bus with a crowd of wet, grumbling people, a cheery voice welcomed us, "Good morning, happy people!" I looked up and almost fell backward in astonishment. It was the bus driver.

This man exuded joy. He smiled at us, called out street intersections, and reminded passengers to watch out for puddles.

A genial mood filled the wet, steamy bus; sullen-looking folks began smiling; tense-looking people relaxed. As I prepared to get off at my stop, I complimented the driver on his good humor.

He flashed a big grin. "Well, mister, when I start my day, I know I can choose to be happy or be blue. And some days, like today, there don't seem nothing to feel good about. But when I act happy, my body catches up and I feel happy."

Yes, I thought, as he closed the door and his bus rumbled away, there's a happy man who has really got out of himself.

Good things do happen when you get out of yourself, despite those days when, as the bus driver said, "There don't seem nothing to feel good about."

There are times, I admit, when I find it difficult to get out of myself. I'll never forget the day I boarded an airplane at La Guardia bound for O'Hare in Chicago. I still can't believe this whole episode actually happened. But it's absolutely true. I sat down and soon a young fellow, whom I judged to be in his early twenties, flopped down in the seat beside me. He was what we older folks called a "hippie": long scraggly hair, jeans that hadn't seen a washing machine in months, and a raggedy jacket festooned with strange symbols. I found myself edging away from him, and when he flung open a newspaper I was grateful he didn't want to talk. But after the plane took off, he suddenly crumpled the newspaper and flung it to the floor. "G——— d——— lousy world!" he snarled loudly.

Well, when someone does a thing like this, it's obvious he's seeking attention. And, in my experience, this usually means he wants help, whether he consciously realizes it or not. Frankly, I was in no mood to talk with him. But I knew I had to get out of myself.

It happened to be a beautiful day, bright blue sky with a few floaty cumulus clouds and golden sunshine. I indicated all this with my thumb. "Not all that bad," I commented. The young man only glared and sullenly stared ahead. Good, I thought to myself, I did my part.

But I wasn't to escape that easily.

He turned back to me. "Mister, you and others like you are so far out of it, you don't know the time of day."

I glanced at my watch and said, "It's two twenty-five."

He ignored my pleasantry and, obviously noting my old-fashioned haircut, pressed on. "I mean you're all like sheep, dressed like each other, wear the same clothes, believe what the government tells you . . . That's why the world is in such a mess today. Besides," he asked, "why do you wear your hair so short?"

"Because I am a rebel," I snapped. "Nobody is going to tell me how to cut my hair. Nobody.

"Are you any different?" I pursued. "How come I've seen a thousand people like you this week, dirty jeans, long hair, spouting the same stuff, listening to the same antiestablishment leaders? You really make me laugh."

He took a deep breath, started to say something, then broke out in a laugh. "OK, OK, you got me. I guess we're even." He settled back and began to talk. Like most young people, he was quite intelligent and we really began, in his terms, "rapping." We actually had a good time.

After a while he was quiet for a moment, then asked, "Mister, are you really happy or are you putting on an act, like most folks seem to do these days?"

"Yes," I said, "I'm happy, really happy. I have had the time of my life all my life."

"So," he pressed. "So, you're happy. How do you get that way?"

I could sense a bit of disbelief, a bit of challenge in his tone. "Do you really want to know, or are you just talking?"

He settled back and said quietly, "Yes, I really want to know because you . . . you really do seem happy."

"Well, I'll tell you," I said, "but don't give me any argument. Take it or leave it. Hang on to your seat because this may rock you. But I can tell you in one word of five letters—Jesus."

I was going to tell him what Jesus meant to me, what He could do for him, but by this time our plane was rolling up to the gate at O'Hare. The young fellow put out his hand and we shook. Then to my surprise he said, "Give me your card." He stuck it in his jacket pocket and moved toward the exit. He said something in a low voice but I had sharp ears and caught it: "Who knows? Maybe I'll try that sometime."

Some years later I happened to be in Chicago's O'Hare Airport waiting to board a plane when a man introduced himself to me as a pastor from downstate Illinois.

"You meet so many people, Dr. Peale," he said, "that I'm sure you've forgotten this one; but do you recall a hippie who sat with you on a flight to O'Hare several years ago, who asked you how come you were so happy?"

"I sure do," I said, wondering how this pastor happened to connect me to that hippie. "I always regretted we didn't have more of a chance to talk. Why do you ask? Do you know the young man?"

The pastor smiled. "Yes, I know him well. He came from a churchgoing family, went on to college, and became a real rebel, repudiating his faith. He didn't even believe in himself. But something you said to him and the way you said it started a turnaround process. Now he is back into faith. Oh, he still asks questions. But I can tell you, he's happy, really happy."

By now my curiosity was really aroused and I started to speak, but the pastor continued: "*I* was that young man, Dr. Peale," he said, adding with a laugh, "and I don't blame you for not recognizing me. I admit I looked quite different then."

"But what was it I said?" I pressed.

" 'Jesus,' " he answered quietly. "Only one word: 'Jesus.' "

"You know," he continued, "in my frame of mind those days, if you had tried to give me a sermon I would have turned you off quicker than a faucet. But you took the time to be friendly, though you gave it to me straight. Then, when we were parting and I asked you what made you so happy, you answered with one word: 'Jesus.' Well, that put the ball in *my* court. Made me think back to what I had rejected. And now . . ." he smiled, "we're both in the same business."

As he hurried to catch his plane I found myself being thankful for the impulse to get out of myself that day long ago when I first met that young man.

Each of us can expect astonishing results when we

seize the opportunity to help someone else. And in

the right spirit, it makes us feel good.

CHAPTER 7

RUNNING ON EMPTY

■   ■   ■

A GROWING PROPORTION OF OUR COUNTRY'S POPU-lation has me concerned. Of course, we are always troubled about the poor and homeless. But the group I'm talking about now is called the baby boomers. These are people born between 1946 and 1964. And many of them are extra-talented. They have it made jobwise. But a lot of them say they are empty and I think that is just too bad and something should be done about it.

In an article entitled "Big Baby Boomers" and subtitled "The generation that was born to be wild now has to figure out how to be middle-aged," F. J. Kalm III calls the onetime baby boomers the "new fogies" and says they are aging, tired, and conservative.

"The new fogies," he says, "embrace security, safety, the family. They lower their hemlines, they don double-breasted suits. They try to look wealthy. And gray hair is hip."

So what's wrong with that? But wait, there's more.

Kalm quotes researcher Jan Andrew as saying, "When the baby boomers first entered the job market, everyone expected raises and everybody expected to be successful. Now they've discovered that the number of people who actually reach the prize is small."

Others who have studied the later careers of this group tell us that many have made it financially but are "empty" on the inside. These men and women are estimated to number between seventy-six and eighty million, approximately one third of our country's total population. They are Americans all, fathers and mothers, some early grandparents. What I'm particularly concerned about is this pervasive "empty feeling" that so many of them say they have. (Of course, I know some sixty- and seventy-year-olds who have the same complaint.) Here are three recent encounters I had, one woman and two men.

I met the young woman in a famous restaurant in San Francisco, where I had recently spoken before an annual sales convention. As I was finishing my meal, she came up to my table and complimented me on my talk. I could sense she had something more on her mind.

"Sit down and have a cup of coffee," I invited.

She accepted, and we talked. A woman in her early thirties, she told me about her company and her job. I was impressed.

Then, putting down her coffee cup, she looked at me seriously and said, "Dr. Peale, I'm terribly unhappy."

I wasn't surprised. After some sixty-five years of ministering to people, I can usually tell something about them. It shows in their eyes, their body movements and voice inflections.

"Tell me about it," I said.

Thereupon, she poured out the following.

"I was reared in a traditional Jewish family. Dad and Mom were wonderful, loving, upright people with a strong faith in God. But somewhere in college I lost that faith."

She looked down at her coffee cup.

"I got in with a sophisticated crowd, some of them from religious Jewish families like mine. But the classes, the professors, the bull sessions were all so negative, so cynical, so downbeat. Before long we all became turned off."

Her eyes were imploring. "But I never found anything, Dr. Peale, to take the place of that solid, satisfying feeling my faith had given me. I feel empty, just plain empty."

"Have you talked with your rabbi?" I suggested.

She gave a nervous laugh. "Oh, he wouldn't understand," she said. "He is a nice man, but he wouldn't have the foggiest idea how to help me." She sighed and sipped her coffee. "Oh, well, maybe someday this empty feeling will go away.

"You know," she continued, "it isn't just the religious thing that confuses me. It's this, well . . ." she looked away "this 'new morality.' Somehow it doesn't . . ."

She shrugged and didn't continue.

"Hmmmm," I mused, "that must have been a terrific college you attended, with an all-time superior faculty."

She looked up in surprise. "It is a good school with a fine faculty, but why do you assume it's all that great?"

"Because before college you had some really great teachers, marvelous intellects like Isaiah, Jeremiah, and Moses himself. Then to have some college professors persuade you to repudiate their teachings makes me think they were 'some faculty.'" I smiled wryly. "Did they also put down Socrates, Plato, and Aristotle?"

She laughed. "Touché. You're pretty smart yourself, getting at it that way. I must say I like you, Dr. Peale."

"Well, I return the compliment, for I like you, too," I smiled. I leaned back in my chair and looked at her seriously. "You know, I think you're much too intelligent to fall for such small minds versus the really greats."

She looked amused. "Then what are you going to say, Dr. Peale, when I tell you I went to a Christian college?"

I grinned. No wonder this young lady was head of an important department in her firm.

"Touché, too," I responded. "When Christians take a flop, as Mayor La Guardia used to say, 'it's a beaut.' Tell you what," I continued, "go home and read Genesis, Isaiah, Jeremiah, Ezekiel, the Proverbs, and the Psalms."

She wrote these names down on a notepad retrieved from her purse.

"I guarantee that those books will turn you back on again," I said, "but there's something more you must do . . . more than just reading them."

She looked up questioningly.

"*Believe* what you read," I emphasized. "Remember, those teachings have sustained Jews, Christians, and others whose faith is based in part on Old Testament writings, for thousands and thousands of years. If they weren't true, they would not have stood that test of time.

"And take another suggestion as sound advice from a Christian minister, young lady," I added. She looked up while putting her notepad back in her purse. I leaned forward and said, "Start loving your rabbi. I'm sure he's OK."

She smiled, picked up her purse, and stood to leave. "I must admit I feel better already, Dr. Peale. But . . ." a frown crossed her brow "I'm still confused. I'll have to do some thinking."

"Do plenty of that," I agreed. "The more real thinking, the more reading you do of those eternal truths written by some of the greatest psychologists and thinkers of all time, the more quickly you'll regain that solid, satisfying self-confidence and faith." I stood and shook hands with her. "I'll also send in your direction some good positive Protestant prayers asking that you find peace and happiness. You know," I said as we shook hands good-bye, "it's out there, waiting for you to simply accept and *believe.*"

Sometime later I received a note from her on her firm's stationery. "I did what you advised, Dr. Peale, and I'm working my way back." Then she added, "I told my rabbi about your advice and you'll never guess what he said: 'That man would have made a good rabbi.'"

Quite a compliment, I thought. When I asked her permission to use this incident in this book, she agreed, but asked that her name not be used, for personal reasons.

Weeks after this experience I was in Las Vegas to speak at a national business convention when I met another baby boomer. After my talk I was shaking hands with many of the attendees when a youngish-looking couple greeted me. They seemed quite charming. The husband took me aside, put his hand affectionately on my shoulder, and said, "You seem like an old friend, Dr. Peale. I read your book *The Power of Positive Thinking* when I was a young boy and really went for it. I had all kinds of enthusiasm and faith.

"But I've got to admit something." He hesitated, then added, "Our minister started criticizing you. He said your writing wasn't theologically sound, that we should not be misled by it. Your books, he said, were only success books, how to make big money, how to lift yourself by your own bootstraps kind of thing. Well, I listened to him and stopped reading your books."

He shook his head. "Maybe I was dumb in doing that. But somewhere along the way I've lost that enthusiasm I had as a kid. I don't have faith or self-confidence anymore, at least not the kind you talked about."

He looked at me helplessly. "Maybe it's simply the world, Dr. Peale. With all the crime, the shenanigans on Wall Street, the crazy things going on in the Middle East and Central America, maybe my old minister was right in saying you can't look at the world through rose-colored glasses.

"I have a good job in a large city, but I know it's a dog-eat-dog world, Dr. Peale. I guess you could say I feel negative about everything. Really, I have nothing much to live for except Phyllis here," he said, indicating his wife. "She's a wonderful person, a positive thinker, and a real Christian, but, let's face it, I'm empty. I don't think there's *anything* one can really believe in anymore."

My heart went out to this young man. He actually *looked* empty.

"Why not go back to your hometown pastor and tell him how empty you feel," I suggested. "I'm sure he's an understanding man. He'll help you."

The man shook his head. "How could I? He's the one who threw cold water on all that enthusiasm I had as a kid."

"Oh, I'm sure he didn't mean to do that," I countered.

"Perhaps he thought he was protecting your faith. Maybe he lacked understanding. But give him a break. All of us at one time or another probably have steered someone the wrong way.

"You are aware," I continued, "that Jesus Christ was the most positive thinker this world has ever seen. His teachings—such as asking God for help and *believing* you'll receive it, turning the other cheek, forgiving your enemies, and letting Him take over your worries—run so counter to this world's way of thinking that we humans find them hard to believe. So don't blame your old minister too much."

And now I put my hand on *his* shoulder. "At any rate, my friend, you'll never find peace with that resentment in your mind."

Then I remembered what I told the young Jewish lady about reading the Bible.

"Just don't let one man call the shots for you. Read the great writers of the Old Testament; then study Matthew, Mark, Luke, and John, and don't skip St. Paul either. I believe all of that will help you get back on the right track."

He promised he would, and I believe he did get back on track.

He now seems to be a believer in life and values. For when you compare the ageless truths of the great saints with the superficial thinking of "get mine" and "do unto others *before* they do unto you" in vogue today, the difference is what you might call impressive.

It wasn't long after I met this young man that I happened on a report in the esteemed *Journal of the American Medical Association*. It caught my eye because it was about baby boomers. Both the young woman in San Francisco and the young man in Las Vegas fit in this category.

According to the report, Dr. Gerald Kierman, of Cornell University Medical College in New York, and a colleague reviewed studies over the past five years of forty thousand people in ten major countries. It showed that baby boomers were four to five times more likely to be depressed than those born earlier or later.

This was true in industrialized countries such as the United States, Sweden, Germany, and Canada. Dr. Kierman believed this was because in such urban areas, close-knit family ties, a key source of social support, tend to be weaker. "You might say that depression is part of the price we pay for urbanization," he said.

I thought of the young Jewish woman and Christian man who, though rising rapidly to the top in their professions, had lost their basic faith. I continued praying that both would find the basic belief that so strongly anchored generations of their families before them.

After reading that American Medical Association report, I wasn't really surprised by the attitude of the third person I met. For he was another baby boomer, a thirty-two-year-old executive of a Hollywood film company. He had come to New York to supervise the filming of episodes in my book *The Power of Positive Thinking* for a VCR tape for home, business, church, and school use.

I must admit I was a bit shocked when in our first interview he said, "Now, I prefer that we not use the word 'God' in this tape; let's substitute the word 'good.'"

When I demurred, he explained. "I'm from a strong Protestant family. Indeed, my grandfather was a minister. But frankly, I'm turned off by that God stuff. So let's not burden the viewers with something I find hard to believe."

After a lifetime of preaching on His behalf, I wasn't about to let someone substitute a simple adjective for the name of God. And we went ahead with the filming on that basis.

Well, as a good professional will do, this man took the time to study our activities and find out what historical concepts and current thinking he was working with. In time, our faith got to him and this self-confessed "turned off" person became very turned on.

In his enthusiasm, he discovered some studies by public-school educators who found that practically all children are positive-minded with a healthy sense of self-esteem when they enter kindergarten. But when they finish the fourth grade, 80 to 85 percent of these same children have become negative-minded and lost their self-esteem.

The reason? In those five years the world "gets to them." The children, beaten down by harsh negativism, hurt by forced competition, cut by unfair comparisons, have been crushed. The educators also feel that teenagers who succumb to sex, drugs, alcohol, absenteeism, violence, and suicide are not "bad" kids but are trying to compensate for a low self-esteem.

Accordingly, this spiritually rejuvenated Hollywood film man persuaded the governor of West Virginia and his superintendent of education to adopt a positive-thinking program into kindergarten and the first four grades of their state's elementary schools.

It has been so successful in building healthy self-esteem among those children that the program has also been adopted by the elementary schools of Kentucky and is planned for many other states.

As a result, this brilliant young man, Mark Lambert, formerly a self-confessed "turned off," has become very turned on.

It's because of him and others like him that I am writing this book. I cannot keep from liking people and believing in their immense possibilities. Unfortunately, many are so terribly unhappy. I know this too well because they write to me. And these sad letters come by the hundreds from people of all ages. Obviously, many are good thinkers, and in some cases, I've had to agree that being turned off by certain circumstances was a valid reaction. The trouble is that most such people have not found a replacement for their lost faith or belief when they became turned off.

Many have "made it" materially but still are unhappy because they are "disappointed," "dissatisfied," and "empty." Some add: "How can there be a good God, or even *any* God?"

A large number of these people hold diplomas from top universities. They have been adjudged educated thinkers, philosophers, upcoming business geniuses. And yet they are discontented, unhappy. And this in the United States of America, the greatest country in the world, with the finest governmental and economic system known. Yet in this land of opportunity, all some can come up with is, "Oh, what the hell!"

When I expostulated on this to a learned acquaintance, he shook his head. "Norman, the world is going to pot in a handbasket and there's nothing anyone can do about it, much less you or I."

Well, I react to this kind of statement like a bull to a red flag. Yet *who* am I to be thinking *I* can do anything about it? What qualifies *me?*

For starters I've lived in this wonderful country now for ninety-two years. Born in a beautiful little southern Ohio village, growing up in Cincinnati, and living for over sixty years in New York City, I've had close relationships with all sorts of Americans. I think they are the greatest. And I dislike hearing any of them talk defeatism.

There are those who have been church members all their lives, who have been successful in business, and who devote themselves to charitable and other good works, yet still feel "empty." What about them?

Such a person was Jack Eckerd of Clearwater, Florida, who founded one of the nation's most successful drugstore chains. In 1982, some twelve hundred Eckerd drugstores were serving families in fifteen states. Jack was a tough cookie who had built his business with guts and determination.

On top of this, he had distinguished himself in good works. In 1968, the Jack and Ruth Eckerd Foundation began a therapeutic wilderness/camping program for children with emotional problems. The foundation also ran a youth training school. Jack chaired a successful prisoner industries rehabilitation program. He had headed the General Services Administration under President Ford and was successful in Florida politics. Besides, the National Conference of Christians and Jews had named him an "Outstanding Citizen."

Then why did a voice within Jack seem to keep on asking: *With all that you have and all you've accomplished, why then the empty feeling, Jack?*

"I tried to brush away the thought," he relates. "It had been haunting me for the past several years—an emptiness, a void that success and giving of myself had never filled."

Jack had been a longtime church member. "I didn't really participate," he says. "I'd sit in church planning a store for a new location I'd looked at last week. I was in the water, but I wasn't swimming."

Then Jack was invited to a Bible study meeting one of his neighbors had, but he went more out of curiosity. "For some reason, the whole thing irritated me, especially those cars clogging up the driveways," he confessed. "Who were those men, anyway, I wondered. Probably a bunch of kooks."

However, Jack was intrigued at the Bible study meeting. "Along with the Bible reading, the men did a lot of talking about personal problems," he said. "As we discussed a Scripture lesson, the men would often tell how it directly related to a difficulty they were facing. Their openness surprised me.

"It was the reverse of my world, in which many of us put up a hard front," he continued. "We did not dare let the other guy know our real feelings, figuring he'd take advantage of us. But these men were honest and frank. It did something to me. Little by little, I found myself opening up, too. And when we all held hands and prayed together, I experienced a companionship I'd never felt before.

"Then one morning we were studying First Corinthians, chapter 13, verse 3: 'If I give all I possess to the poor and surrender my body to the flames, but have not love, I gain nothing.' I had read these words before, but now they hit me. They told me that it didn't matter how much I helped needy children, worked for prison reform, or served my country; if I didn't have love, none of it meant anything," he said.

"It made me take a close look at myself. I began to see a man who was inclined to keep a wall around himself. But that verse had opened a chink in the wall. And as we continued studying, the chink became larger. For it became more and more apparent that if I was going to achieve the wholeness I sought, I would have to have that love St. Paul was talking about. And to get it I would have to turn myself over to Jesus. That was a tough decision. It wasn't easy for someone who'd been a fighter all of his life to become a submitter, and tougher still to switch from decision-making to following.

"While brooding about it, I met Chuck Colson, who heads Prison Fellowship ministries. I liked him immediately, so I didn't resent it when, a year later, he said, 'I can't understand you business executives who are used to making major decisions. Then along comes the most important decision you will ever make, and you equivocate. You sit on the fence. What's the problem, Jack?' "

Jack Eckerd said it all "boiled down to my continuing to call the shots and living with that empty feeling, or getting out of the way and letting Jesus take over.

"I gave up. He wouldn't let me off the hook. Lightning didn't strike. The earth did not shake. I didn't experience anything as dramatic as Paul did on the road to Damascus, but I did begin to sense a deep peace I'd never had before, and that old, empty place, like a dry well within me, slowly began to fill."

From then on, Jack Eckerd's life became even more exciting. He found himself having a new empathy and compassion for others, which was reflected by his growing work in prison reform and drug treatment and educational programs. He was instrumental in removing obscene magazines from Eckerd drugstores and became even more active in his foundation and other charitable works.

"That old phrase *born again* is no misnomer," he says. "I feel like a new man, with a new vitality and zest for living that has made each day even more exciting. Now I'm seventy-seven, but each year gets better. That's not to say I don't have problems and a few aches. Of course I do. But He gives me the strength to face them."

In his book *The Greatest Risk of All* Walter Anderson, editor of *Parade* magazine, makes this significant statement:

"Be assured, it's not possible for human beings to be empty vessels. No person who has ever lived has been an unbeliever, despite what they may argue. Everyone believes in something. It might be God or not God, manifest greed for money or power, a career or a friend, science, a principle—*something*. Whatever it is we place before our lives is what we turn toward.

A story told to me by a friend, Father Joseph Kelly, might be useful here. It's about a young priest who began to doubt his vocation.

"One afternoon in the dead of winter, he passed a small boy—homeless, skinny, his jacket threadbare, his tiny body huddled over a street grate as he tried to absorb the heat from the subway tunnel below.

" 'God!' the priest exclaimed, his frustration at a boil. He looked back at the shivering child. 'God,' he demanded, 'why do you allow this? Why don't you do something about it? Don't you give a damn?'

"In his mind, to his astonishment, he heard for the first time what he knew was the voice of his Lord:

" 'I do care,' he was told, 'and I have done something about it. I created *you.* '

"*Choose* what you believe.

"We need to remember that the wise God put us here to help that suffering child. We are His hands, His feet, His voice. And we can choose to believe this or not. There is no such thing as unbelief. For we all believe in something. Either we believe in love, virtue, and hope. Or we believe in hate, evil, and hopelessness."

Happy people, and I think they are smart, too, choose love, virtue, and hope. And I have had more than a little experience with both kinds of people in my many years in New York City. I was there practicing my profession during the Great Depression, World War II, the turbulent sixties, the Vietnam War, indeed, most of the disturbing events of our twentieth century.

And it seems like I've run into a lot of baby boomers, ex-hippies, and yuppies in recent years. Take Ben, for example. He was always at church, he with his long hair and bushy beard, jeans and sneakers. He did condescend to wear a jacket to church, but I never did see him with a necktie. Probably he never learned to tie one. He was a likable character, engaging. But he had the tendency to become a pain in the neck because of his incessant questioning. "You said this morning . . ." and then he wanted to know what was meant and how come, et cetera.

But since I've always admired an active mind and admired real thinkers, I patiently tried to answer Ben's questions. Obviously, he was trying to learn, but my answers led to more questions, and Ben became, let us say, somewhat trying.

His questions related largely to himself, to his life. He was concerned about bettering himself and getting along successfully in the world. I figured that here was a creative student of the five things necessary to a better life: *think, learn, try, work, and believe.* But even so, I almost hated to see Ben coming.

One day I had to drive to Allentown, Pennsylvania, where I was scheduled for a speech before a central Pennsylvania sales rally. About 2 P.M. I left my office to get into my car to drive to Allentown, figuring I would think through and finalize my speech on the way. I am an ad lib speaker and don't fuss with notes. As I slid behind the wheel I heard a familiar voice call out, "Hey, Doc, wait a minute." You guessed: It was Ben, who, sticking his head in the car, asked where I was going.

Then, uninvited, he opened the door and plunked down beside me. "Mind if I go along?" he asked blithely. "We can have a good talk."

I wasn't what you might call enthusiastic but said, "OK, Ben, but here are the ground rules and you must promise to observe them. I've got to think about my speech en route and it's only about one hundred miles. If you will keep still on the way there, I'll talk on the way home."

"Sure thing," he agreed.

I must say he did pretty well. A couple of times he started to speak, but I put my finger to my lips and he subsided. But when, after the meeting, we started back to New York, he began talking and it was again mostly questions about how could he really get somewhere in life. He wondered about his slow progress. "I've read all your books and still I get practically nowhere." So we talked as we drove through the moonlit night.

Finally, we approached an attractive roadside restaurant, and I said, "Ben, I'm starved and you must be, too. How about stopping here for a hamburger and french fries and a big slab of apple pie?"

"À la mode," he said with alacrity. Soon we were sitting at the counter, with Ben still thinking and talking—and learning, as it subsequently turned out.

Suddenly Ben brought his fist down in an enormous blow on the counter, making the dishes jump and clatter, and he yelled out,

"I've got it, I've got it!" Other diners were startled and looked our way, and I exclaimed, "You've got what?"

"I've got the answer!" he exclaimed. "The reason I don't get ahead is me, myself."

"Boy," I said, "I never knew there was such power in a hamburger."

Afterward in the parking lot, standing by the car that moonlit night somewhere in New Jersey, Ben said in a new voice for him, "Norman [and he had never called me by my first name before, only 'Doc'] I want to commit myself to God. I want to follow Jesus. Bless me now will you, please?"

I was deeply touched by his sincerity. He bowed his head and I put my hand upon it and said, "Dear God, receive my friend Ben into a new life with You by his side. Give Ben peace and joy and guide and strengthen him every day, always. In the name of our Lord and Saviour Jesus Christ. Amen."

Ben shook my hand with a firm grip, then said, "I'll never forget this."

As we drove home I realized that something momentous had happened to him. I don't know how or why. It must have been a combination of things, including our talks and arguments and his fighting the acceptance of help. But in that moment of time his questioning was answered. He became a real believer, not only in God but in himself also. Subsequently, he worked at his job as never before, utilized latent skills he had never really put to use, and went on to a power-filled life. Ben's long held emptiness was filled. He was joyful and excited. He had reverses and sorrows, to be sure, but he was now an overcomer. He married and his company transferred him miles away as a manager of their office in a large city. So he passed out of my life, but not out of my memory.

He was a man who used the five principles to gain a successful life. The same five creative principles can be employed to achieve good results in every phase of our total experience.

But remember that these principles must rest on a solid foundation of faith in God. This, of course, is the meaning of the fifth principle. For without this assurance, the other four principles become empty in themselves.

- ▶ Think

- ▶ Learn

- ▶ Try

- ▶ Work

- ▶ Believe

And be a success in life!

CHAPTER 8

TURNED ON TO A JOY-PACKED LIFESTYLE

■   ■   ■

I WANT TO REACH MORE SELF-CONFESSED "EMPTY" people and help them find the joy of successful living. In this respect, I happen to be a firm believer in the greatest Scientist of all on the full and triumphant life, Who succinctly explained His mission in the world as follows: "I am come that they might have life and that they might have it more abundantly" or "in all its fullness" (John 10:10). And fullness is, of course, the opposite of emptiness. I have found personally that following the great Genius and the way of living He taught fills up all possible inner empty places. And He fills them with joy and excitement, immeasurably increasing the ability to get things done and done with excellence.

Let me relate a most remarkable experience in which this pervasive emptiness was filled.

It was a cold and bleak winter day in December just shortly before Christmas. Darkness had fallen early, as it does at that time of year. We were preparing to close our offices on Twenty-ninth Street in Manhattan when my secretary came in and said, "There's a man in the outer office who seems under great stress and demands to see you. And," she added, "he is rather elegantly dressed, but I confess I am a bit afraid of him. He seems sort of, well, tense. Shall I tell him you can't be disturbed?"

When you are in the business of trying to help all kinds of people, especially in New York City, you must be prepared for just about anything, but fear isn't a good reaction at any time. "Bring him in," I said. And, as a result, I had one of the most extraordinary experiences of my counseling career.

This man did have a sort of wild gleam in his eyes. "Look," he said, "I heard your speech to the National Realtors Convention at the New York Hilton today and I said to myself, 'Even if he is a minister, he seems like a levelheaded, commonsense guy and wouldn't give me a lot of that God and Jesus stuff.'"

With this as an opener, he proceeded to tell me he was an alcoholic "and I am fed up to my ear with myself." He admitted to being a rebel in the sixties and later made a fortune in real estate. "But what did it get me?" he asked, confessing that though he had most of the things he wanted that money could buy, he felt "empty on the inside." After he poured out quite a tale of woe, I said, "You sure have built up a lot of negatives in your young life. You can't be a day over thirty."

"Thirty-two, and I'm a flop. I've spent my life getting nowhere but making money and failing at everything else. I'm empty, I tell you. You seem to have answers. Do something for me, for God's sake."

"OK. But I'm no wonder worker, far from it," I assured him. "And I haven't the know-how to help you, I'm sorry to say; but I know Who can and will. He is somebody you obviously don't like."

"Who?" he demanded.

"God. Ask Him to help you. He knows you through and through; He loves you and can make things better for you by making you better."

He jumped to his feet. "So you're just like all the rest of the religious fanatics. I hoped something better from you, but all you can come up with is this God and Jesus stuff." So saying, he stomped out without so much as a good-bye. All I could do was to send a prayer after him.

About a half hour later my secretary put her head in the door. "He's back and even more upset."

"Who's back?" I inquired.

"That man who went out angry."

When he came in he paced up and down. "What I want to know is, am I going nuts? Am I off my rocker? Tell me!"

I got him to sit down and tell me what happened, and he related the following almost incredible story, especially coming from a seemingly hard-boiled, sophisticated New Yorker. After leaving my office he had blindly turned west on Twenty-ninth Street, crossing Broadway and then Sixth Avenue, stamping along muttering angrily to himself, "God, God, Jesus, Jesus. That's all they know, that's all they have to say—nothing but God, God, God—oh, God." Then something happened. Though it was dark, suddenly the street between Sixth and Seventh avenues seemed full of light. The people passing had faces that were lighted up and appeared to be very beautiful. Then the sidewalk began "undulating," moving up and down. And light was over everything, "a kind of unearthly light."

He leaned forward in his chair, his face filled with something like awe. "What happened to me? I feel sort of peaceful and—and —clean. What happened to me out there and why?"

"I don't know," I said. "I honestly don't know." I hesitated to tell him what I thought for fear of again turning him off. "I can only say I read a book once. I forget the title and who wrote it, but it was about mystical experiences."

"What's a mystical experience?"

"Again, I don't exactly know, except that it's, I guess, something extrasensory, out of this world, or seeming to be. I can't speak much from experience," I continued, "but when my mother, who lived in a small town upstate, died suddenly, I was standing by that desk over there in shock, resting my hands on the Bible, and I felt distinctly two soft hands cupped on my head.

"But I would say you have had an experience with Someone you seem to dislike, named God. It may be that even if you don't like Him, He loves you and has revealed Himself in this unusual manner."

"But I didn't hear any voice," he said, "just light and beauty and power pushing me up in the undulation of that sidewalk. Did a miracle happen to me? If so, why me?"

"I don't know. Seems unlikely, doesn't it? But God often goes for unlikely people. I think God wants you."

"Do you mean I'm going to die?"

"Not necessarily; maybe He wants you to live, really live His way—full of joy."

He grasped my hand. "Thank you, oh, thank you, Norman," he said fervently.

"But I didn't do anything, nothing at all," I protested.

"But you were kind to me, and I know I was boorish, yet you were kind to me."

"All I did was to send a prayer after you."

What was the subsequent story of this man whom I only knew briefly thereafter? One thing was unforgettable. A confirmed alcoholic, he was completely relieved of this disease, never even had the desire again.

He became kindly, outgoing, and was an insatiable human helper, excited and enthusiastic about life. He was filled to overflowing with joy. People loved him. Then one night when he was forty-seven years old he suddenly died. From what I understand, he was happy right up to the end.

Some may say it was such a short life. But to that I say, it's not always the number of one's years, but the quality that counts. And after this experience his remaining years were exuberant, happy, vibrant. One thing is for sure, I will never forget him. He surely did have his emptiness filled. I've never had quite that same type of experience with anyone else. But less dramatic cases have resulted in empty feelings giving way to a remarkable fullness of life.

I cite this unusual experience not to suggest that your emptiness necessarily can be filled in this superdramatic manner. The Creator, Who made everything that scientists have ever discovered, as well as the wonders yet to be found, does not use seemingly "miraculous" methods very often. He seems to expect us to utilize that miracle thing called the mind He has built into all of us, the power of thought.

To think our way out of failure, adversity, and negativism, and then to fill our empty personalities with the joy and excitement and wonder of life itself might be called a miracle, considering the extent of change it involves.

Attesting to this is one of the many letters I treasure; it came from Vito A. Celender, who is in the beauty-supplies business in Pittsburgh.

Dear Doctor Peale:

Years ago in a hotel in Johnstown, Pennsylvania, I was planning out a sales call on a client the next day. I was, to say the least, apprehensive since this was my first call.

It was in the mid seventies, and I was just coming out of the so-called hippie era or whatever era that was. Anyway, I had with me a copy of PLUS, *your positive-thinking magazine, which turned me around. It told me and made me believe that if God is for me, who could be against me? Even today I think of that when I need to get ready for a sales presentation or to teach my children to have confidence for a special occasion.*

So what I'm trying to say is Thank You! Dr. Peale, you made a giant difference in my life and now, I hope, my children's lives as well. I've wanted to write you this note 1,000 times.

Again thanks.

                                                        Vito

One of my greatest satisfactions is receiving letters like this. And there are thousands, each one truly stimulating. And each shows a life turned around, a person suffering from despair who has found joy and traded his emptiness for a rich, fulfilled life.

I was once a guest on a radio talk show in San Francisco. I don't like talk shows, because you never know what kind of questions you're going to get and you never know what kind of an answer you're going to give. On this show, a man came on and asked, "Dr. Peale, is that you?"

"Yes, sir, that's right."

"You're sure it's you?"

"As far as I know it's me."

"You always talk about positive thinking, don't you?"

"Not always."

"Well," he continued, "I don't buy that positive thinking stuff! I have a problem you can't get around. You might as well fold up on this because you can't handle it."

I replied, "If that is the case, why go further with it?"

"But I want to get an answer. Here is the question: I'm fifty-two years of age and out of a job. You know yourself that no man fifty-two years old can get a job. Furthermore, I don't have any brains. I haven't had any good experience. I haven't had any education and nobody likes me. What are you going to tell me to do about that?"

I then asked, "How do you know you haven't any brains?"

"When I was a young child, I was told I didn't have any brains. The brains in the family all went to my brother."

"Who told you that?"

"My brother."

"But you sound to me like you have brains."

Then I continued, "Are you telling me that no one fifty-two can get a job? I hired a man last week who is fifty-nine years old. The trouble is, you're overwhelmed. If you get underwhelmed, I know you can get a job." Then I took another angle: "Who did you say doesn't like you?"

"Nobody likes me."

"You're off base on that one, for I like you. Do you like yourself?"

"I never thought about that."

"If you will get to liking yourself, you will realize that you have what it takes to get a job and do a great job." Then I added, "You must love your neighbor as yourself. But you can't love your neighbor until you love yourself."

Finally, he asked, "Will you pray for me?"

"Now you're talking! Of course, I'll pray for you, and you pray for yourself."

Then he asked, "Is that positive thinking?"

"No, that's faith in yourself and faith in a good God, but it certainly isn't *negative* thinking."

About six weeks later, I had a note from this man saying he had a job. He said, "It isn't much of a job but, believe me, by the time I get through with it, I'll make a terrific job out of it!"

That's the way to think and talk! Take what you can get, and do the best you can with it. Work at it until it becomes something great. There are negative-talking, miserable, defeated, unhappy, discouraged people everywhere. It isn't necessary to be that way, either about yourself or about your country or about the time in which you live. So say to yourself and to your husband or wife, "You know something, honey, from now on I am underwhelmed."

Of course, you may shake him or her up for a while, but he or she will get used to it. *Underwhelmed* is the word.

Once you become underwhelmed, get excited about life. If you are not excited, you can get excited. And how? The answer is: Act as if you are excited. This is one of the greatest psychological principles ever enunciated. So if you're full of fear and you want to be full of courage instead, you must act as if you do have courage, and, in due course, you will be courageous.

Interestingly, there are many people leading empty lives who are satisfied with the ordinary. Unfortunately, not until their later years, sometimes too late, do they realize what they are missing.

I know of one such man who, in his earlier years, did not realize how empty his life was until he had a fortunate confrontation aboard a ship. His name is Peter Grace. Chief executive officer of W.R. Grace & Co., a worldwide corporation, he is a businessman, a philanthropist, and has served three U.S. Presidents in advisory capacities, most recently as chairman of the President's Private Sector Survey on Cost Control, also known as the Grace Commission.

But as Peter Grace tells his story, he, as a young man, was in no way interested in serving others in the business world. For after graduating from Yale, he looked forward to many years of fun in athletics. He had devoted himself to becoming a hockey goalie, to captaining a prize-winning polo team, and to becoming a winning golfer.

However, his discerning father challenged him to take a job with one of the firm's South American operations in Peru. Peter prayed to God for guidance and the answer he got was "Go." He didn't want to hear it, but one cold November day in 1938 he found himself on the deck on an ocean liner leaving New York harbor for South America.

"I was utterly miserable," he says. "I felt as low as the ice floes in the turgid waters around the pier pilings." Not only was he leaving a life of fun and games, but at the last minute one of his best friends, who was to accompany him, couldn't make the trip.

As the ship's whistle boomed a farewell and its bow headed into the gray Atlantic, a hand clasped Peter Grace's shoulder.

"I turned to look into the smiling face of a priest," he said.

"Curly white hair framed cherubic cheeks, pink in the ocean wind."

"Aren't you Peter Grace?" the priest asked in a warm, friendly voice.

Peter answered yes, hesitantly. And the priest introduced himself as Father O'Hara, who at the time was president of the University of Notre Dame. Soon the two were in conversation, and the priest, sensing Peter Grace's troubled mood, asked if he could dine with him the rest of the voyage.

"The first meal was the beginning of another kind of voyage for me," says Peter Grace. "I had never met anyone like Father John O'Hara."

The priest's father had been a U.S. consulate officer, and Father O'Hara had grown up in South America, knew the language, and related the rich history behind each port where their ship stopped.

"But my thoughts seemed to interest him most," says Peter, "and we talked long past dessert. I confessed my resentment at giving up an exciting life for what seemed to be a drab responsibility."

The priest shared something of himself, too. He told how often accepting new responsibilities was difficult, adding, "God knows what's best for us, son, much more than we do."

Without Peter really realizing it, the priest began lifting his sights to a higher horizon, and Peter began to see life in a new way. "I came to see the ship as a world of its own," he said. "Once, members of the ship's crew had been only dim background figures, but now I began to see them differently. Each of them had a job to do, and I was able to appreciate their contribution to the functioning of our little world."

Peter saw that without such men and women as the dining stewards, the engine-room wipers, the navigators, and the purser, all diligently filling their own particular responsibilities day in and day out, their ship would never reach its destination. And he began to think about what sort of contribution he had been making to his world.

"A Bible story came back to me," he says, "the parable about the three men whose master gave them talents to invest. The first two multiplied theirs and were commended, but the third buried his and was punished. I used to think the third man was fearful of losing what was entrusted to him, but now my talks with Father

O'Hara had given me a new perspective. The third man wasn't afraid; he simply didn't want the responsibility.

"That was it, I realized. It was about time I assumed my own responsibility.

"That was Father O'Hara's gift to me—helping me to see my place in a world where people had to depend on one another. Now I knew that no matter what I faced in my new job in Peru, or whatever contribution I could eventually make to our world, it would be a lot more fulfilling than the life of fun and games I had left back in New York."

Yes, Peter had learned how to turn an empty life, albeit one quite attractive to him at the time, into a rich, fulfilled life of serving others. In heading W.R. Grace, Peter has been challenged by some tough situations. And he'll be the first to tell you that putting one's self on the line for the greater good can be difficult. But everything worth accomplishing is tough and requires will, purpose, goals, stumbling, falling, picking oneself up, and resolutely going forward again despite all setbacks. But Peter Grace will tell you that the rewards of joy and satisfaction are well worth it.

I have been visited by many people describing themselves as "turned off and empty." Sometimes they come to argue and debate, but more often to seek help.

Some have been outright hostile. I remember one case in particular. While I was shaking hands with people following a meeting, a young man refused my welcoming hand.

"When can I talk with you privately?" he demanded. "Or, I suppose," he smirked, "you're all booked up."

He was what I call an emergency case.

"How about right now?" I shot back. Leaving the folks waiting to greet me, I took his arm and led him to my office. He said his name was Jim. I offered him a chair, but he angrily paced back and forth in front of my desk, ventilating his gripes against the church.

"I came from upstate as you did," he barked, "and I've heard all the hogwash you ministers hand out. And I'm telling you"—he pointed to his neck—"I'm fed up to here! It's the same old stuff and

you're worse than those guys upstate because you spout this positive thinking stuff."

"You live here in the city?" I asked quietly.

"Yes, I work downtown."

"What do you do?"

He looked at me out of the corner of his eye. "Oh, I have a good
job." He laughed sarcastically. "Why do you ask? Looking for a
contribution? Well, I have nothing for the church. It's never helped
me."

As we talked, others tried to get into my office, and I could see
my secretary fluttering about. But I felt it best to let this young
man talk. Finally, he noticed it. "Hey," he said, "how come you're
giving me all this time?"

"Well," I replied, "maybe you don't realize it, but this institution
called a church is also a hospital for the mixed-up and screwed up
and you seem to be one of the most interesting specimens afflicted
with this spiritual and mental disease I've seen lately. I want to
give you plenty of time to spew it all out so I can learn better as a
mental-spiritual doctor how to treat your kind of trouble which,
I'm afraid, can be terminal."

"So I'm just a cadaver to you," he scowled.

I tried not to smile. "You've even got your terms mixed up. A
cadaver can't talk. All his hate has died with him. Oh no, my
friend, you're no cadaver. You are a live patient that I'd like to take
on. But you don't seem to like me, and when you engage a doctor
you've got to like him if he's going to do you any good."

"OK, if you're so smart, what's my trouble?"

It was the breakthrough I'd hoped for.

"Just off the cuff, I'd say 'failure to use a good sharp mind.'"

That stopped him for a moment; then, seizing another tack, he
shot back, "What about all that sin stuff?"

"We're all sinners, my friend, but more to the point right now is
that the only sin I see in you is with a good mind you act like a
dummy. In my opinion, some of the worst sins are hate, resentment, and hostility. And judging from your attitude, you must
have enormous guilt feelings."

He stopped his pacing and looked at me.

"I respect, even admire your mind," I continued, "but if you've
come here to a church which you try to make me think you loathe,

and expect me to do something for you, forget it. I'm not the one you need."

He stared at me, his mouth open. "You, a big-shot minister with all the know-how and yet you say you can't help me. Then who can?"

"Well, though I know it sounds simplistic and your tendency will be to fight my suggestion, I can refer you to someone who can turn you back on," I said calmly. "He will take all that irritation out of your good mind and fill that empty feeling with a sense of real peace and satisfaction. But this doctor is expensive."

"Oh, don't worry about that," he interrupted.

I was silent for a moment, then said, "He wants *all* you've got. He wants you, yourself, in payment."

The young man stared at me, turned and went to the window, where he stood for a moment. Then he said softly, "You mean Jesus."

"Smart boy," I said quietly.

He turned from the window, walked to the chair before my desk, and slumped down. For a while he seemed to be looking at something a long distance away; then he faced me.

"Dr. Peale, I knew about Jesus before I came here. I used to believe in Him when I was younger. But somewhere along the way, getting through college, making it in the business world, I've lost contact with Him."

Jim didn't realize it, but at that moment, he began to come full circle from his turned-off emptiness. In our talks in succeeding weeks he became mentally and emotionally reorganized. He stopped fighting what he knew and felt was the truth. He began to find himself again. He learned that *believing* is how we become the person we are meant to be. He became a believer in life, in himself, in the present, the future, and in his relationships with others.

Jim became full of spiritual vitality as few people I've dealt with, becoming turned on to a joy-filled life.

And he still has it after a dozen years. Recently, I was in a city out West and a big husky fellow came up and gave me a hug that nearly crushed the breath out of me.

It was Jim. "Still handing out that hogwash, Rev?" he said with a broad smile. And he aimed an affectionate blow at me, which I deftly evaded.

Yes, the turned-off are being turned on. The empty are being filled. Those millions of baby boomers and others in search of something in which to believe are being rewarded in their quest. Moreover, in recent years, open-minded scientists and researchers have been conducting studies on attitudes and feelings and faith. And their thrilling conclusions prove once again that wise men like Isaiah, Jeremiah, and Moses, like Matthew, Mark, Luke, and John—like Jesus—were right, then and now.

So stop fighting the *truth* . . .

and discover untold joys.

CHAPTER 9

LET GO OF FEAR AND AFFIRM FAITH

■   ■   ■

Let me tell you of a time when fear was dominant in the United States. During the Great Depression of the thirties I was minister of a Fifth Avenue church in New York City. I think I'm safe in saying that no sadder time ever happened in the big city. People walked the streets futiley looking for work. It was a generally accepted fact that no one over thirty could get a job. Formerly affluent people lined up at soup kitchens which had been set up on what had been thought of as the best streets in town. Shops closed, factories were shut down.

Everyone lucky enough to be employed suffered several cuts in salary. The usual negative thinkers who always come out of the cracks in times of adversity went about declaring that the country was through. I attended a Rotary Club luncheon where the speaker, reputed to be one of the best financial oracles of the time, declared that "we will never again have prosperity in the United States." My respect for "oracles" has been tinged with skepticism ever since.

A pall of gloom and fear hung over the entire city. Since I always directed my talks to people and their needs, an ever increasing procession came to listen to our positive assertions that the nation *would* live, that God *was* still with us, that better days would come. People asked for private counseling in such numbers that we were hard-pressed to see them all.

I was totally unprepared to counsel people in desperate straits, being less than ten years out of theology school, where no courses had been offered in the field of psychological science. But I was lucky in doing two things right: I cared, and I listened. But still I needed help. Accordingly, I went to the general secretary of the New York County Medical Society and asked if he could refer me to a psychiatrist who was also a spiritually sensitive person. He soon introduced me to one of the greatest human beings I ever knew, the late Dr. Smiley Blanton, one of the best-known and most highly respected psychiatrists of that era. He was a very intelligent man whose eyes gleamed behind horn-rimmed glasses.

I told him of my predicament of being faced with incalculable human problems and of my lack of training, and asked if he would give me some help. His response was most surprising. He asked if I believed in prayer. He said that he had been praying for a long time that someday he might meet a pastor with whom he might "team up in a merger, so to speak, of psychological science and the science of pastoral therapy."

For this we were both criticized, he by other psychiatrists and I by many ministers, for at the time there was mutual suspicion between clergy and psychiatrists. Anyway, together we established the Institutes of Religion and Health, which became one of the most highly respected mental health clinics and training institutions of the twentieth century, now called the Blanton Peale Institute.

Dr. Blanton joined me in counseling people and one day said, "What we are seeing in these people is nothing short of a plague. They are sick in their minds, and it is showing up in an array of physical symptoms."

"And what is this plague, Doctor?" I asked.

"Fear, just plain old fear." And he added, "Anxiety is the great modern plague."

I was surprised and asked if fear actually could make people sick physically. "Indeed it can, and it is now doing so in epidemic proportions." I recall one thing the doctor said: "Fear is the most subtle and destructive of all human diseases." This sort of talk, then new to me, was discouraging, considering the enormity of the problem of widespread unreasoning fear. And I asked almost desperately, "What can we do about it?"

Dr. Blanton looked at me calmly. I knew him to be a highly educated, scientific man. Formerly he had worked with Freud in Vienna. Later he was associated with The College of Physicians and Surgeons in London, and still later was on the faculty of the University of Wisconsin.

"Son," he said, "there are two enormous powers operating in the world and one of them is fear. It is the greatest power of all, save one, and that is faith or believing. Faith is the most powerful of all forces. It alone is greater than fear; and faith, firmly held, can cancel out fear. Faith works wonders." Dr. Blanton was born and reared in the mountains of Tennessee. Educated at Vanderbilt University, he was, in his own estimate, "still a hillbilly Methodist reared and grounded in the faith."

"Just give 'em faith, Norman, just give 'em faith. Teach them to believe. That's the only medicine that can cure the disease of fear. But it can; never doubt it."

"Faith in what, Dr. Blanton?"

" 'Faith in what,' you ask me, and you a minister of religion? You ask me 'faith in what?' You should correct your language to 'faith in *Whom.*' Why, of course, the answer is faith in the good Lord God. Just a moment until I read you something." He picked up a Bible from my desk and turned quickly to a page, so quickly that I knew it was a well-known page to him. "I'm reading from the best-loved Psalm, the Twenty-third: 'Yea, though I walk through the valley of the shadow of death, I will fear no evil; for thou art with me; thy rod and thy staff they comfort me.'

"And get a load of this," Dr. Blanton continued, flipping over the pages to Psalm 34, verse 4. "Just listen to this: 'I sought the Lord, and he heard me, and delivered me from all my fears.' Did you get that? Not some of my fears, but *all* my fears. That is what we must be—believers—and we must make believers of these poor fear-ridden people. Once they have faith they will be well in their minds and in their bodies, too."

This impressed me, for here was a graduate with honors from leading medical schools, one who enjoyed the highest ranking in the specialty of psychiatry, and he had retained the faith of his childhood and was using it in scientific practice. My admiration of his attitude knew no bounds when he commented, "We learn when truth is held before us. One of the wisest and most profound truths I heard long ago in a backwoods Sunday school. It is this: 'And now abideth faith, hope and love, these three; but the greatest of these is love' (I Corinthians 13:13). When we give that prescription to a patient we give him the blueprint of health and happiness."

Apparently, this was uppermost in Smiley's mind, for he telephoned me one day saying that he was referring a patient to me. "This man is very religious, the old-style kind, and at heart, as you know, I'm of the same variety. But he has a lurking suspicion of psychiatrists as some peculiar kind of person to be avoided. But when I told him I am associated with you, a preacher, I could see that he was impressed. He will, I believe, accept your prescription for fear, for that is his problem and it is threatening his ruin. So give him faith." When he gave me the name of the patient, I was flabbergasted. It was one of the top industrialists of the country at the time. Let's call him Mr. Jones.

When Mr. Jones came, he revealed his executive capacity at once by clearly describing his trouble. All his business life he had possessed the ability to think a problem through and make a decision; and, judging by his success, his batting average for right decisions was a very high percentage. Therefore he had risen to the top of a large and successful company. But of late it seemed that his decision-making ability had left him; and then, after finally making a decision, he was tortured with fear that it was erroneous.

He said, "I know that my associates are aware of my difficulty and are covering for me, but this state of affairs cannot go on. And my health is being affected. I must have help."

To my question as to whether fear had previously ever been a problem, he said he had lacked self-confidence as a teenager. But he had conquered it, or thought he had. But since he was given this top responsibility, it had returned in more virulent form than ever before.

I studied him with pity, for this had been my personal story also, and I told him so. "Well, how did you get on top of your fears?" he asked.

"I visualized sliding fear out of my mind and then sliding faith in until I could hear it click into place."

"You mean just like a mechanism?" he asked.

"Yes. Then I clicked in hope and love. Do you know the three words?"

"Sure. Faith, hope, and love."

I wrote out a "prescription" for him. When making a decision, he was to think it out, then pray for God's guidance, then *believe* he had such guidance. He was to act at once on the basis of his thinking and guidance, make the decision, put it in the hands of God, and forget it.

"Do you know Mr. Kraft of the cheese company?" I asked.

"I do; he is a top businessman and a fine fellow."

"Well, he told me that in the early days of his business he himself delivered cheese driving a wagon. He had a horse named 'Paddy.' As he clogged along he talked his problem aloud and Paddy would flick his ears in response. If he had to make a decision, say, by Thursday noon, he would think it over and talk it over with God. Then what came dominantly and steadily into his mind he would take as his answer.

"Mr. Kraft told me, 'Decisions arrived at by this method proved to be right decisions by a very high percentage.'"

Mr. Jones responded, "This makes sense. I will try the same technique." After working at this for several weeks he reported progress. His fears finally subsided so that he was able to think clearly. His health likewise improved. "Fear nearly ruined me; but when I began really drawing upon faith, it proved stronger than fear," he declared.

The next time fear knocks on the door of your mind, ask yourself what is the worst that could happen. Then ask if it has ever happened to you. And what are the chances of it happening now? Aren't the chances that the worst will not happen far greater than the slim chance that it will?

During the Vietnam War, President Nixon asked me to go and speak to the troops at the front, to encourage those on the battlefield, and to visit the wounded in the hospitals.

At first, I shrank from this assignment. "Mr. President," I said, "may I remind you that I am over thirty, and isn't there a so-called generation gap?"

His reply was characteristic. "Where you are going, there is no generation gap between real men."

"Well," I asked, "what do you want me to say to our men at the front?"

"Tell them the same thing you always preach in church; just talk to them like that. And, for the wounded, go sit on their beds and pray with them."

It was really touching. So I went.

In Vietnam, a split-second schedule had been prepared for me. My rank on the field was that of a brigadier general, with a colonel as my aide, a helicopter for transportation, and two planes to protect us while in the air.

I spoke to the troops in many areas. But the time that shall linger in my memory was when we were asked to conduct a memorial service for the 7th Marines in a front-exposed position. We arrived by helicopter at Hill 55. It had been swept by gunfire, so there was absolutely no vegetation anywhere around. The hill was banked with sandbags and other forms of protection. Soldiers were sleeping in tents because they were in the field.

I was met by General Simpson, a grizzled U.S. Marine. I liked him at first sight, for he was what you call a man. He had a gruff exterior, but underneath the kindest, most loving heart. He took me into the little shack to meet the field chaplains. What men! I have met few to equal them.

I asked a Roman Catholic chaplain, "What's your job, Chaplain?"

"Twice a week, I go twenty miles into the jungle to a far-removed post to give the Blessed Sacrament to a half-dozen men."

"Isn't that dangerous?"

"Yes," he answered. "But that's the way it is."

"Did you volunteer to come over here and do this?"

"Of course I did."

"And why?" I asked.

His answer told it all. "As a pastor, I dedicated my life to serve the Blessed Lord Jesus and His children wherever and whenever they were in great need."

Then the general escorted me, amid about eight hundred men, to a small, improvised altar. Above the altar, waving in the breeze, was the American flag and the South Vietnamese flag. In the distance, I could see B-52 bombers dropping bombs in the jungle, for this was the infiltration route. The separate hills in the line of vision were named Arizona Territory, Dodge City, Charley's Ridge, and other Americanisms.

Finally, my eyes rested on eight rifles, thrust into the ground on their bayonets. And on the butt of each rifle was a helmet, symbolic of eight comrades who had died in the battle of Pipestone Canyon. We could see Pipestone Canyon in the distance.

The men were sitting on the ground facing me, and I said to the general, "I don't know that I can handle this, General. I'm not in the same world with these boys. I'm a civilian, an older man."

"I'm older, too, Doctor. These are my boys." He gave me the impression that he was just like a father. And to my question, he answered: "What shall you speak to them about, you ask me? Look, talk to them about God and immortality. And speak to me about that, too, for some of these boys may themselves be dead a few days from now. This may be the last time they will hear about God."

This was my opportunity to talk to young Americans about the greatest truth in the world: that our Savior promised us life for now and eternity. As I talked, I became aware of the intensity with which they followed every word, hanging on to each syllable as if it were life itself. And I tried to make my message the Word of Life. Even though a strong breeze was whipping the flags, there was a hush over us all.

Then a magnificent black sergeant arose and sang, as I've never heard it sung before or since, "How Great Thou Art." Then the men sang the Marine Hymn. Taps were played and the benediction was pronounced.

General Simpson walked with me to the helicopter while every man in that vast assemblage stood at attention. I boarded the helicopter. Glancing back, I saw that the entire regiment was at salute, including the general. I asked myself, "What are they saluting? They're certainly not saluting me, for I'm only a civilian pastor." Then I realized that they were saluting the deepest truth that had ever been implanted in their thoughts and lives: the love of God and the hope of immortality.

As I stood in the doorway of the helicopter, I had an overwhelming desire to look intently at them all. I wanted to preserve that scene forever in my consciousness so that I would never forget it. They were still at salute, framed by the circling hills.

Now, I'm not a saluting type of person, and certainly not of the military. So I did just what any old American would do. I waved to them. And suddenly an astonishing thing happened; from the general on down, they all broke the salute and became American boys as they waved to a pastor who had come from America, their homeland, to talk to them about God and eternity.

As I took my seat and buckled my seatbelt, I looked around at the men in the helicopter. They all were doing what I was doing, whisking away tears, for we had been, for a few moments, under the spell of immortality.

One of the most inspirational men I have known was William H. Danforth, founder of the Ralston Purina Company. He wrote a little book called *I Dare You*, which had a very beneficial effect on me, as well as upon thousands of others. When Mr. Danforth was a young boy, he was sickly. But he had the good fortune one year to have a teacher who was a positive thinker. He taught his students the fine old American doctrine that they could be anything they wanted to be if they would work hard to achieve their goal, had strong character, plus faith in God and in themselves. The teacher was particularly drawn to young Bill Danforth, for he sensed the sickly little fellow's potential.

"I dare you, William, to be the healthiest boy in this school. You can be. I dare you to be what you can be." This challenge awakened the love of battle in this frail boy. He began to apply all the rules of health to himself by eating good body-building food. He never smoked nor drank, never took into his body anything that would not build physical strength. In the end he outlived every classmate.

One day when he was eighty-six years old, he took me to lunch in a local hotel. As we were about to separate after lunch I happened to ask what exercises he was using to keep in such obviously good shape. We were standing in the rather crowded lobby. "I'll show you," he said. "Take off your coat." And there in that public hotel lobby, to the delight of the crowd that gathered around, he demonstrated his vigorous exercises, which included lying down on the floor, I alongside him, waving legs in the air and doing push-ups. The crowd applauded, for in that city citizens loved him.

"And keep talking about positive thinking, for to have a sound, healthy body you've got to have a sound, healthy mind," he said in parting, giving me a handclasp that I felt for minutes afterward. It is an indisputable fact that healthy-mindedness leads to good physical health.

Oswald Chambers, the great Scottish thinker, echoes this: "Health is the balance between physical life and external nature, and it is maintained only by sufficient vitality on the inside against things on the outside. Everything outside my physical life is designed to put me to death. Things which keep me going when I am alive, disintegrate me when I am dead. If I have enough fighting power, I produce the balance of health. The same is true of the mental life. If I want to maintain a vigorous mental life, I have to fight, and in that way the mental balance called positive believing is produced.

"Morally, it is the same. Everything that does not partake of the nature of virtue is the enemy of virtue in me, and it depends on what moral caliber I have whether I overcome and produce virtue. Immediately I fight, I am moral in that particular. No man is virtuous because he cannot help it; virtue is acquired."

Lynn Andrews, author of *Medicine Woman*, says, "The life force pours out of you through the holes you create in your life through addiction. The worst are emotional addictions such as addiction to sadness, to chaos, to a feeling that we are not good enough."

And Carl Simonton, M.D., coauthor of *Getting Well Again*, asserts, "Health is the natural state of humanity. When we are in harmony, we feel better, feel more joy, and feel healthier. I see healing as a positive feedback system and illness as a form of negative feedback."

All of which supports our thesis that much illness derives from an unhealthy mental pattern.

Right thinking is ever supportive of health and it is a natural restorative. As Hippocrates, mentor of physicians, who lived from 460–370 B.C., said, "The natural healing force within each one of us is the greatest force in getting well."

The mind, properly controlled, can do just about everything. You can think your way through adversity, you can think your way through problems. It is a superpowerful instrument which so few use to maximum. And if the mind thinks with a believing attitude one can do amazing things.

Regardless of how much trouble you are having, how hard the going seems to be, keep your thoughts on a high and positive level. Be a believer, a strong positive believer—and do it no matter how difficult, how unreasonable a situation may appear to be. Do not let yourself ever believe in the dismal pronouncements of Samuel Butler that life is "one long process of getting tired," or with Sigmund Freud that "the chief duty of a human being is to endure life." Believe that life is something to take hold of and master by getting on top of it. Always remember, there is more strength in you than you have ever realized or even imagined. Certainly, nothing can keep you down if you are determined to get on top of things and stay there. Draw upon your fantastic inner power, for it is there, waiting to be used. Fantastic is the only adequate description of that power. And always hold the thought that you can, if you think you can.

Take as an example this story, which I saw in a newspaper.

A farmer stood in front of his barn, watching a light truck move rapidly across his land. His fourteen-year-old son was at the wheel. The boy was too young to get a license, but he was car crazy —and seemed plenty capable of handling one. So he had been given permission to drive the pickup truck around the farm, staying strictly off the public road.

But suddenly, to his horror, the father saw the truck overturn into a ditch. Racing to the spot, he saw there was water standing in the ditch and that the boy, pinned under the truck, was lying with his head partially submerged.

This farmer was a small man. According to the newspaper account, he stood five feet seven and weighed 155 pounds. But without an instant's hesitation he jumped down into the ditch, put his hands under the truck, lifting it just enough so that a farmhand who came running up could pull the unconscious boy out from under.

The local doctor came at once, examined the boy, treated him for bruises, and pronounced him otherwise unhurt.

Meanwhile, the father started wondering. He had lifted that truck without stopping to consider if he could. Out of curiosity he tried again. He couldn't budge it. The doctor said it was a miracle.

He explained that the physical organism sometimes reacts to an emergency by sending an enormous discharge of adrenaline through the body, giving extra power. That was the only explanation he could offer.

Now, of course, the capacity to deliver that much adrenaline had to be there in the glands. Nothing could have activated what wasn't there. A person normally has a great deal of latent physical power in reserve.

But experiences of this kind tell us an even more important fact: Something happened to the farmer physically to produce that surge of supernormal strength. But it was more than a physical reaction. Mental and spiritual forces were involved. His mind-response, when he saw that his son might die, motivated him to rescue with no thought but to get that truck off the boy. Such a crisis summons the amazing latent powers with what you might call spiritual adrenaline, and if the situation calls for enhanced physical strength, the mental state produces it. Believers draw upon extra power reserves.

One of my friends, Beverly Kelly, was publicity director for the Ringling Bros. and Barnum & Bailey Circus.

When it opened in Madison Square Garden every year he would ask me to go with him to a performance. Once I asked, "Bev, how do you like this job?" His answer was a classic: "It's lots better than working."

Pointing up to where "daredevils" were performing, "swinging with the greatest of ease" on the high bars, he said, "That reminds me of something you could use in a speech or a book," and he related the following circus story, which illustrates a rule of success.

A young fellow was thrilled by high-bar performances and wanted to be such a performer himself. He went through all the training and instruction. Then came the day when, for the first time, he was to perform before a packed house. He looked at the bars up high and suddenly saw himself falling to the floor of the Garden. He became terrified and exclaimed to his instructor, "I can't do it. I just can't."

The instructor knew that he could do it. He was simply suffering from an attack of jitters, so replied calmly, "You can do it, son, and here's how. Throw your heart over the bar and your body will follow."

That story told by Bev Kelly has often helped me when facing a big crowd before a speech. It has helped others when facing a crisis: "Throw your heart over the bar and your body will follow."

There is within every person an incredible power. It is almost divine, as if befitting a child of God, which is what we all are. And this power heals and keeps us in health of body, mind, and soul.

To close this chapter, let me quote some wise words from a truly great book by my friend Bernie S. Siegel, M.D., titled *Peace, Love and Healing.*

Bernie says, "I got to this perfect core-self through meditation. But, however you get there, you'll know when you have arrived at that still, quiet place at the center of your being where mind and body are unified. It's like coming home . . . And home is where the healing can begin—within your true, unique and authentic self."

Everything worthwhile accomplishing is tough and requires will, purpose, goals, stumbling, falling, picking oneself up and going forward despite all setbacks, resolutely going forward. But the objective of getting through with that killjoy empty feeling and substituting a fullness of joy and satisfaction is well worth all the difficulty necessary to attain it.

And to start the change, fix in mind a four-word fact. Repeat many times a day until you believe it:

THINGS CAN BE BETTER

THINGS CAN BE BETTER

. . . Until that wonderful day arrives when you exclaim, "THINGS ARE BETTER!"

When you keep your thoughts high and pray

for God's guidance, that day is never far-off.

CHAPTER 10

MORE ABOUT THE HEALING
POWER WITHIN THE MIND

■   ■   ■

Nᴇᴡ MEDICAL DISCOVERIES HAVE RECENTLY been announced that will help a person become healthier and happier as quickly as it takes to change one's mind. For the scientists have discovered the mind's effect upon the body. Many scientists now say that achieving good health includes not only physical culture, but, perhaps even more important, mental culture.

Of course, the principles behind these discoveries are as old as time. Ministers, priests, and rabbis have been teaching them for centuries. It is just that medical research, after long study, has put its stamp of approval on these principles as effective and practical.

I have already referred to this new science, called psychoimmunology, earlier in this book. It was the subject of a recent *New York Times* article:*

> *Psychologists and immunologists are producing surprising new evidence that altering a patient's mental state can boost the immune system.*
>
> *The findings are the early fruits of a combination of psychology and immunology, two fields that in the past have had virtually nothing to do with each other. The resulting*

* Aprii 20, 1989

*discipline, psychoimmunology, seeks to discover the mecha-
nism that links a person's emotional life with the ups and
downs of the immune system, the body's line of defense
against bacteria, virus and cancer.*

I draw here again from that great medical man Bernie S. Siegel
and his book *Peace, Love and Healing.* He wrote:
"The more we learn about mind and body as a unity the more
difficult it becomes to consider them separately. What's in your
mind is often quite literally or 'anatomically' what is in your body.
Anything that offers hope has the potential to health."

A few years ago a man was referred to me for counseling by my
doctor, Louis Bishop, who was well aware of the above principles.
The man dragged himself into my office, slumped in a chair, and
lackadaisically drawled, "Funny thing, I haven't been feeling good,
under par and all that stuff. You and I happen to have the same
doctor. He gave me the usual checkup, then said, 'Better go see
Norman Peale.' "

The man leaned back in his chair and, with a quizzical look,
said, "Now, I ask you, why would a recognized medical expert like
Dr. Bishop send one of his patients to see a writer of books and,
beyond that, a minister? It doesn't make sense, if you ask me; but,
anyway, here I am."

"Does seem strange," I replied, "and Louis Bishop is perfectly
qualified to handle your case." After a pause, I added, "Perhaps he
wanted you to know something that you might not want to hear."

He shifted in his chair and looked a bit puzzled. We sat eyeing
each other for a few moments. Then I said, "Tell me whom you
hate and why."

He reddened, sat up straight for the first time, then growled,
"None of your business, and what's *that* got to do with it, anyway?"

"It *is* my business," I pressed. "That's why the doctor sent you to
me. I know Louis's methods. Apparently he thinks the trouble that
causes your low levels of energy and physical sluggishness is located in your mind."

He started to interrupt, but I held up my hand and continued.
"Besides, when you go to Dr. Bishop for a diagnosis, he puts you in
an examining room and tells you to take off all your clothes down

to your shorts. I am in the business of examining minds, so you will have to unclothe your thought processes if we are to return you to health."

I could see he was a little puzzled by my logic and I concluded with, "When we get your mind healed, with that physique of yours you will be one of the healthiest men in town."

Finally, realizing what I was driving at, he capitulated and, evidently convinced of the efficacy of the mind-body relationship in health, he started unloading his hate of another fellow, a former friend. With his face darkening, he poured out a mass of resentment that took nearly an hour to exorcise. When he finished, he went right on to other hates and I concluded that he had wasted a tremendous amount of physical energy over his many resentments.

When finally he ran down in this catharsis, I asked, "Is that all?" He quickly remembered one other whom he vindictively labeled an "S.O.B." This consumed another ten minutes. But finally, breathing deeper and more relaxed than when he first came into my office, he told me that was all.

"I am all cleaned out," he said. Then he did what may seem a strange thing. He stood up to his full height, stretched his arms above his head as far as he could reach, and exclaimed, "You know something? I feel good!" He hesitated. ". . . I feel *real* good."

I responded that his good feelings were natural since he had unloaded off his mind a mass of sickening emotion which he had been carrying for a long time. He went away walking tall, truly a different man, but not before I let him know that we were not through with his case.

"At least one more examination is required," I said. "Then I will give you a mental 'prescription' to aid in your acquiring robust health." He didn't argue, and as he left I told my office assistant to make another appointment within three days. I didn't want my "patient" to have a relapse.

When he appeared for the next treatment and promised prescription, he said he had been feeling better "than in a long time."

"Good," I said. "Now we will start the second stage of your treatment. It is a five-part prescription."

1. *Forgive each person that you have hated: say the name aloud. Say, "I totally forgive ——." Forgiveness is the curative medicine for hate.*

"That's hard to swallow," he commented.

"But the swallowing is part of the cure," I answered. So he named the persons, one by one, and affirmed his forgiveness of each one.

2. *Pray aloud for each formerly hated person, and in that prayer say, "Give me what it takes to love—— (naming each one)."*

He objected that he had never prayed publicly. "I'm not the public," I said and gave him the words to say: "Heavenly Father, I pray for——. And I'm really sincere and not a phony. I even ask you to help me to love——." He did this, but reluctantly, and said, "I feel like a lousy hypocrite."

"You are in a state of change," I explained.

3. *Now reflect and decide whether you have ever done a wrong to any person. Decide what, if anything, you can do to make amends. Go to any length in trying to heal the breach. If after a sincere attempt the other person rejects your advances, love him or her, anyway, and forget it. And when you say your prayers, put this relationship in God's hands. He will take care of it.*

"You believe in God, don't you?" I asked.

"Sure I do. I'm a Presbyterian, but maybe an absentee one," he admitted.

"Better find the in-depth help that brings God into the solution of everyday problems," I suggested.

4. *Ask God to forgive you for your bad disposition. And ask Him to help you improve it.*
5. *Finally, level with God. If you have any other weaknesses, ask Him to cure you, as you have been relieved of hate.*

In saying good-bye, I said, "You don't need me anymore, unless you fall from Grace."

"What does that mean?" he asked.

"Discuss that with your Presbyterian minister," I said.

He had me write the five points down so he could take them with him. Already I could see a new light in his eyes. Then, as he rose to leave, he said fervently, "How can I ever thank you?"

"Don't try," I replied. "Thank God. He did it."

Some weeks later, while I was in Dr. Louis Bishop's office getting my semiannual checkup, he said, "Remember that fellow I sent to you [naming him]? Whatever you did for him, it worked. He is now in normal health, has a good attitude, and is going strong."

I cite this case because it graphically demonstrates the relation of mental health to physical health. Some others to which I have given the same treatment did not experience improved health as fully. The reason was a lack of faith and no intense desire to get better. The desire to get better is very important and is needed in order to build up real faith. There is much truth in the statement, "If you have faith even as a grain of mustard seed, nothing shall be impossible unto you" (Matthew 17:20). It isn't so much the quantity of the faith as the quality of one's belief. The man Dr. Bishop sent to me had the capacity to believe.

This positive belief or expectation that things will be better was given medical credence by Dr. Willard A. Krehl, emeritus professor of medicine at Thomas Jefferson University in Philadelphia, when he said:

". . . a person's expectation is an important part of taking any medication—even vitamins and aspirin.

"Good physicians intuitively know this and it is the reason they tend to give patients not only prescriptions but also reassuring words, 'This will make you better.' "

Krehl recalls that he once met a physician who had aspirin in "six different colors . . . to take advantage of the placebo effect. If a patient said the blue pill didn't help, he gave the patient a red pill —or another color—and it might help. Nobody can ignore the placebo effect. If you think you'll be helped, the odds are increased that you will be."

Dr. Krehl, who also has a doctoral degree in biochemistry, says,

"This expectation extends into the cancer field, where bad news is always traumatic. Your immediate attitude is negative. You're afraid you're going to die. But how you feel can make a great difference in how you live.

"Medicine must be given with a strong spiritual support," stresses Dr. Krehl. "The patient must develop a sense of faith not only in the doctor and the medication but, most important, within him- or herself, saying: 'By golly, I'm going to beat this thing.'

"This is particularly true of cancer," he adds. "I believe that strong nutritional support along with faith in this support will not harm and certainly may be of help. A natural cell is stronger than a cancer cell. Strengthening it in its natural environment will give it a greater chance to overwhelm the cancer cell.

"You can think your way into sickness," he concludes, "and you can think your way out of sickness."

An article in the March 12, 1990, issue of *Time* magazine entitled "Can the Mind Help Cure Disease?" discusses the role of emotions in medical prevention or treatment of disease and points to "modern science's discovery of innovative ways to measure the mind's impact on the body's health." The article cites, among others, Dr. N. Herbert Spector, a neurophysiologist at the National Institutes of Health, who says that when researchers can pin down the appropriate clinical uses for mind-body therapies, the result will be "a revolution in medical practice."

The article goes on to outline the results of psychotherapy and relaxation in recent studies involving breast cancer patients, hypertension patients, and even sufferers of the common cold. However, the article makes clear, not all in the medical community fully espouse these techniques, fearing that some patients might abandon standard medical treatment. "Physicians walk a very fine line between promising more than we know and destroying a person's hope," says Sandra Levy, a psychologist at the Pittsburgh Cancer Institute. "We know mental health helps [but] we cannot go beyond that."

In his latest book, *Head First: The Biology of Hope,* Norman Cousins documents numerous recent strides in the field of mind-

body research. In discussing the relationship between mental attitude and the diagnosis of a health problem, he writes:

> *A colleague in the medical school told me about a woman
> who had gone in for a complete checkup and learned that
> one of her kidneys was totally nonfunctional. The shock
> produced instant deafness. With sustained and prolonged
> psychotherapy over several months her hearing was re-
> stored. What troubled my colleague was that the infirmity
> need not have happened. The routine nature of the way the
> diagnosis was communicated produced a health problem
> hardly less severe than the original deficiency.*
>
> *Most of the patients I am asked to see are cancer sufferers
> but also every serious disease is represented in the total
> group. What is most striking about these cases is that the
> illness worsened coincident with the diagnosis.*
>
> *Why should these patients experience a severe downturn
> in their condition coincident with the diagnosis? Why
> should bad news make them worse? Was it possible that, the
> moment they had a label to attach to their symptoms, the
> ability of their bodies to respond to a challenge was signifi-
> cantly diminished? . . .*
>
> *This being the case, I have attempted, whenever possible,
> to bring newly diagnosed patients together with persons
> who have come through similar illness . . . The specific
> evidence that recovery is possible acts like a tonic and actu-
> ally enhances the prospects for effective medical treatment.*

I have chosen to feature a cure of hate in this chapter, for it
seems to be one of the most corrosive mental disturbances. No
wonder the greatest physician who ever lived and healed taught
people to love one another. Love is the best curative and health-
producing medicine and is, of course, a product of the mind.

A country doctor, prominent in the American Medical Association, discussed with me the physical effects of hate. He told me
that it actually ought to be called a disease, a virulent one. A patient of his, a mean and bitter "old cuss," hated so viciously that
his color became sallow and his breath foul. When he died, the

doctor thought of writing on the death certificate "grudgitis" as the cause of death. "But those bureaucrats at town hall," he said, "would have thought I was balmy. Actually, though, that is what he died of, 'grudgitis.'

This physician, who certainly knew his stuff, was right; for I have seen people go steadily downhill physically, until some took a big dose of forgiveness and love. Then the decline was arrested and they lived happy lives into old age.

Here's an interesting case. A letter came from a young woman who said bitterly that she hated money for what it did to people like herself who didn't have enough. (She'd been laid off from her automotive-company job.) She also hated money for what she claimed it often did to people who had too much. She said that America had become a dollar-worshiping society, and she blamed money for that. She even misquoted the Bible. "Money is the root of all evil!" she wrote, underscoring every word. (Actually, the Bible says, "The *love* of money is the root of all evil"—I Timothy 6:10—quite a different thing.)

"Stop seeing yourself as the helpless victim of an imaginary villain called money," I wrote her in reply. "If you personalize money so vehemently and hate it so intensely, you certainly won't ever attract it, because your unconscious mind will be programmed to repel and reject it."

I urged her to image herself as a well-balanced, intelligent person whose mind was able to take charge of her emotions. "Calm down," I wrote. "Be objective. Stop all this hate business. Hold the image of yourself as someone determined to remove all these turbulent, confusing emotions from your mind. Nothing is going to go right for you until you do."

Anger is just one emotion that money problems can generate. Another is fear. Not long ago, I was on a call-in radio program. One woman who called said to me, "I wish you'd tell me what to do about bill collectors. I'm terrified of them."

"Well," I said to her, "I happen to know a couple of bill collectors and both have told me how nervous *they* are when they come to a home to talk about nonpayment of bills. They say they get tense and tongue-tied and hot and cold all over."

The woman said, "I can't believe it!"

"It's true," I told her. "A bill collector is also a human being, and he is not trying to harass you or be mean to you or put you in jail. He's just representing a business person who has to get money to keep on selling merchandise to people like yourself. His main objective is to get you to work out a payment plan.

"So here's a suggestion. The next time a bill collector comes to your door, change the picture you have in your mind of what the interview is going to be like. Instead of seeing yourself as embarrassed and angry and evasive, and him as hostile and threatening, visualize a meeting between a nice person who has a job to do and a nice person who happens to have some unpaid bills. See both of you working out a solution together in a friendly way. And here's another suggestion: Before you open the door, say a quick prayer for the poor fellow, because he's probably just as nervous as you are."

"Well," she said, "I certainly never thought of praying for a bill collector. But I'll try."

Imaging is one of many techniques that can help people in financial difficulty. My wife Ruth and I have worked out a few simple, effective suggestions.

The first is: *Don't panic.* If you find anxiety getting the upper hand, image peace of mind. The simple act of praying creates an image of your problems being brought to the source of all wisdom, and that is tremendously reassuring and comforting. Then read the Twenty-third Psalm. When you come to those marvelous words, "I will fear no evil: for thou art with me . . ." (verse 4), run them through your mind at least twenty times. Repeat them to yourself during the day if you feel your anxiety returning. Write them on a piece of paper and tape it on your bathroom mirror, where you will see it first thing every morning. Saturate yourself with this idea.

Then, when you have your emotions under control, *get organized.* This is Ruth's favorite bit of advice because she is highly organized. Make a list of all your debts, everything you owe. Make another list of essential expenses. Add up all sources of income and see what you can count on. It's amazing how many people really don't know exactly how much they owe or what their basic expenses are. Visualize yourself living within your income with a fraction left over for debt reduction. Paint that image vividly in your mind.

A final suggestion is *think*. If you'll sit down and really think, you'll come up with ideas or insights that can change everything.

I've always liked William Saroyan's story about the time when, as a struggling young writer, discouraged and almost broke, he decided to ask a rich uncle in a nearby city for a loan. With his last bit of cash, Saroyan sent his uncle a telegram. Back came a reply of just three words: HAVE HEAD EXAMINED.

Once he got over the shock of this seemingly sardonic refusal, Saroyan pondered the message. Gradually he began to see what his uncle was saying: You don't need a loan. Look inside your head. That's where you'll find a solution in a new idea.

Thus challenged, Saroyan sat down, thought up a plot for a short story, wrote it, sold it, and was on his way to a brilliant career as a playwright and novelist.

Let me recall another case history illustrating how the substitution of positive goodwill for hate-resentment resulted in healthy well-being. A friend, whom I'll call Phil, was executive vice president of a prominent manufacturing company in a Midwestern city. He had come up fast and the responsibilities assigned to him really made him operating head without the title of CEO. The president of the company, at whose recommendation this man had been advanced, was nearing retirement, and it was generally thought that our friend would be named to succeed him.

But when the president retired, the board of directors brought in a well-qualified executive from outside the company and named him president and CEO. Phil was devastated and resentful of "the dirty crowd of double-dealers" and less complimentary appellations. Phil began to hate until it affected his work, his sleep, and an obvious physical decline set in. This latter became a matter of concern to his friends, and he had many. He would walk the streets seething within over the way he had been "double-crossed." He haunted his club, where he had been a popular member, but so unpleasant had he become that even old friends avoided him. Out of long habit and a sense of loyalty, Phil showed up regularly for work and did his job mechanically, though the verve and enthusiasm were lacking.

Then it so happened that I had an engagement in Philadelphia. I took the train, went into the dining car for a late lunch, and there at a table sat my friend Phil. I sat down across from him and ordered lunch. He was drinking coffee, cup after cup, and I noted he was chain-smoking cigarettes, lighting one from the butt of another. "Good thing you are a teetotaler," I said. "If it was whiskey you were drinking like that, you'd pass out."

I noticed then that his hands were shaking so that the coffee sometimes spilled. His state of health was obviously pathetic. I knew him to be a religious man, so I said, "Phil, I've heard about your situation and I'm sorry. Maybe the good Lord brought us together on this train, for He wants you well again." He started then to recount the whole unhappy story, using terms such as "double-crossers," "phonies," "enemies," "skunks."

"Listen, old friend, I know the entire story. I have to get off this train at Philadelphia and so let's get down to business. You can't go on as you are or you will ruin yourself. Where are you headed now?"

"Home," he said, "I took this train so I could think."

"OK. Let's think now," I said, adding, "Phil, your hand is shaking like an aspen leaf. You drink cup after cup of coffee. You chain-smoke cigarettes. You're breaking up. All the signs are there. Tell me how you feel, and level with me."

"Awful, just awful." Then he started on what I supposed would be a long spiel on how bad he felt. "Chuck it," I said. "Let's talk about how you can regain your good health and feel better." He looked at me appealingly.

"Phil, you are a dear friend and I'm going to give it to you straight," I pressed on. "Hate and resentment are ruining you. Even if you were given a raw deal, that isn't the new president's fault. He's an innocent party."

Phil squashed out his cigarette and shrugged. "I suppose you're right, Norman. And I realize I'm hurting myself. But I just can't get out of this mood."

"Well, I'm no medical man," I answered, "but I have made a study of the body-mind relationship and I'm certain that if you simply accept the situation, you'll get well. I'm also sure it will be good for your future business career."

"Accept it?" he asked, looking up in disbelief.

"Yes," I said. I suggested that he go into the new president's office and say, and mean it, that he wanted to know how he could be helpful. Then give the jobs assigned to him all he had of loyalty, experience, and enthusiasm. Phil sat quietly listening to these suggestions, then said, "I suppose you're right. But it will be hard to do."

"So what?" I replied. "You're man enough to do a hard but sensible thing."

We were then pulling into the Philadelphia station. He held out his hand. "Thanks, Norman. I'll try."

A week later Phil phoned to tell me what happened. He did approach the new president. "It was hard to do, Norman," he said, "but you know what he said to me? 'I need you, Phil. You know this business like no one else. Thanks so much.'" I was elated to hear the old spark back in Phil's voice. The sequel to this story is that Phil and the new president became real coworkers and, in time, friends. The president did a good job, so good in fact that in five years he was offered a better position with another company and left the post vacant. Whom do you think was then selected by the board to head the company? You're right. Phil got the appointment and served effectively until the age of mandatory retirement.

He took me out to lunch one day when I was in his city and he was still active. "I owe you a great deal, Norman," he said, "but really you are not all that smart. All that advice you gave me is in the Bible and I had just forgotten it." We both laughed. Later we walked up the street together. I watched Phil as he strode toward his office, a strong man, healthy in body, healthy in mind.

Our generation would do well to more completely practice the mind-body technique of well-being. Exercises are fine; I do them, too. And take medications when prescribed. But always add the mental well-being principle. Always think healthy.

Many people feel this is something new. But haven't wise men and women realized for a long time the power of the mind over the body?

I have never forgotten a doctor who took care of our family in Ohio many years ago. And it must have been a long time ago, for I remember that he drove a horse and buggy to make calls. He was summoned because I complained of a stomachache, occasioned, no doubt, by a boy's habit of eating green apples. He looked at my tongue, poked at my stomach, then solemnly wrote a prescription, handing me a pill with instructions to start with that.

Before departing he rumpled my hair, saying, "A stomachache, sonny, is not as bad as a mental pain in your head. Keep your thoughts healthy."

That incident occurred perhaps eighty years ago, but the memory of it has remained with me ever since. I grew up in a family of ministers and medical doctors, and remember that not a few members of the medical profession knew that how a patient thinks has a lot to do with how he or she feels. So the mind-body concept has long antecedents in human experience.

One other incident particularly stayed in my memory, and I mention it here, for if you seize upon the same idea, I believe you will feel better and be healthier. One day years ago when I was at the *Detroit Journal*, I went into Grove Patterson's office and routinely asked, "How are you, Mr. Patterson?" "Terrific, I feel wonderful," he replied vigorously, adding, "If I felt otherwise, I wouldn't tell you. I think and talk health and you'll be smart if you do the same, for what you think about your body has a lot to do with how you feel." He pointed a long ink-stained finger to emphasize the point. (His finger always seemed to have ink on it.)

That incident in the old newspaper offices on Jefferson Avenue took place no less than seventy years ago, but the scene is indelibly etched on my mind. Grove Patterson was for all his life a strong, healthy man of prodigious energy; and he was also one of the most intelligent persons I ever knew.

A third experience that persuaded me that one can have better health if he thinks better thoughts, has positive attitudes, and controls mental enemies such as hate, fear, and other negatives took place one never-to-be-forgotten day in Chicago. It was in the old Sherman House, a great hotel which then stood at Clark and Randolph. The managers were Frank Bering and his brother Gus. These men grew up in the small village of Lynchburg, Ohio, along with my mother and father. They were particularly nostalgic about Lynchburg and would never charge me for room or meals at the Sherman House. So naturally I always stayed there on my frequent trips to Chicago to speak at conventions. That city was the undisputed national convention city in those days.

Gus, then part owner, was still managing the hotel at age eighty-seven and he was healthy, energetic, and mentally competent. One day I was there to speak to a convention of the National Standard Parts Association and watched Gus with admiration as he moved around, directing operations. I stopped him and asked, "How old are you, Gus?"

"What's the matter, isn't your room satisfactory and the service OK?"

"Oh, sure, it's perfect, as always."

"Well, then what's the difference how old I am?"

"I know how old you are, anyway, for you went to high school with my mother," I replied.

"Well, why bring it up?" growled Gus. Then he punched me in the chest and it was a solid blow, too, but it was his way of showing affection. "Let me give some advice, son; live your life and forget your age and always think health." With that, he punched me again and strode off masterfully. A man sitting nearby heard this interchange and asked, "How old is that man?"

"Eighty-seven," I replied, "and still running this hotel."

"He sure is."

"Incredible," he muttered, "absolutely incredible."

But you see, incredible things can happen to anyone who mentally takes charge, constantly sending healthy thoughts circulating, vibrating, and pulsating through the physical system. The general rule seems to be—and for a fact is—think right and feel right.

I believe that a positive-thinking person can, by the power of the mind, affirm and visualize health for many years beyond the average life span computed by insurance companies. This I believe because I have practiced affirmative health principles successfully to my present age of ninety-two years.

For example, I use an affirmation regarding blood pressure. The last two times my blood pressure was taken by a physician it registered 130 over 70. The affirmation I have used successfully was suggested by Dr. J. A. S. Sage, who was influenced by Dr. Niehams, the well-known Swiss physician. It goes somewhat as follows and should be affirmed aloud and repeated several times:

"My living body cells, which are always intelligently directed, are now making my arteries, veins, and tissues soft and flexible as in youth. My heart is strong and healthy and my blood pressure is within a normal range."

With this affirmation, I consciously visualize the entire body as functioning normally, picturing it as so doing from head to foot. In addition to this mental affirmation and visualization, I moderate my food intake, exercise regularly, principally by walking, and strictly keep all thoughts of resentment out of my mind.

By doing and writing about such procedures, I realize I may open myself to criticism. However, I was reared in a strict scientific tradition and was a long time in arriving at the foregoing suggestions. All I can say is these mental practices have worked and therefore I pass them along.

My friend the late Dr. Maxwell Maltz said, "The most important psychological discovery of this century is the discovery of the self-image." As we visualize ourselves in harmony with the laws of health, these laws are less impeded in doing their perfect work in our physical bodies.

The primary step to take in living long and having good physical health is to keep the mind active and healthy. This may be accomplished by becoming a strong believer, believing in yourself, in the future, in people, and in the watchful and loving care of God. And that includes positive thoughts which cast out pessimism. William Clarence Lieb, M.D., told me, "Experience has taught me to regard pessimism as a major symptom of early fossilization. It usually arrives with the first minor symptoms of physical decline."

So the way to health is certainly good medical attention, lack of stress, exercise, sensible eating, regular checkups, and, for sure, an attitude of love and healthy-mindedness.

The rise of psychological and psychiatric treatment and the development of religio-psychiatric healing centers, such as the Blanton Peale Institute in New York, illustrate the effect of mental attitudes on health.

Condition your life so that you are able at all times and under all circumstances to preserve your tranquillity and peace of mind. Take to heart the words of the wise Marcus Aurelius: "I affirm that tranquillity is nothing else than the good ordering of the mind. Constantly, then, give to thyself this retreat, and renew thyself."

▶ Remember the healing powers of love and forgiveness.

▶ Cultivate good will over hate and resentment.

▶ Healthy-mindedness and care for our physical well-being must work together.

CHAPTER 11

YOUR COMEBACK POWER

∎   ∎   ∎

MANY SUCCESSFUL PEOPLE I HAVE KNOWN HAD
one thing in common: They all had what it took to overcome setbacks. And what was the quality? It might be called comeback
power.

Our country was built by people who believed that things would
always be better. Even in times of adversity, such as war or economic depression, it has been characteristic of the American, by
nature positive in attitude, never to doubt that better days were
just ahead. And so the better times came. But they were achieved
by Americans thinking so, by believing in them, by trying and
working, by never giving up.

Everyone has to learn to look for better things if he or she expects better things to come. And they *will* come if one strongly
expects them to come. Expectation, the pure kind, has powerful
magnetic attraction. And this means you must be positive about
outcomes that may look like dead ends. Take, for example, the
experience of Tommy Herr, second baseman for the Minnesota
Twins, who told us at *Guideposts* magazine about how he suffered
a deep "low time" in his career when he was playing for the St.
Louis Cardinals.

It started on April 22, 1988, in St. Louis's Busch Stadium when someone tapped Tommy on the shoulder, saying, "Whitey wants to see ya."

"Whitey" is Whitey Herzog, the legendary manager of the Cardinals. Tommy, who had played in three World Series for Whitey and the Cards, made his way back to the team office, wondering what his boss wanted.

"As soon as I stepped through the door I knew something big was up," he said, for General Manager Dal Maxvill was standing behind Whitey, who was seated at his desk.

Whitey asked Tom to sit down. "I looked at Whitey and then at Dal questioningly," says Tommy, adding, "I felt my stomach start to lurch. Oh no, I thought. Not me!"

"Tommy," Whitey began in a tired, even tone, "you've been a fine player for me for nearly eight seasons. You've given the Cards everything we've asked of you. But . . ."

That "but" stopped Tommy's heart.

"But," continued Whitey, drawing a deep breath, "we've traded you to the Minnesota Twins for Tom Brunansky."

For an instant, time seemed to stand still for Tommy. "I kept trying to define and redefine the word 'trade' in my head. I knew exactly what it meant: to exchange, to swap, to get rid of. I just wanted it to mean something different this one time. I wanted to make believe I was being asked my opinion of such a wild idea, not being told that it was a done deal."

The general manager tried to explain why the move was good for both the players and the teams, how the Cards desperately needed a power-hitting right fielder like Brunansky.

"My eyes rested on a picture on the wall behind him—my picture—hanging along with some of the other veterans of pennant-winning and world championship Cardinal teams," said Tommy. "I wondered if Whitey would take down my picture now."

The thirty-two-year-old Tommy Herr couldn't believe he was no longer a Cardinal. He had started his career with the team. He expected to finish it in St. Louis as well. "I was in my prime as a ball player," he said.

Dal Maxvill wound up the meeting, saying, "I think you understand management's position. The Twins would like you to report in time for tomorrow night's game against the Cleveland Indians in Minneapolis. Good luck, Tom."

"I just wanted to get out of that office. Lick my wounds," said Tommy. "Whitey was looking at me blankly. What emotion was he masking? I knew this wasn't easy for him either. Almost as if in slow-motion replay, he stretched out his hand to mine."

The hardest part, Tommy says, was letting his wife, Kim, and children know about the trade. "We're going to Minnesota," he told his wife.

"Well," she replied, catching her breath, "I know this must be God's will, Tommy."

"I know I am part of God's great plan," said Tommy, "but my ego had taken a major broadside. All my life I've triumphed at sports. I'm not accustomed to being told to pack my bags. I'm always the guy everyone wants . . ."

Tommy's first few games with the Twins were a disaster. He was feeling desperate. Finally he got a hit. Four, in fact. A huge weight seemed to lift off his shoulders and he began feeling more comfortable at second base in the Twins' dome. He began to like the Twin Cities, he thought the fans were incredible, and his enthusiasm came bouncing back.

"It still hurts a little to think about the trade," says Tommy. "But dwelling on rejection is not good. I had to get over it and go to work on the baseball diamond like the veteran I am. In this game your time in the sun is very short. Besides, the Twins gave up a good player because they wanted me. I hadn't thought too much about that.

"I can see now that the trade wasn't personal," he concludes. "Baseball is a business as well as a sport, and the Cards' decision was a business decision, an even exchange, one good player for another."

Yes, Tommy Herr let his comeback power bring him back, all the way back and beyond.

The Creator built into you this marvelous power. It's really wonderful: One should always remember that he or she has it when everything seems to crash. Whatever you call it, "comeback power" or "rebound power," it is in your personality all the time, even in the worst of times. That is why things can always be better. You have it in you to make them better. Never forget that.

When we are trying to adjust to things that go wrong, we need to recognize that most of what is going wrong usually comes from within ourselves. If you claim that someone else is the cause of your problem, you are, in effect, saying that your destiny is out of your control.

We ourselves are almost always the cause of things going wrong. Of course, this does not include the sorrows and tragedies that are beyond all human control. But when things start going wrong with me personally, I always analyze my inner condition. I ask myself, "What am I doing to make these things happen?" A good, sharp, honest analysis will often reveal the truth.

If I may use another analogy from sports, I remember a major-league baseball pitcher telling me what he did when he was in a slump. (This applies to every person. No matter what your line of work, you can get into a slump.) Well, this pitcher was wise. In one of the periods when he was "going good," as he put it, he had movies taken of himself in action. In slow motion, he could see every move he made—where he put his foot, how he held the ball, how he delivered the pitch.

The next time he went into a slump, he had more movies taken, so that he could see exactly what he was doing that was wrong. Then he had the two pictures run simultaneously in slow motion, and he carefully studied the differences. He discovered that when he was in a slump, invariably he pushed his left foot forward on the pitcher's mound about three inches more than when he was pitching well.

This being the case, you might think that the cure would be simple; if he pulled his foot back three inches, the pitcher would correct the fault. But he was smarter than that; he asked himself what made him push the foot three inches forward. And he had to acknowledge that it was because he was overly anxious; he was afraid; consequently, he overpressed, and his foot crept forward and disturbed his normal pitching positions. So to cure the situation, he practiced getting calm and quiet in mind, imaging himself, getting the old harmony back. Being a religious man, he prayed and asked God that he might be in tune with Him. The foot came back to the proper place on the mound. And the ball was delivered properly. The slump ended.

Now, wouldn't it be wonderful if we could all take movies of ourselves during our good and bad periods and compare them? What you *can* do is take a mental picture of yourself. When you are on top of life and things are going smoothly, study what you're doing right, and hold it in your consciousness until it becomes a natural part of yourself. And when things go wrong, study yourself, asking honestly what is wrong with yourself. Then start correcting it.

You, my friendly reader, when coming to this chapter headed "Your Comeback Power," may have some doubts, especially if things have gone bad, really bad. "How can I ever make a comeback?" you may ask. "It's impossible to start over again." This is when negative thinking starts taking hold. And that is the precise moment to pull yourself up and take charge of your life. Affirm, *I'm going to make a comeback beginning now!* From this moment on, I'm thinking upward, visualizing upward, moving upward. I'm on my way back and I'm going to exceed everything I've done in the past, so help me God." Your comeback will be all the way back and beyond as you picture it in your mind.

The following story of Phyllis Diller (as told by John McCollister in the April 1989 issue of *The Saturday Evening Post*) tells how she achieved her thrilling comeback.

> *Thirty-six years ago, America's most well-known female comic didn't feel much like laughing. Phyllis Diller, a middle-aged housewife in Alameda, California, had hit rock bottom.*
>
> *"It was awful," she remembers. "My husband was fired from his job. We owed back mortgage payments. We knew that any day we would lose our home. The local grocer wouldn't give us food or credit. The power company threatened to turn off the electricity."*
>
> *Pressures at home became unbearable. Phyllis had to get away to someplace where she could sort things out. She walked—alone—around her neighborhood. She passed an open church and, on impulse, went inside.*
>
> *"Empty churches are a retreat for me," she says. "Even today, whenever I really want to think, I visit an empty church. The vibes, especially in a large cathedral, are pow-*

erful. An empty church is the one place I can go to get in touch with the 'inner me.' "

As she meditated there in solitude, she realized she was being dominated by negative-thinking people and negative circumstances. She made a private vow not to allow this to happen to her again.

"It seemed as though God Himself wanted me to get that message," she says. "Of course, my life didn't turn around instantly. But that new conviction got me pointed in the right direction. I had read books on the subject of self-motivation, but putting it to practice is much different. My first step was to realize that I had to stop wallowing in self-pity and negative thoughts about what a hard time I was having.

"I had a new confidence," she says. "I went out and got a job in a local radio station. Sure, I still got scared at times, but I faced all my fears eyeball-to-eyeball and never let them get the best of me."

She learned to hate the word "quit."

Just two years after her low point she resigned from her job at the radio station to pursue a career as a stand-up comic. When she handed in her two-week notice, her station manager promised to keep her job open in case she failed to make it. Without hesitation, Phyllis promised him, "I shall not return."

She was nervous, scared, and unsure of herself at her audition. But she galvanized her gumption, walked onto the stage, and gave it her best. She passed the test and was signed to perform for two weeks.

Her act was filled with jokes about the one subject she knew best—being a housewife. Patrons howled with laughter. Many returned to hear more. The owner was pleased enough to extend her contract. Diller stayed for nearly two years.

Phyllis Diller went on to become a national success. "So what?" you say. "I'm not a Phyllis Diller." The answer is, neither did Phyllis think she was, but she began to practice positive thinking. She **became a believer in herself and discovered talents reposing** within just waiting to be activated. You cannot really know what super accomplishments are waiting inside you. Release them. That's why we list the five creative principles: think, learn, try, work, believe. And be joyful. They work magic for those who believe in God, who believe in themselves, and who believe in the future.

You may not become a national celebrity on your comeback trail, but things can become better, much better, and that is our goal, to achieve the better life and live there with joy.

Here is another story of comeback power, of the many I could tell. It is recounted by Dianne Hales, in an article entitled "Starting Over" in the May 1988 issue of *McCall's*, and features Carol, widowed and suffering other misfortunes, who made her comeback by trying, working, believing, and thinking positive thoughts.

> *On an icy February day in 1981, a tractor trailer skidded across a highway, smashed into a car and killed the driver instantly. In that terrible moment, Carol lost her husband, her sense of security in the world and her plans for the future. At the age of 42, she was going to have to start again.*
>
> *"I had three children in grade school. I hadn't worked in twelve years. I knew nothing about making or managing money," she recalls. "At night I'd lie in bed and fight back the panic that just about overwhelmed me. But every morning I got up and told myself to just keep putting one foot ahead of the other." She took the first job she could get, as a sales clerk in a dress store. On weekends and evenings, she studied real estate. "We weren't penniless, but I needed to support my family, and I didn't have the time to go back and finish college."*
>
> *As soon as she got her Realtor's license, Carol began working with non-stop energy and determination. She became the county's "real-estate rookie of the year," selling more houses than any other new agent in her area. "Fear was my biggest motivation," she says. Within five years she was one of the top sales agents in the state. In the process of building her business, she built a new life for herself and her children and discovered capabilities she never suspected*

*she had. "It was the hardest thing I've ever done," she says.
"But I'm a stronger, wiser person because of what I've been
through."*

We all know people who have suffered similar losses or setbacks. Some, like Carol, bounce back to find new meaning in life.
Others, hit no harder by fate, never scramble to their feet again.
They wrap themselves in self-pity, drink, live in the past, sink into
depression. Why do some individuals thrive after a setback when
others barely survive? Experts in adult development have identified the following characteristic in people who make successful
comebacks from crises:

"The critical thing is self-esteem," says David Chiriboga, Ph.D., a
specialist in human development at the University of Texas Medical School in Galveston. "If that's intact, you can weather any
storm."

Be a maximizer. When you want to do something that seems
impossible your biggest obstacle may be a low self-esteem. If you
have an inferior feeling about yourself, you are a minimizer.
Never be a minimizer! Always be a maximizer! Everyone has
greater powers than we ever realize.

Develop a positive mental attitude toward the bottom. I have
often had to deal with glum and discouraged people who have
said, "I've hit bottom and there is no hope." To one such man I
replied, "Congratulations. Having hit bottom, you can go no
lower; the only direction is up. So start thinking *up*." He did, and
after a time new ideas came that helped him to move up well
above the bottom.

"Now," he said, "I'm actually glad to know that the bottom is
down there to shield me from further decline in the future." He
had actually turned the bottom into an asset!

I remember during my many years as pastor in New York City,
there were in the congregation a large number of visitors from out
of town—buyers, salespeople, financial executives, managers, and
CEO's—men and women from all over the country. I noticed a
particular face in the crowd every now and then, a striking face
because it showed pain and misery.

It was a man aged forty or forty-five, so I estimated. This face
rather haunted me because it was so obviously the face of a very

unhappy man. But he never came to shake hands with me, as many visitors did each week.

But I happened to encounter him on the sidewalk and in the brief conversation he said, "I would like to talk with you sometime if you can give me an appointment." We fixed a time and he came and sat, nervously clasping his hands. Finally he said, "I've got to talk. I can't handle it anymore. Is this conversation absolutely confidential?"

"Absolutely and you'd better get whatever it is off your mind," I replied.

Then he told me that he was the financial man for a manufacturing business in a far-off location in the United States. He had been living beyond his means. He didn't blame his wife, whom he loved devotedly, but I had a suspicion that she and their two children figured Daddy would give them everything they wanted. So he accumulated debts.

"Dr. Peale, I had lived honestly all my life, but I had to have more money and, God help me, I siphoned it off our company."

"How much have you 'siphoned off?'" I asked.

He flushed and obviously it went hard with him to discuss his dishonesty. But he finally said, "A bit over $200,000. I know the exact amount to the last cent." And then he added, "My boss, our president, has been like a father to me, the kindest, most caring man in the world. He has given me every opportunity since I went to work and I'm—" he hesitated "—a dirty, thieving, no-good crook."

"Could you siphon back in the amount you have taken?"

Sadly he shook his head. "I've thought of that, but I'm about strapped. I'd have to sell my house and my wife and children would have to know why."

"Then," I said, "it comes down to this: Have you got what it takes to be completely honest now? If you have, your comeback power will, I think, come to your aid and get you over this situation. But what I'm about to suggest will take every bit of manhood you've got in you. And that you have strength is shown by how you are suffering."

"With God's help I'll do anything you advise," he said in almost a whisper.

"OK, here's my suggestion. Go back home and go to your presi-

dent and tell him just what you have done and promise to pay
back every cent and submit your resignation. If he is the kind of
man you describe him as being, I think he will do what is necessary for the company; but he will think of you, also. He may be
tough, though."

He went back and told his president everything. Later, he reported on the interview. "My president just sat back listening to all
the lousy story. And when I had finished he was silent for a long
time. Finally he got up and stood looking out the window. Then he
came and, looking down at me, he said, in his kind voice, "You
poor fellow. I'm so sorry for you, Bill." (That isn't his real name.)
"It's hard for a good man to be a thief. You must be suffering hell.
Of course, you will repay your company. I'm taking you out of
your financial job. I think you will do well in sales. Your salary
will be less and you can add to it by commission. You've got to
reduce your lifestyle. But frugality may be good for you and the
family. And, Bill, this is just between you and me."

"And what did you say?" I asked.

"I told him that he was the best man who ever lived and I would
try to be a good salesman. I couldn't say more, I was too choked
up."

The rest of the story is that Bill paid it all back and made good in
sales. He had comeback power, which he used to the full.

Believe that you can, you can, you can. Personalize that word
"can" and say it aloud every day: "I can, I can, I can." Success is
lurking in your mind. Let it out. Let it come to life. Think it out,
pray it out, believe it out. Phyllis Schneider, in an article called
"Career Charisma" in *Working Woman* magazine, May 1988, cor-
roborates the power of positive thinking.

> *The real winners in business and in life, the women and*
> *men who are tapped for golden career opportunities, have*
> *something extra.*
> *The people with charmed careers have a way of looking*
> *at the world that makes top management feel they can do*
> *almost any job superbly, that imbues everybody with whom*
> *they work with a kind of enthusiastic, winning spirit. Their*
> *success is as much a matter of attitude as of hard work and*

talent. They are optimists. That optimism is astonishingly powerful, and it can be cultivated.

Although Norman Vincent Peale has championed the virtues of "positive thinking" for more than 35 years, only recently have serious researchers started to explore the ways optimism affects not only one's health and longevity but career success as well.

A number of studies confirm what Peale intuitively knew was correct: The optimist almost invariably has an edge over less enthusiastic colleagues.

So practice thinking comeback power. Such positive thinking will summon that force you possess from the inner resources of your nature.

▶ Believe that you have it in you. Never doubt it.

▶ Your comeback power is always there, ready to work for you when needed.

▶ Just be a believer, a real believer.

CHAPTER 12

THE OLD,
EVER NEW SECRET OF
SUCCESS

■   ■   ■

IN 1931, A REMARKABLE MOTIVATIONAL BOOK WAS published. The author was Vash Young, one of the most successful insurance producers of that era. The book, *A Fortune to Share*, became a very popular and widely read book of that time. I read my copy at least once a year for quite a while.

Then I put it on a top shelf in my library and there it remained until 1989. One day, while searching for another book, I saw *A Fortune to Share* and took it down, opened it to page one, and started reading. It gripped me and held me enthralled by its simple, commonsense philosophy of success, which is as true and factual today as it was in the thirties and forties.

The impressive story is that of a man who was failing but came upon a commonsense and workable secret, and by it vaulted to immense success. The ideas put forth in the book must have penetrated deeply into my consciousness, for it is, in a sense, a forerunner of my own book, published twenty-one years later, *The Power of Positive Thinking*.

Since perhaps most of you never read it, let me draw a bit on this book that helped to turn many failures into successes over fifty years ago. These principles can do the same for you now. The author wrote:

"I am one of those lucky fellows who inherited a great fortune, which came to me after years of poverty and reckless living."

The great fortune Vash Young received was a new idea that led to success. He describes the idea thus:

> Start sharing myself with others. What a simple idea! But I found there is enough of myself to go around no matter how many others take a cut. It is not the kind of wealth that is affected by bank failure, stock-market crashes, or business depression.
>
> The man who brought me riches inherent in this idea resembled me in every outward way. As a matter of fact, he was my former self. I had given up a fruitless struggle and died. The autopsy showed my former self had died of selfishness, pessimism, fear, worry, indecision, vain regrets, stewing about business, irritability, envy, false desires, negative thinking, and other complications.
>
> My new self took this inheritance, this new positive idea into the business world, and made me successful beyond my fondest hopes. I started giving myself away, and soon discovered that the more I gave the more I had. Men and women of great affairs began coming to me, bringing business with them. It often happens that the man who pursues the dollar too diligently finds it hard to catch; but if he pursues some other and better goal, dollars come around to see what sort of fellow he is.
>
> The old Vash Young was an advertising salesman who was doing nothing worth speaking of. Then he became an insurance salesman, starting from scratch in the most highly competitive of occupations. It looked like seven lean years ahead. An acquaintance of mine, learning that I had cut loose from regular pay checks and had started out on a precarious commission basis with less than a hundred dollars, and with a wife and daughter to care for, was decidedly alarmed. "Vash, you are in a hell of a fix!" said he.
>
> Outwardly, I was. But inwardly I was in a heaven of a fix, for I had challenged negative thinking to a death battle, and had won the preliminary skirmish. There is no finer sensa-

*tion in life than that which comes with victory over one's
self. It feels good to go fronting into a hard wind, winning
against its power; but it feels a thousand times better to go
forward to a goal of inward achievement, brushing aside
all your old internal enemies as you advance . . .*

*Doubts tried to creep into my mind, but every time a neg-
ative thought came to me, I stopped, mentally if not physically, challenged it, thrust it out of my consciousness and
thought of something worthwhile. This is a habit any one
can acquire. At first the unwholesome thoughts of fear, negativism and the like will struggle, but they are not strong
enough to win. Crowd them out of your mind. Think of
something positive.*

Vash Young did, and went on to claim victory.

Suppose you owned a factory. Would you manufacture only
goods that you—or anyone else—do not want, do not need, and
cannot use? Would you deliberately operate your factory in such a
way as to make it definitely harmful to you, the owner? Well, then,
consider that you do own a factory, a thought factory. It is inside
you, and you are both owner and superintendent. Nothing can
happen in that factory without your approval. Nothing can go into
it, neither raw materials nor partly manufactured goods, except
with your permission. Nothing can come out of it except the products that you yourself design.

"A thought factory! That's what you have inside you," Vash
Young said. Take a look at your products. Fear, worry, impatience,
anger, doubt. Are you proud of them? Not a bit of it! Your factory
is capable of taking the raw materials of experience, mingling
them with faith, love, courage, and compassion, and thus becoming a plant worth operating. Your thought factory should produce
positive, self-confident thoughts which naturally lead to positive,
successful results.

Another industrial pioneer who knew how to run his thought
factory successfully, as well as ship-building yards and other man-

ufacturing plants, was Henry J. Kaiser. Here are his five rules for
being successful.

First: *Know yourself and decide what you want to
             make out of your life. Then write down your
             goals and a plan to reach them.*
Second: *Use the great powers you can tap through faith in
             God, the hidden energies of your soul and your
             subconscious mind.*
Third: *Love people and serve them.*
Fourth: *Develop positive traits of character and personal-
             ity.*
Fifth: *Work! Put your life's plan into determined action.
             Go after what you want with all that's in you!*

I remembered these rules when a father came up to speak to me
after I addressed a convention of businessmen in Pittsburgh. He
referred to the talk I had just given and then said, "Dr. Peale, I
have a gut feeling that you could get my son turned around; and
that would be a miracle." I reminded him that I was not a miracle
worker, that I dealt only in time-tested ideas that, if followed,
could turn a person from failure to success. "That is all I try to
do," I said.

"That's plenty," he replied. "My son is an attractive and smart
fellow, but he fails at everything he undertakes; every job he gets
results finally in failure. And my son is now twenty-nine years old.
And," he added, "he was an honor student in college. Maybe he
shot his wad there. I've seen good students who amounted to nothing after they graduated. He is willing to see anybody I suggest. He
has already been to the best psychiatrist."

"Well," I replied, "I'll see him, but I'm a simple soul with simple,
though workable, ideas. Is your son big enough to be simple, or
does he go only for the complex?"

"I don't know, but maybe you can reach him. I pray you will."

"OK. Keep the prayers going. I'll take a whack at him."

When the son came to my office, he proved to be a polite and
rather gracious young man. He was impressive physically but
soon began to put himself down. "My father asked you to talk with

me, didn't he? He is one of the business leaders in this city. He wants me to be like him, and, frankly, I haven't the ability."

"But in college . . ." I put in.

"Oh, that was a fluke," he quickly said. "I just repeated back what the professors wanted. I haven't got any creative brains. Guess I'm good for nothing." This was all said in the first five minutes of the conversation.

"Low self-esteem," I commented.

"Yes, the psychiatrist told me that and charged me $150 for the information."

"Look," I said, "I do not want to embarrass you, but we've been together for about five minutes and you have volunteered the following negatives:

1. *You haven't your father's ability.*
2. *Your honors in college were a fluke.*
3. *You haven't a creative brain.*
4. *You're good for nothing.*
5. *You admit to low self-esteem.*

"Now I put it to you, an educated man, how can you expect to succeed at a job with all those adverse self-concepts working against you? I rather guess that subconsciously you have been competing with your father and given up on yourself. Did it ever occur to you that you are the only person with whom you should compete? Have you ever thought of being truly yourself? Why not try adding up your assets.

1. *Fine physique.*
2. *Polite.*
3. *Gracious.*
4. *Personable.*
5. *Got a good brain for something other than for what your father does.*

Then I told him Henry J. Kaiser's rules for success.

"That is the end of this interview," I said in conclusion. "I'm sorry, but I must get a plane back to New York. But I want to see you again soon."

I gave him a date two weeks hence in my office in New York City. "But," I said, "before that interview, I want you to find a guy who is really down-and-out and try to help him. Approach him in the way I've taken you on. I also want you to think about what you would like to do as a major life work and tell me about it when next we meet."

At the second interview he said, "I ran into a classmate, Alvin, whom I hadn't seen since college. He told me he was dragging bottom. His father is a professor and wanted Alvin to be a professor also, but all Alvin was able to get in college was a B— average, so his father said he could never accumulate the degrees necessary for a professorship. But Alvin's a whiz at music, and I found that he would like to go into that. So I told him to be a man and do what he wanted to do. And I've got him adding up his assets to counteract his negativism like you did with me. I'm going to help that guy make something of himself," he added enthusiastically.

"And what would *you* like to do?" I asked.

"Well, I have a friend who is in the head-hunting business. He brings executives to companies in the $100,000 to $300,000 salary range and is doing real well at it. He says I would be a natural in that business, recommending executives to upper management. He wants me to come in with him to learn the business. Maybe later I could start up such a business for myself." He was enthusiastic when telling me this, but then the steam seemed to go out of him when he said, "But, of course, Dad would turn thumbs down."

"What about that advice you gave your classmate to be a man?"

"I know, I've thought of that," he said wistfully, looking down at the floor. Suddenly, he straightened up, looked me in the eye, and said, "You know, I believe I'll do it, anyway! Do you really think I have what it takes? Imagine my locating top executives!" His new tone of voice made me feel he could hardly wait to get started.

I gave him this advice. "Start imaging and visualizing yourself as one of the finest top executive placement experts in the country. You can do it!"

By his reaction I could see that we had found the key to this young man. And he did actually become what he visualized.

Some years later I spoke at a business luncheon in the Duquesne

Club in Pittsburgh and his father came up afterward. "Remember me?" he asked. Then he added, "We sure did hit the jackpot with my son. He's the best in that business. No firm in this town would think of hiring a top executive except through him."

I replied, "I'm not surprised."

Later that day I called to see the young man in his impressive suite of offices. Seated behind a big desk he said, "You know all those ideas you gave me? Well, I've found where you got them." He reached in his center drawer and drew out a Bible. "You got 'em right out of this book," he said.

"Smart fellow," I declared.

"They certainly work," he affirmed, putting the book back in the drawer. "I keep it handy," he explained.

Of course, the certain way to success involves other principles as well: the think principle, the work principle, the study principle. A person who thinks about his or her job, how to perform it better, is bound to be promoted to better and more important jobs. For example, the late well-known banker Gates W. McGarrah was a friend of mine. He held a top post in the Morgan banking interest in the Wall Street area. At one time he was head of the International Bank with headquarters at Basel, Switzerland.

I asked him one day how he got the start which eventuated in his becoming one of the great bankers of the world. "It's simple," he replied. "I came of a poor but religious family upstate. And I had to leave school and go to work. So I walked into the bank in the village where we lived and asked for a job because I wanted to be a banker.

"The banker looked at me. 'Are you willing to work?' he asked. 'Yes, sir, I am.' 'Well, the only job we have is to open up and sweep and dust, and,' he added, 'clean the spittoons, too. Most customers chew tobacco. It also includes cleaning the toilets, also emptying wastebaskets. The last boy we had was no good. How about you?' 'You've described the job. Sir, you can trust me to do it well,' I asserted confidently."

The bank opened at nine o'clock, but everybody reported to work by eight-thirty. Gates showed up at six. He planned his cleaning campaign, vowing, "I'm going to be the best cleaner in New York State."

The thing that bothered him the most was the brass spittoons. Just wiping them left them smeared. So he went to his mother about it. She recommended brass polish, but that was an unaccustomed outlay for the bank. So out of the ten dollars he got on Saturday he bought some brass polish. The spittoons gleamed. The bank's president said, "Good boy, Gates. We never had such beautiful spittoons."

Gates hung around after work asking questions of the other employees about the banking business. He did his own work better than anybody had ever done it before. But he didn't limit his thinking to his cleaning job. He thought and studied banking. He worked hard and intelligently, thinking and studying always. One day the president called him in. "Good boy, Gates. Can you train a cleaning boy to do your job as well as you? I've got a better position for you."

"I'll supervise him, sir," said Gates. And he was on his way to Wall Street and an outstanding career.

The sure way to success is so simple, but it requires character, guts, persistence, the mastery of lower jobs to be ready for the better ones.

Concluding his narrative, Mr. McGarrah repeated once again, "I'm proud that I was the best cleaner in any bank in the State of New York." He definitely felt that doing every job well, plus thinking, studying, working, contributed to his total success.

At a hotel in Europe, I once met a pleasant-faced, good-natured German boy named Hans who had already made some wise choices in life. He was the hotel restaurant's busboy. Hans had an outgoing and enthusiastic personality. He was alert to everyone's needs and eager to be helpful, not only to the guests, but to his fellow workers as well. He liked responsibility.

From our talks, I learned that Hans had a specific goal. He wanted to become maitre d' of a great European hotel. He had decided to be the best possible busboy, because he knew that this was the first step in reaching his objective.

To reach his goal, he knew it was necessary to go to London for the essential training in his field. "London seems a long way off, especially since I have no money," he said to me.

"You're on the right track," I told him. "You've chosen the profession you wish to enter, and you've made the first step in climbing the ladder by giving your present job all you've got." I gave Hans this advice. "Hold in your mind a picture of reaching your goal. Image yourself running one of Europe's most distinguished hotel dining rooms. Image the terrific job you're going to do!"

I gave him a copy of the German edition of *The Power of Positive Thinking*. "You are already a positive thinker," I said, "but I want you to read this book and learn the wisdom of choosing to put your life in God's hands."

Several years later, when Ruth and I were guests in an elegant London restaurant of a prestigious hotel, the headwaiter said something that touched off my memory of Hans. I looked closer and he smiled. "Dr. Peale," he said, "I'm Hans, and I'm still practicing positive thinking."

I was pleased to learn that he had made it to London and was attaining his goal. All because of the choices he had made!

I had a friend who worked in the Ford Motor Company plant in Dearborn, Michigan, during the time the original Henry Ford was active. He told me about a workman on the assembly line who was also a thinker. Instead of complaining about the monotony of assembly-line production, he gave it creative thought and on his own began to perform a certain process differently, more efficiently.

One day, engrossed in thought, he failed to notice Henry Ford standing by his side peering at his procedure. Mr. Ford did not criticize him for varying the process, but simply asked, "Why?"

He, too, became engrossed in examining the variation. Finally he said, "You have demonstrated a better way of doing things. You are a thoughtful and constructive man." It is not surprising that he moved up in the Ford organization. The worker and the thinker and the giver always go ahead. That is the sure way to success.

In Seoul, Korea, in January of 1990 I was invited by my friend Mr. In Gyung Go to visit his language school. There were seven thousand young men and women studying eight languages.

"Why so many students of languages?" I asked, greatly impressed.

Mr. Go replied, "Because young people in Seoul realize they will spend their lives in an international world. Frankly, they want to get ahead, to achieve success. They believe that one way to do that is to be proficient in languages."

I found the atmosphere in that language school to be dynamic and stimulating and decided it was because everyone was practicing self-improvement and each had a goal.

Then I spent a few days with a good friend, Joseph Dunkle, in Tokyo. He is an American who served in Japan during World War II, liked it, married Yuki, a charming Japanese woman, and stayed.

Joe has successfully developed a cookie business called Aunt Stella's Cookies. He caters to the Japanese preference for crisp cookies and his business has boomed, with approximately sixty stores. Joe is the first American to be on the board of directors of two Japanese companies. He speaks the Japanese language fluently.

Joe is a thinker, always considering and discussing positive ideas about the future. While I was on my recent trip, as we talked of the business success of the Japanese, Joe said, "OK, call it aggressiveness or perseverance of the Japanese. But my observation is that Americans formerly created wealth with enthusiasm and hard work. Now, instead, they are churning wealth. And the Japanese are now the ones using wealth creatively."

What a keen analysis.

Grandma Moses was born in 1860 on a farm in Greenwich, New York. She spent the next seventy-five years with a genius for painting locked within her. At the age of seventy-six, she picked up a paintbrush and unlocked that genius. By the time of her death, she had completed more than one thousand nostalgic scenes of rural life, many of them displayed in some of the world's greatest museums.

Her talent was there all those years, lying dormant. It was not until her thinking changed, until she discovered her native talent, that she found fulfillment in painting.

Change your thoughts. Open your mind to new ideas and see how your life changes for the better.

▶ Ask yourself: "How can I expect to succeed if I have a negative self-concept?"

▶ List your assets when you're feeling hopeless or inadequate.

▶ Do every job—no matter how "small"—with care and enthusiasm.

▶ Go after your goal with faith—and image yourself achieving it.

CHAPTER 13

YOUR CENSOR KNOWS—TRUST IT

■   ■   ■

THERE IS A FASCINATING DEVICE BUILT WITHIN each of us that never ceases to amaze me. Like an automated radio beacon, it continually sends messages to us which, if listened to and followed, enhance our lives immeasurably. If we disregard these messages, we can crash and perhaps fail.

Your censor is persistently powerful, always awake, and invariably factual. It has an uncanny facility for discerning the right path among the many options facing you. It tells you clearly—both consciously and unconsciously—whether a thought or action is right or wrong. It does not deal in "ifs" or "buts." It does not ever argue a matter, or rationalize a decision. Its conclusions are never gray; they are only wrong or right.

Your censor likes you and is working for you. It wants only success and happiness for you. But it will not compromise and go along with you when something you want to do is wrong, or when you can't see why it isn't okay and argue that everyone else is doing it. The only standard your censor has is simply: Is it right? And the reason it is unchanging in its messages to you is that it wants to shield you from failure and the misery that results from wrong thinking and wrong action. Your censor is not a killjoy. It is a *builder* of joy! It is *for* you, not *against* you. It is your friend. And if you listen to its friendly counsel, and always accept its wise advice, you will have the best in life and be successful as a person, and happy, too.

What happens when you do not heed your censor's sensible counsel? It creates within you a vague, dissatisfied feeling. It may even be the low-grade, but persistent, self-disgust you feel when you commit a wrong; or it may be a gnawing regret when you are presented with an opportunity, but don't think you are up to it and so let it go by, wishing forever after that you had had the nerve to do it.

What, really, is this thing I call a "censor?" Is it conscience? No, I believe it is more basic, for conscience is something acquired by religious teaching, whereas the censor works in even unlearned or irreligious people. Some might argue that it's the accumulated experience of all your forebears, passed down almost like instinct. I also believe it is not only a natural part of a human being, but also something God put in each of us in order to hear His voice. All are endowed with it.

A sensitivity to right and wrong is in all people, for even the most ignorant have a bell that rings inside them when they act meanly or dishonestly or cruelly to a fellow being, or when they shy away from an opportunity.

Most of what I know about the censor I learned from my old friend and colleague Dr. Smiley Blanton. He talked about the censor often, and I came to trust him as an authority on the matter.

A definition for "censor" in a dictionary goes something like this: "Censor—the force that represses unacceptable ideas, impulses, and feelings and prevents them from reaching the conscious mind." The word comes from the title of two wise magistrates of ancient Rome who not only took the census, but regulated public behavior for the good of all.

The most famous and heroic of these was the Roman statesman Cato the Censor (234–149 B.C.). He was renowned for his devotion to simplicity of life, honesty, courage, loyalty to family and country, sexual morality, and ability to endure hardship.

If the absence of trouble resulting from wrong actions means something to you, if the inexpressible satisfaction of feeling good about yourself appeals to you, go for another principle: *Do only what you know to be right if you want to gain real happiness.*

This is one of the safest principles for making things go well for you. People who think that this concept is outmoded, or who assume they can have an easy, bendable moral attitude and get away with it forever, always find otherwise. Adherence to a proven moral code does not guarantee sweetness and light. But it does promise an enveloping feeling of rightness much more surely than when we bend the laws for pleasure.

Sometimes we try to fool ourselves when our censor advises us not to do something, and the consequences are always bad. I'll never forget the story of Iron Eyes Cody, the movie and TV star you may remember from the famous TV spot for the "Keep America Beautiful" campaign. He was the Indian in a canoe with the single tear rolling down his cheek when he saw our polluted waters.

Iron Eyes used to relate an old Indian legend about a young lad who ignored the censor's voice within him.

"Many years ago, Indian youths would go away in solitude to prepare for manhood. One such youth hiked into a beautiful valley, green with trees, bright with flowers. There he fasted. But on the third day, as he looked up at the surrounding mountains, he noticed one tall, rugged peak, capped with dazzling snow.

"*I will test myself against that mountain*, he thought. He put on his buffalo-hide shirt, threw his blanket over his shoulders, and set off to climb the peak.

"When he reached the top he stood on the rim of the world. He could see forever, and his heart swelled with pride. Then he heard a rustle at his feet, and looking down, he saw a snake. Before he could move, the snake spoke:

" 'I am about to die,' said the snake. 'It is too cold for me up here and I am freezing. There is no food and I am starving. Put me under your shirt and take me down the valley.'

" 'No,' said the youth. 'I am forewarned. I know your kind. You are a rattlesnake. If I pick you up, you will bite, and your bite will kill me.'

" 'Not so,' said the snake. 'I will treat you differently. If you do this for me, you will be special. I will not harm you.'

"The youth resisted awhile, but this was a very persuasive snake with beautiful markings. At last the youth tucked it under his shirt and carried it down to the valley. There he laid it gently on the grass, when suddenly the snake coiled, rattled, and leapt, biting him on the leg.

" 'But you promised—' cried the youth.

" 'You knew what I was when you picked me up,' said the snake as it slithered away.

"And now, wherever I go," says Iron Eyes, "I tell that story. I tell it especially to the young people of this nation who might be tempted by drugs. I want them to remember the words of the snake: *You knew what I was when you picked me up.*"

Yes, tragedy can result when we don't listen to our censor. For, as I said, it always has our good at heart. An interesting example of what can happen when someone pays attention to his censor, despite the world's argument, was told by Donald Seibert, who was chairman of the board of J. C. Penney stores for many years.

It happened in 1946 when he was a young man recently discharged from World War II military service. Newly married with a six-week-old daughter, he was trying to pick up the pieces of his life. The little family was in desperate financial straits, and when he was offered a summer job in May of that year, playing the piano in an eight-piece orchestra at a resort on Chautauqua Lake in western New York State, he jumped at the chance.

He and his wife and baby daughter joined up with the other seven band members at Bemus Point. For living quarters they leased, for the summer, rooms at a resort near the pavilion where they would play. Their landlord depended on the rent for support of his own family.

The summer started out well as patrons thronged the pavilion to listen to "The Rhythmaires" with "The Romantic Vocals of Donny Seibert." But then in mid July chilly, rainy weather set in that just wouldn't go away. Business got so bad that the pavilion owner couldn't pay the band members' salaries on time. Their landlord listened sympathetically and said they could pay him their rent when things got better. But the weather worsened.

One by one, the band members slipped away in the middle of the night. Finally, only Don and his family were left. It would have been simple for him to disappear, too, and leave the landlord holding the bag.

"You've got to look out for Number One," said one band member to Don before he took off. *He was right,* Don thought, *I have to look out for Number One.*

But then he listened to his censor. God, he realized, was Number One.

God had helped his wife through a dangerous childbirth; God had sustained his family this far. "And He was the one Who directed us to love our neighbor as ourselves," said Don.

The next morning the landlord was surprised to find Don Seibert still there.

"You . . . you didn't leave?" he asked.

"No," said Don, "we're staying on to the end of our lease."

Don asked if he could pay off the rent by working at the resort. So he cleaned tourist cabins, changed beds, and washed sheets. By the time Labor Day came he still owed the landlord $150.

So Don got a job at a nearby grape-juice processing plant for 75 cents an hour. He had to rise at 4:30 A.M. to be there on time. It was rough work, hauling the heavy canvas juice filters from the presses and washing them. The temperature neared 130 degrees and Don's fingers cracked open from the acid in the juice. But for some reason he found himself working with enthusiasm.

Finally, in October he was able to pay up the last of the lease. The landlord had tears in his eyes. "It's not the money," he said, gratefully thanking Don. "It's just so reassuring to know that there are people in the world who are as good as their word." Then he added, "You'll go far, son. You'll go far."

Yes, Don Seibert did go far.

Not long after that he got a job as a shoe clerk with J.C. Penney in Bradford, Pennsylvania. He kept listening to his censor and made his way from assistant store manager to manager and on up the ladder to become chairman of the board.

But I know of a man, I'll call him Tom, who did not listen to his censor. He was a district sales manager for a large office-supplies company. He often hosted dinners for his individual salesmen where they discussed business. However, company policy forbade him paying for his salesmen's dinner tabs.

Other district managers advised him to put down a phony name on his expense account. His censor left him feeling uneasy about doing this, but a fellow district manager argued, "Everybody does it."

So that's what Tom did. "One season I used up the whole roster of the New York Yankees for phony names," he said.

Then Tom was offered a better job with another firm and he took it. In his new job, he often took customers to dinner. Of course, he had a legitimate reason for picking up the tab. However, Tom's old habit was so ingrained in him that he continued putting down phony names.

One day a large corporation took over his firm in a merger. Tom went along doing things as usual. That is, until six months later when his boss called him in.

"Tom, new management has had their comptrollers checking into every phase of our financial operations and they found something amiss with your expense accounts. What's going on?"

Tom admitted what he had been doing and, under the circumstances, he had no choice but to resign.

"It was a lesson I'll never forget," said Tom, who now is working with a firm in another part of the country. "Something sort of whispered at me when I started putting down phony names. I should have listened to that little voice [censor] within instead of the other guy."

Of course, there are many others in similar circumstances who don't get caught. They seem to get away with it. But someone knows! The censor knows; it never forgets, and it continuously reacts. And why? Because it represents the best in every human being. And for some reason, known only to the Creator, that best will not tolerate being flouted.

Our censor can produce good feelings, very good feelings. I once called an air-conditioner company and asked if the firm handled a certain make which I had become convinced was the best in the business. My high opinion of this product was based on the perfect air conditioning in a hotel room where I stayed overnight in superhot weather. So I was sold on this make and model.

The company sent one around with a salesman. Well, he gave me a moderate, sensible explanation of air conditioners, climate variation, and humidity control, which amounted to this: "We think this make and model is one of the best available and its record of performance seems to be pretty good. But it's probably no better an air conditioner than I am a man, and I try to be a good man. I don't really aspire to be the best man in the world, but I do believe that this is a good air conditioner. And if you take care of it and handle it right, I think it will be giving you satisfaction five years from now."

Well, I looked with admiration at that quiet, sensible, honest man. His censor was obviously in good working order. Actually, I bought *him* rather than the air conditioner. It's long past five years, and the air conditioner is still going strong. While we were completing the purchase, we got to talking, and I complimented him on his forthrightness. "Well, I try to do what I believe is right," he said, somewhat abashed, "and that's the only way I can feel good about myself."

Noticing my Rotary Club pin, he told me he was also a Rotarian. A while later I met a member of his club and asked if he knew this air-conditioner salesman. "Do I know him! Well, I should say I do," said the man. "He is one of the most decent and happiest men I know. He has a lot on the ball and is," he added, "a terrific salesman, too."

How Reggie Jackson, the famous ball player, let his censor help him in adverse circumstances during a crucial World Series game in 1973 has always intrigued me.

He was the star outfielder of the Oakland Athletics at the time. And during the Series he received a death threat.

"At first I had tried to laugh it off," he said. "But then I thought of Martin Luther King, of John and Robert Kennedy. Their killings didn't make sense either."

His club assured him there would be bodyguards, the FBI promised to be on hand, and the whole park would be kept under surveillance.

"Even so, what could they do for a man standing all alone out there on the diamond?" he questioned. "I began to visualize a fanatic on a roof overlooking the park. He's holding a high-powered rifle. I'm in the batter's box waiting for the pitch. He lines up the cross hairs of the telescopic sight and slowly squeezes the trigger . . ."

Reggie realized he could never play ball with that fear inside him. It would be more crippling than a pulled hamstring muscle.

Then he remembered his father. His dad had run a little tailor shop in Wyncote, Pennsylvania, where Reggie grew up. His father had played semi-pro ball and taught Reggie much of what he knew about baseball. He had also taught his son a most important lesson when he caught him swiping candy bars at the local grocery store.

"Play square with your fellow man—no lying, no cheating or stealing—and The Man Upstairs will take care of you," he told Reggie.

"Dad's simple beliefs became the basis of my faith," Reggie said. "Not only did I never steal again, but I learned to respond to that inner voice that told me whether I was doing right or wrong."

From his father's guidance, Reggie said he gained a deep inner peace, a sense of protection, an assurance that all would be well and "if I tried to play square with the other guy, God would take care of me."

When he advanced in the major leagues, he admits he made mistakes, losing his temper, throwing his cap or bat.

"Finally, though, I began to grow up," he says. "And each year I enjoyed baseball more. When I could jump on a 'heater' or fast ball and hit a long 'dinger' or home run, it gave me an overwhelming sensation.

"I found there was only one way to play—*hard*. If I didn't grab a base when I could, I felt I was shortchanging myself, my family, my team, the owners, fans—and that Man Upstairs."

Well, I don't have to tell you what Reggie did about that death threat.

"Thinking back to my father's assurance that The Man Upstairs would take care of me, I was suddenly able to shrug off the death threat and I was filled then with a renewed sense of that deep inner peace."

The next day Reggie was in the batter's box facing a fireball pitcher. The crowd was going wild and Reggie had his mind only on that ball.

Whack!

"I was rounding third when the realization struck me," he said. "I had forgotten all about the death threat. I knew Dad was watching our game on television back home and he must have heard about the threat against my life. I looked up to where the TV cameras were and waved. I know he got the message."

Another man who obviously pays attention to his censor is Judge Joseph A. Wapner, who has a wide television following on *The People's Court*, in which real people bring real cases before him. His judgments are based on twenty years' experience on the bench of the superior and municipal courts of California.

Judge Wapner belongs to a men's Bible study group at his synagogue, Valley Beth Shalom. And he claims that one of the most offbeat memories from his career relates to Leviticus 19:11, which reads in part ". . . neither deal falsely, neither lie one to another."

"When I was a judge of the Municipal Court of Los Angeles," he says, "I was obliged on my very first day to judge a defendant's claims literally with my own eyes. The man, whom I'll call Mr. Tobin, was charged with speeding on Olympic Boulevard, where the limit was thirty-five miles per hour. The policeman said he had followed Mr. Tobin's 1949 Cadillac and clocked it at sixty.

" 'Your honor,' pleaded Mr. Tobin, 'my car is broken. It won't go over thirty-five!'

"The policeman laughed out loud.

" 'All right,' I told Mr. Tobin. 'If you'll wait until I finish my other cases, I'll ride in your car myself. If it won't go over thirty-five, you win.'

"Later, during our lunch break, my bailiff got behind the wheel, with Mr. Tobin and me as passengers.

"No matter how hard the bailiff pressed down on the accelerator, that car wouldn't go over thirty-five. The transmission was broken.

"I returned to court, banged my gavel lightly, and ruled, 'Not guilty.'

"That case taught me an invaluable lesson: Like the great Solomon, look for the truth with your own eyes and ears and good sense. Don't trust others when your own common sense tells you something's wrong."

Yes, our common sense could be another definition of censor.

An interesting synonym of the word is *doorkeeper*. Beverly Garland, the Hollywood actress, has her own motto, which she uses: "Stand porter to your mind." She says that when she was a child, her father taught her those five words that she has used all her life, in her acting career, as a mother, in her business activities.

"If I complained that I was afraid of the dark, or if I seemed worried about meeting new people, Dad would say, 'Stand porter to your mind.'

"Nowadays this phrase might seem old-fashioned, but it still makes sense," she says. "A porter is a gatekeeper, someone who stands at a door letting people in or out. Dad would get me to picture myself stopping destructive thoughts—such as fear—at the door, but saying, 'Come in,' to faith and love and self-assurance.

"As an actress, before I went on camera, I'd make sure anxiety stayed out and confidence in my ability came in. And as a mother, when I was anxious about my children, I would try not to let worry in, but would fill my mind with trust—in them and in God.

"Of course, there were always times I'd forget those words," she admits.

"I remember one time in particular. In 1972, my husband, Fillmore Crank, and I opened the doors to our own hotel, the Beverly Garland in North Hollywood. This was a new business venture for us, and it was a lot more complicated and personally demanding than we, in our naiveté, had figured.

"We were on call twenty-four hours a day. Something was always going wrong. Plumbing got clogged, electricity went on the blink, food wasn't delivered, employees called in sick. Once, a flu epidemic suddenly left us with no maids. Fillmore gave me a choice: Scrub floors or do the laundry. For ten days I folded enough king-size sheets and pillowcases to blanket the whole state of California.

"Then there was the energy crisis. The price of gasoline doubled, and tourism in California dropped. How could we fill our beds? What if we kept losing money? What if the hotel didn't catch on? What if we failed? Here I was at the front desk of a seven-story, 262-room hotel, and those old uninvited guests, fear and worry, were sneaking in. But I caught them just in time. I stood porter.

"I stood in the door of my mind and sent fear packing. The Bible tells us, 'Perfect love casteth out fear' (I John 4:18). That's how to stand porter.

"These days at the hotel (which is thriving, I am happy to say),

whenever fear tries to register, I just smile and point to the sign
that reads NO VACANCY."

That makes sense, doesn't it, and that's a wonderful sign to put
up yourself when fear or negative thinking tries to push past your
censor: "No Vacancy."

An old boyhood friend of mine was a master at letting the censor control. He is now deceased. But the other day I received a
letter from a young woman, whom I have never met, who told me
that she is his granddaughter. She said she never knew her grandfather but had heard so much about him and wanted to know
more. She had been told that I was a close friend of his and would
I tell her what I knew about him.

His name was Forest R. Dietrick, but he was always called Sport
Dietrick and, though some years older, he was a close friend when
our family lived in Bellefontaine, Ohio. I answered his granddaughter's letter telling her she was in a really great family tradition. Her grandfather was a great man by every standard, a man
who lived every minute by his censor. He was forthright, scrupu-
lously honest, of stalwart character, always outgoing and happy,
even boisterously so.

I first knew him when he pressed clothes in a dry-cleaning establishment and I was home from college for the summer. The last
time I saw him he was president of the leading bank in Worthington, Ohio, a suburb of Columbus. It was there that one of the finest
hours of his life took place and I told his granddaughter about it. It
was during the deepest financial depression we, in the United
States, ever had. Franklin D. Roosevelt was President and coined
one of the greatest phrases ever struck off by a public official: "The
only thing we have to fear is fear itself."

At the time banks were closing all over the country. And one day
some depositors of the bank in Worthington became nervous and
withdrew their deposits. This stimulated others and a crowd began
gathering outside. It could have precipitated a run on the bank.
Sport Dietrick, correctly appraising the situation, went outside,
climbed up on a box, and in his strong voice said to the apprehensive people, "Your bank will pay you every dollar you have entrusted to us. We are in good shape. Take my word for it."

They all knew that his word was as good as gold. For they knew he was as honest as the day is long. He had what is known in American history as character. No one even asked a question. Someone in the crowd called out, "If you say so, Sport." And the crowd quietly dispersed. Not a soul lost anything in Sport's bank. No wonder he is in my memory as one of the happiest men I have ever known. He was good in a he-man way, through and through.

His granddaughter's letter got me thinking about the other boys in our crowd in Bellefontaine. All of them seemed to pay close attention to their censor. There was Bob Cooke, who became a businessman in Los Angeles, John Scarf, who became a surgeon in Boston, Hike Newell, who ended up as a great business success in Cincinnati, Glen Hill, who eventually became one of the top insurance men of Ohio, and many others.

But my closest friend was Sammy Kaufman. I always waited for him at the corner, and we went to school together and came home together. It's been many years, but I can still see the sort of rolling gait with which he walked and that thousand-watt smile of his. Bellefontaine was a Methodist-Presbyterian town. There were not enough Jewish families to support a temple or synagogue and the Kaufmans attended my church, the First Methodist, of which my father was pastor. Dad was a big-souled man, a thoroughgoing Christian, and he loved all people. As a result, the few Jewish and Roman Catholic citizens in our town and even the handful of self-proclaimed atheists felt comfortable with him.

Sammy's family was wealthier than ours, and when the bicycle craze came, his father got him one. It was a red beauty with a bell and a light on the front. Sammy was the soul of generosity, and I do believe I rode the bicycle as much as he did.

We always ended up in Rich's shop for a chocolate sundae with nuts and a cherry on top. Well, Sammy went to one college and I to another, and he ended up in Cleveland a rich man, head of a big sweater manufacturing business. And his sweaters were good quality, even as Sammy was, for he always paid close attention to that inner voice. He supplied me with sweaters for years. All I could give him in return were the books I wrote. Out of his big heart he proclaimed them all good. Whenever I was in Cleveland or he in New York, we got together as in the old days.

The last time I saw him was in New York, and I took him to lunch at the Metropolitan Club. It was one of those poignant get-togethers that only old friends can know. We had a table by the window looking out on Fifth Avenue and Central Park. Sammy was thinner and I was concerned by the way he looked, but the wonderful old smile was still there.

"What's the matter with college students nowadays?" Sammy asked. It was at the time some were burning flags and draft cards. "They say they're turned off by the establishment, meaning the country, and some say they are turned off from God Himself. Why," he continued, "this is a wonderful country, the best in all history, and how could they turn against God, Who has been so good to them?"

But then we agreed they may have had reasons for their gripes and they represented only a part of the young people and, even if they were turned off, it was up to us to get them turned on again, and we ended on a positive note.

"What will you have for dessert, Sammy, our old favorite? A chocolate sundae with nuts and a cherry on top?" He grinned that big smile and we both ordered one. "Don't tell my doctor," he said. As we finished our dessert, Sammy said, "It's good to be with you again, old friend. This chocolate sundae was good, but not quite up to Rich's store back in Bellefontaine, don't you agree? Those were the days."

We separated at the corner of Fifth Avenue and Sixtieth Street with an embrace and a handclasp. I watched him until he was lost in the crowd as he made his way to the Plaza Hotel. He walked slowly now, quite unlike the way he would come flashing up North Detroit Street in Bellefontaine on "our bicycle" long ago. He turned around to wave and the same old thousand-watt smile was on his face until he was lost in the crowd. Sammy died soon after, but for me he will always live in memory. He had what it took to be happy, a genuine, loving nature, a clear conscience, and a caring soul. And he was also, in his sincere way, a real man of God. His strong faith was a powerful reason he was one of the most unforgettable and best-loved friends I've had in life.

But when bad luck or adversity strikes, not once but repeatedly, how are you expected to trust your censor? Well, let's see!

I knew of a man named Jay from Rhode Island who had many hard knocks and rebounded from each one. But, you see, he had what it took to be happy, even so. He was a man who listened closely to that inner voice.

Just out of college he was offered a job with a sales company which seemed to have excellent prospects of success. However, the company folded in two years and Jay lost his job. But he wasn't out of work for long. He bounced back and soon had another job selling for a specialty company. He did well, got a couple of promotions, was making good money. Then he was in an automobile accident and laid up in the hospital and at home for months. The company carried him for three months, then had to hire a replacement, who also did well. He did so well that the company couldn't let him go. Jay was offered an office job that paid less than half of what he earned selling.

He took the job in good humor, listened to his censor, and just kept on being happy. He bounced back and proceeded to do the office job so well that he was advanced to supervisor with increased pay. Being so good-natured, he was popular with both sexes and soon wedding bells were ringing. Then his company made him sales manager, with an advanced salary plus percentage. All went well for several years, then adversity struck again. This time it was real adversity. His wife, whom he loved devotedly, died and Jay was left alone. But he took this blow chin up, throwing himself into his work.

Then he made an apparent mistake. Another company, impressed by Jay, lured him away with an offer he couldn't refuse. Was he listening to his censor then? I don't know. He didn't know it at the time he was hired, but this company had a management team that was getting all they possibly could out of it. Then they sold the company and the managers got out just in time. To save expenses, the new owners had to let a large number of employees go and they adopted the policy that all who had come aboard in the last three years had to go, which, you guessed it, included Jay. He stood up to this hard knock and in time bounced back again.

At the time an insurance company asked Jay to give a talk at an agents' breakfast on what he had learned in his sales experience. Officials of the company were impressed with his sales methodology and his positive approach and persuaded him to become a producer. So Jay bounced back again, and as far as I know, that was his last bounce back. Associates say he is one of the best insurance producers in the company.

I first heard about Jay when I spoke at his company's convention. "What gave Jay this bounce back, this comeback ability?" I asked.

"Resilience," was the answer, "a nondiscouraging attitude, positive thinking, a subscriber to the old idea that every knock can be turned into a boost."

"Quite a guy," I commented. "And he remained genuinely happy through it all?"

"Never thought of quitting," one said. Another man summed it all up. "You guys are missing the real point about Jay. He is a confirmed, enthusiastic believer."

Despite everything, this man had the basic secret of success. He always kept his censor in tune.

So doing what you know to be right pays off in increasing your chances of success and happiness. And you do have what it takes to be happy if you use your faith, Catholic, Jewish, or Protestant. And if you are saying, "But I have no faith," I like you, anyway. You and I are friends. So I urge you, in your own way, start on the search for believing and get for yourself the surest guarantee of success and lasting happiness. You, too, have what it takes to be happy and confident in the face of adverse circumstances.

► I repeat: Do only what you know to be right to gain real happiness.

LIVING IS BELIEVING—POSITIVELY!

$\blacksquare$ $\qquad\qquad$ $\blacksquare$ $\qquad\qquad$ $\blacksquare$

Out of a rather long life, with almost seventy years of speaking, writing, and preaching, I have come to a definite conclusion. It is that all of us, you who are reading this book and everyone else living and breathing, have been put on this Earth for a definite purpose. I believe Almighty God the Creator has a plan for our lives, and if we know and follow that plan, we will be happy and fulfilled.

This doesn't always happen, of course. Somewhere along the way a person may fail. And a principal reason for this, I feel, is a lack of believing. Those who are real believers don't often fail, for they have recoup ability.

Believing does make the difference in the quality of our living. That is the reason this book was written.

Let me tell you a story about a little Puerto Rican boy who found his true calling in life by believing. Juan Antonio Rodriguez was born in the little town of Río Piedras of a poor family. Sometimes he and his five brothers and sisters ate a real meal only twice a week. Sometimes there was only coffee on the table. At age seven he was plowing sugarcane fields behind a team of oxen. But he had believing parents who taught him he could do anything if he became a believer.

Then little Juan found a job caddying at a nearby country club.

Soon he had made his own golf club by using a piece of pipe plus the end of a guava limb. With it he began hitting bottle caps around an imaginary course. Juan got pretty good at it. During his early years one of the men he used to caddy for gave him a set of golf clubs. By the time Juan was in the United States Army, he had come to believe that he was destined to be a professional golfer. And his first goal would be to buy a house for his mother, who by then had moved to New York and was living in a tenement.

By 1960 Juan, now known as Chi Chi Rodriguez, got started in the Professional Golfing Association tournament. Within three years his mother moved into her new home. Then Chi Chi met someone who added a new dimension to his already strong belief system.

While playing at the Sleepy Hollow Country Club in New York, he met none other than my old friend Dr. Smiley Blanton, who was a club member.

"Smiley Blanton was in his late seventies and I in my twenties," Chi Chi recalls, "but when we'd walk the course together, laughing and talking, those years between us didn't exist. He usually shot in the low eighties and could drive a ball two hundred yards off the tee. I learned a lot from him. About life. About golf. He taught me that when I prepared to tee off, I must concentrate on the pin, not on the sand traps and water hazards in between.

" 'Be positive,' he'd tell me. 'Your body can do only what your brain sees, Chi Chi. If you think of the negatives, you'll be drawn to them. But if you keep your goal foremost in mind, you'll aim for it.' "

Chi Chi became even more of a believer and went on to win eight PGA tournaments. Then, reaching age fifty in 1985, he joined the Senior PGA tour and has since become a top winner in its tournaments, earning *Golf Digest*'s title of "Senior Player of the Year."

Today he passes on his philosophy of believing to troubled, abused, and poor children through his Chi Chi Rodriguez Youth Foundation, in Clearwater, Florida. "I tell them it's a lesson they can apply to any challenge they face. 'First,' I say, 'communicate with God. Listen to Him, and when you feel His direction, don't willy-wally around. *Obey!*

" 'The Lord sees a lot farther down the course than we do,' he advises them. 'Life is full of hazards and traps. But if you keep your eye on the pin and follow through with all your might, you'll be champion at everything you do, even if you don't win every time.' "

Chi Chi is fulfilling God's plan for his life. For he is a *believer*.

Another sports leader who is an enthusiastic believer is Tommy Lasorda, energetic manager of the Los Angeles Dodgers National League baseball team.

"You've got to keep on believing," he says in a *Fortune* magazine article of July 1989. "Winning the World Series in 1988 was positive proof of what you can obtain in life if you really believe in yourself. Those twenty-four players all believed in themselves. It is not the strongest man who wins. It's the one who wants it just a little bit more than the next and keeps on believing."

That checks with my longtime friend John Galbreath, of Columbus, Ohio. He was another who started out as a poor boy and became one of the nation's most successful business leaders.

"What must one do to become successful?" a newspaper reporter once asked him.

"Be a believer," John answered. "Have an intense desire to attain a specified goal; work, work, work and always keep believing."

Believe in yourself as intelligent and capable. Believe in your purpose in life. Believe in God, Who put you here to fulfill that purpose.

Some may sniff at this. "Just telling yourself to believe isn't going to accomplish anything," they may argue.

Well, many Olympic and professional athletes know that one's believing power is as important as weight lifting, wind sprints, and situps, even *more* so.

For example, Elizabeth Manley, the famous Canadian figure skater, used to falter in crucial moments, such as when she performed the very difficult triple Lutzes. With the help of her team's psychologist, she spent much time imaging herself performing perfect triple Lutzes to the point where she believed she could do them perfectly. As a result, she went on to win a Silver Medal at the 1988 Winter Olympics.

"We've come to recognize that at the top the difference is minute between a Gold, Silver, or Bronze Medal, or nothing at all. It's become apparent that the ability to be mentally prepared can be the factor that makes the difference," says Robert Helmick of the United States Olympic Committee, "and athletes and coaches have looked for any way to shave off that fraction of a second."

Mentally prepared to win is *believing*, whether you are out to win a gold medal or to earn that promotion in your job.

Ask a team member of the Boston Bruins hockey club if believing makes a difference. In 1988, the Bruins entered the play-offs against the Montreal Canadiens, a team they had not defeated in a play-off series in forty-five years. As before, Boston team members felt helpless. "There was definitely a pretty negative feeling when it came to beating Montreal," said Ken Linseman, the Boston center.

As a result, Dr. Frederick Neff, a clinical psychologist, was hired to set up a mental training program to help team members *believe* they could beat Montreal. For example, anytime they had a negative thought, they were told to immediately replace it with a positive one. Buoyed with a positive belief they could win, the Bruins went on to defeat the Canadiens four games to one and ended up in the Stanley Cup Finals.

"You mean to say that I can change my life as quickly as changing my negative thoughts to positive thoughts?" you may ask.

Well, let's see what other psychologists have to say. Cynthia K. Chandler, counseling psychologist at Indiana State University, and Cheryl A. Kolander, assistant professor at the Department of Health at the University of Louisville in Kentucky, have some interesting observations which appeared in *Education Digest*, January 1989.

> *Beliefs or thoughts held in the mind on a conscious or subconscious level cause the body to respond physiologically or behaviorally.*
>
> *Positive self-communication provides a key to effecting a healthy life-style . . . Students often say negative things about themselves, diminishing positive mental energy. A thought that is in the mind is to some degree believed and can eventually manifest itself in behavior.*
>
> *Thought stopping is an effective response to self-defeating thoughts and emotions. Each time a negative thought comes to mind, students can immediately say to themselves*

"stop." This command acts as a distractor and interrupts
the flow of self-defeating thinking. It is a simple command
that will help break a persistent habit. Thought stopping
can interrupt any type of unpleasant thought. It can aid in
breaking obsessive or fearful thoughts such as thoughts of
failure, inadequacy, panic or anxiety, painful memories, or
recurring impulses such as nail biting or overeating.

Thought stopping can be followed by thought substitu-
tions of positively reassuring or self-accepting statements.
Each negative thought the student stops can be followed by
a positive one. For example, "I'm so stupid" can be stopped
and replaced with "I am smart, and I can do it"; or "I'm a
fool" can be replaced with "I learned something, and I am
wiser because of it." Substitute "I don't have what it takes"
with "I have the courage to give it my best shot."

The psychologists say such positive affirmations should be repeated several times daily, on waking, before going to bed, and at
other times.

Can you actually affect your thinking and very actions by what
you tell yourself? You may wonder. Well, the mind is a very complex thing. Medical science still doesn't understand all of the tech-
nicalities in the way it works.

For example, surgeons and anesthesiologists are finding that patients who have been completely anesthetized do not remember
the operation, but they seem to pick up enough of what is said
around them during surgery to have a bearing on their recovery.

Dr. Carlton Evans, an anesthesiologist at St. Thomas's Hospital
in London, reported in the August 1988 issue of *The Lancet*, a
British medical journal, that anesthetized patients were told such
things as, "You will want to get up and get out of bed to help your
body recover earlier." Those who were given such positive suggestions recovered more quickly and with fewer complications than
those who were not given any such suggestions, he observed.

Indeed, the mind is a wonderful, mysterious power. As a result,
we need not let ourselves be limited as to what we can or cannot
do because we "don't have the strength" or we "are not important"
or "don't have any influence." And this is true at any age.

Kids have to be stimulated to think in a positive way. They have to be given dreams of what they can become. They have to be shown the winning spirit. A mother can say to her child, "You are going to be somebody. You are going to make a great life for yourself."

If children hear this regularly as their personalities begin to form, they will be motivated to become what they can be.

I had a letter recently from the Honorable Ike Skelton, congressman from the state of Missouri. He is in his fourth term, a distinguished member of the United States House of Representatives. He wrote:

> Dear Dr. Peale:
> You will be saddened to hear of the death of my beloved mother. She has gone to be with God. I shall never cease to be grateful for her. She was a friend of yours and so I am writing to tell you of her transition to heaven.

Indeed, I did know Mrs. Skelton. She was a strong, dynamic, powerful, believing woman, a great mother. At age twelve, Ike had an attack of infantile paralysis which left his arms dangling helplessly. His legs recovered satisfactorily and he could function otherwise, except that he could not move his arms. His mother said to him as he sank into despair, "Ike, your life is not in your arms and hands, but in your brain and in your heart. You are going to accomplish everything that you really want to accomplish."

He really wanted to be a runner. He entered Wentworth Military Academy and went out for the track team. But the coach said to him, "Son, you can never be a runner without your arms. They are almost as important in running as your legs."

"Sir, I'm going to be a runner," said Ike.

The first year Ike didn't make it. The second year he didn't make it. The third year he didn't make it either. The fourth year the coach said, "OK, Ike, you're a member of the squad."

Then came the great event of the year. It was the annual meet with their arch-rival, Kemper Academy. Ike said: "Coach, I want to run in the two-mile race, even though I know it is the most grueling of all."

"Son," the coach said, "I'll give you any chance that you wish, because I think you're great. But you really can't compete in that race. However, if it is your heart's desire to run, I'll let you do it. I'm going to fasten your arms to your sides and then you do the best you can."

The first man came in. The second man came in. The third man came in. They all came in. But no Ike. The crowd waited. Finally, there came Ike, way behind, but he finished. And when he crossed the finish line all the students surged down out of the stands and rushed to his side. They didn't put the winner of the race on their shoulders. They put Ike on their shoulders and carried him around the track, shouting his name.

Ike became a lawyer and then a member of the Congress of the United States. Frequently, as he was advancing in his career, I would get a telephone call from Mrs. Skelton. "Help me make him the great man he can be and that I know he will be." And he finally became just that. It was the motivation of his mother that helped make this man what he is today.

Or take this example from Giorgina Reid, "a little old lady," to use her own self-description, who did something the U.S. Army Corps of Engineers could not do. She saved the famous Montauk Lighthouse at the easternmost tip of Long Island, whose flashing light had guided ships to harbor for two centuries.

This noble structure was in danger of falling into the sea. The land it was built on was eroding. Man, with big machines and tons of concrete, was called in to save it, but was failing. It was only a matter of time, experts said, before the ocean would snuff out that historic light.

Mrs. Reid told the Coast Guard that she had a plan that might work. "Let me try to save the lighthouse?" she asked. "They just stared at me, and I knew what they were thinking: *Why, she's nothing but a little old lady.*"

And they were right. "I was little, just four feet eleven inches, and beyond the age of retirement. But so what? A long time ago I found that being little didn't mean you couldn't do a job you set your mind to. I would just have to show them what you can do when you live a lifetime with that attitude."

When Mrs. Reid was a teenager growing up in New York City, she worked part-time in the office of then Congressman Fiorello La Guardia, later the mayor of New York. They used to call that feisty, warm-hearted man 'the Little Flower' because of his first name—and because he was just over five feet tall. "Listen to me," La Guardia said one day as they chanced to be riding up in the elevator. "I know what I'm talking about. Trust in God, believe in yourself, and you can do *anything.*"

"The elevator doors opened," she recalls, "and he stepped out. He may be only five feet two inches tall, I thought, but he's a giant of a man."

One day a newspaper report explained about the plight of the Montauk Lighthouse. Mrs. Reid immediately thought of her own method of erosion control which she and her husband used to save their treasured beach house from falling into the sea. They had built retaining walls from washed-up lumber and stuffed beach reeds and sand between them. The reeds acted as seals preventing the sand from sifting out. Their hollow stems retained rainwater, a miniature underground irrigation system. And when they decayed they blended with the roots of plantings above, holding the soil together like millions of tiny fingers. Mr. and Mrs. Reid were working with nature instead of against it.

"When I first wrote the Coast Guard asking permission to try my plan, they didn't take me very seriously," she said. 'No one can stop the wind, rain, and sea,' they said. How could I succeed where the Army Corps of Engineers had failed? How could a tiny old woman prevail where strong men had been beaten? How could I win where modern science had lost? But they told me to go ahead."

Using her patented system, Giorgina Reid and her husband combed the Long Island shore for washed-up reeds, stuffing them into potato sacks and burying them in terraces on Montauk Point. The Coast Guard was supportive and local residents helped. Again, the system worked.

Today, the Montauk Lighthouse is safe for now and hopefully for future generations, thanks to a "little old lady" who had the power to *believe.*

Believers like Giorgina Reid number into the millions in America. In fact, I feel there are probably more active working believers in our great land than in any country in the world. The freedom of America, the emphasis on the potential in the individual's strength creates a historical climate of thought in which believers thrive.

The pilgrim fathers who came to these shores in the 1600s were believers. Otherwise they would not have left their homeland to venture over the tumultuous Atlantic Ocean with their meager possessions to a little known land. They were believers in a better life in a big free land where they could worship God according to their own conscience and build for the future.

It was believers who trekked west in the prairie schooners, braving the loneliness and dangers of the wilderness, many of them to end in lonely graves along the trail. But they pushed on despite the fiery heat of summer and the cold storms of winter, marching into a better day in which they believed. All through America's history, believers led the way until now we have a united nation from sea to shining sea.

Believers are with us today in ever increasing numbers. And not a few are demonstrating the traditional American way of reaching the top from humble beginnings. Indeed, a national magazine lists one hundred and twenty people who have won a place in what it terms "the national business hall of fame." The people on the list that I know personally worked their way up and every one was a believer, a believer in God, a believer in himself, in our country, in his product, and together they have improved the world for millions of people.

One of those is Conrad Hilton who, born in humble circumstances, built a worldwide hotel empire. He was a believer who went to Mass every day and developed the well-known portrayal of Uncle Sam in prayer during World War II. Also listed is another man who was my friend, Dewitt Wallace, a clergyman's son and devout believer who made *Reader's Digest* a worldwide success, the most read magazine of all time. There was a time when Wally and his wife, Lila, edited the magazine themselves and drove it to the printer in their old car. He originally tried to peddle his concept to publishers in New York who laughed at his "crazy idea."

Joyce C. Hall is another believer who came from a humble home and with a positive attitude created Hallmark, perhaps the greatest greeting card enterprise in American history. Ray Kroc is yet another. After a rather mediocre sales career, at age fifty, he met a couple of brothers named McDonald, became enthusiastic about the hamburger, and pioneered America's fast-food industry. Another friend, Dave Thomas, started as an orphan completely without funds. His first job was washing dishes. He went on to build Wendy's, another popular national hamburger chain.

Still another friend, a confirmed believer, is Tom Monaghan, who was also an orphan, totally without financial resources. He formed Domino's Pizza, another fast-food business. Today Mr. Monaghan is a special kind of missionary, a missionary dedicated to helping make this great country an even better place in which to live, a believer all the way.

Olive Ann Beech, widowed early in life, built the great Beech Aircraft Corporation, which had been started by her husband. She, too, is a highly regarded believer in God, in herself, and in the best in aircraft.

Kemmons Wilson took his family to Washington as a young father living in Tennessee and had difficulty finding garage space for his car. The trip became a chore and he found it expensive staying in downtown hotels. Then an idea came. He was a thinker. So ideas sprang to him. How about a different kind of hotel where a family could drive up to their room door and park without garage costs overnight? So he proceeded to think up Holiday Inns. Mr. Wilson brought in a partner, Wallace Johnson, another positive believer, and together they created the great chain of hotels that pioneered the modern motor inn industry.

The Marriotts, father and son, themselves believers, founded the famed Marriott chain of upper-level hotels and the food service bearing their name. Bill Marriott, Sr., had previously operated a hot dog and root beer stand in Washington, which I at one time patronized. He told me that his first day's profit was a magnificent fifteen dollars.

Believers are aggressive, they are positive. They know that bigness can be created from smallness. A big oak comes from one acorn. Believers are thinkers. They never spend their time being emotional about how badly off they are. They never clutter their minds with negative thoughts. They think positively and think and think and believe. And so ideas come and often those ideas turn into blessings for humanity.

Well, there you have a list of exciting believers and each accomplished something that gave jobs to thousands and added to the well-being of our country.

But the human tendency is to shake one's head saying, those are inspiring stories, but so what? All were gifted superpeople, not an ordinary person like me.

Wrong. All started out as poor people. Ordinary people. But each became extraordinary. How? By thinking and believing, by working, failing, picking themselves up, and trying again and yet again.

Another such person I know personally is a man who was grievously struck down in his youth and made a remarkable comeback. He is Max Cleland, secretary of state of Georgia. When the Vietnam War came, Max enlisted and was sent overseas as a first lieutenant. He rose to the rank of captain. One day a grenade exploded, blasting away both of his legs and his right arm. Medics despaired of his life, but after months of rehabilitation he recovered physically. Though there were deep emotional and mental wounds, Max was spiritually reared and was prepared to meet his tragic and overwhelming crisis. He was able to adjust to a suddenly imposed disability that would have defeated a less mentally and spiritually conditioned person. He reasoned that despite his changed physical condition, he was unchanged in mind and spirit, that he had a superior mind and superior spirit, and he determined to invest them to the hilt in his future.

When fellow Georgian Jimmy Carter became President of the United States, he appointed Max Cleland as director of the Veterans Administration. This department of the federal government was second only to the Pentagon in size and scope, having 236,000 employees and a budget of twenty-two billion dollars. Never had this department of government had a more dedicated and active head. He traveled widely, visiting and inspecting veterans' hospitals and ministering to the needs of men and women who had borne the brunt of war.

After this tour of duty was magnificently accomplished, Max returned to his native state, where citizens elected him secretary of state. From his offices in the historic statehouse in Atlanta, this victor over adversity administers a large staff and discharges the many duties of an important responsibility. His friends, of whom there are many, are certain that Max, now only forty-seven years old, will ascend to even higher office ultimately.

A reason for Secretary Cleland's popularity and the respect in which he is held is his competence. As a person he is well liked and obviously cares for people. A joyous man with an exuberant and infectious laugh, he has the capacity of making others enthusiastic.

Max Cleland's ability to handle the extreme physical adversity which came suddenly to him is derived from his faith in God. But today he is proving that believers can recoup. And he believes God has a plan for his life, just as he also believes there is a plan for each of us. A hand grenade changed Max Cleland's life.

I also knew a young man who blew his success, but got going again. Gene was a personable fellow who made friends easily. High-minded and moral, he was considered thoroughly reliable. He was a top insurance producer. Gregarious, he was a hail-fellow-well-met, and he and his wife, Sylvia, were very popular.

He learned that some of his prospects met late afternoons in a hotel bar where, in the midst of social conviviality, business deals were discussed and some concluded. He did not patronize this place, but concerned that he might be losing some business by not appearing there, he began to show up, ordering only a Perrier water or Coke.

But in the atmosphere of raillery, he allowed himself to be talked into drinking something stronger. It wasn't long before he was drinking heavily. Then Gene began to notice that clients were drifting to other agents. Troubled about these defections, he went to an older agent, the dean of insurance people in his town.

"Gene," the man said, "though I may lose your friendship, I'll level with you. Men like 'drinking buddies.' But our business depends upon our clients' respect, for it relates to their estates, their families, indeed, the lives of their loved ones. A client is likely to shy away from an insurance agent whose character they doubt.

"Gene," the knowledgeable man said, "it isn't so much your drinking that turns them away, they see you as a phony putting on the 'good old boy act' and getting drunk in the process. Better quit coming to those late afternoon get-togethers in the hotel bar and go back to being yourself."

Sadly, the older man's advice came too late. Gene was prone to alcoholism and had never realized it. He found now that he was hooked. To cover it up, he became a secret drinker, at least so he thought, but secret drinking hardly ever remains secret. His habit became a subject of gossip and he lost most of his business. Even old friends gave him a gentle brush-off. He lost the confidence he formerly enjoyed and adversity stared him in the face.

But Gene, despite all, was an intelligent fellow. He recognized the cause of his decline and resolutely faced up to it. He enrolled in an alcoholic-rehabilitation institution and faithfully followed the routine treatment. He then joined Alcoholics Anonymous, went back to church, and employed religious therapy. As a result, he achieved sobriety. And such is the fairness of people that they applauded his determined struggle for rehabilitation, and gradually he began to recoup his business. This true story proves that a person can stand up to self-imposed trouble as well and, whatever the drastic results, can recover. It only required honesty, intense desire, perseverance, and a strong belief that he or she can *do* it.

In fact, believers often are able to turn what appears to be ruinous adversity into an asset on the positive principle that "to every disadvantage there is a corresponding advantage." In every disadvantageous situation the believer pokes around in the ruins for the advantage, the asset or the good that lies there.

In my office I often receive long-distance telephone calls from unknown persons with problems. One was a bright and sharp woman who opened the conversation with a question. "Got a few minutes to think about a situation which seems adverse, but which possibly may contain good?" I liked her approach and sat back in my chair, facing my hands-free telephone. "Go on and tell me about it," I agreed.

"Don't worry. I won't keep you long, and by all means don't assume that you've got a talkative old lady on the wire."

"Ma'am," I responded, "I like you already. Don't feel hurried."

She said that her husband, three years from retirement from his middle management position, had been "temporarily" laid off due to cutbacks in the company. She stated that she had $1.67 in her purse, $220 in the checking account. I wondered if she was going to ask for a loan, but she anticipated me. "Now, don't get the idea

I'm about to ask for money. We've been frugal through the years of good income and have substantial savings, but I don't want to touch them. What would you do in our situation?" she asked.

"I don't know. Let's say a prayer about it over the telephone and ask for guidance and for an idea."

She agreed and I reminded her that the Lord says He is with us always, that when two or three are gathered in His name He is there with them. Afterward she remarked that she felt an idea would be forthcoming, and I had the same feeling. She was a believer, all right. "What are your husband's talents?" I asked.

"He is a terrific salesperson," she replied.

"Is he handy around the house, by any chance?"

"Handy," she exclaimed, "he's a genius! He can fix anything."

Well, I know how difficult it is to get things repaired in this day and age, and I could visualize all the neighbors who had items that needed to be fixed. So I suggested her husband tell his friends and neighbors that he had set up as a superfixer in business. "Bring me anything and it will come back good as new," I suggested as an advertising slogan.

"Oh, he wouldn't charge neighbors," she objected.

"They will be delighted to get that old chair fixed or that old table repaired. You try it and see. And he's got a ready-made agent."

"Who?" she demanded.

"You," I said.

Meekly she said, "You know, I was thinking the same thing." Well, some months later his "agent" called me back to say that her husband did so well at this self-employed business and enjoyed it so thoroughly that he continued "fixing things and never did go back to the company when they sent for him."

This is just one example of the manner in which believers turn adversities into successes.

I recall a man I met in Hong Kong several years ago. I had spoken at the Rotary Club in the Mandarin Hotel and my talk was along the lines of this book, emphasizing believing, thinking, and working as basics of success. This Chinese man came up and said, "I couldn't agree more with your ideas. I know they work, for the same attitude brought me out of poverty right here in Hong Kong."

In the fifties, he had been one of the thousands of refugees from Communist China who had fled to the Crown Colony of Hong Kong where freedom and opportunity were to be found. They had to live for a while in primitive conditions. Families subsisted at government soup kitchens. They huddled under makeshift shelters of old packing boxes and corrugated tin. Later, the government built shelters where families of ten or more lived in one room.

This man said he walked with his wife and four children all the way from Shanghai. We "voted for freedom with our feet," he smiled. "It was very hard going and I had many moments of despair, but I had one way to lift despair from my mind." He reached in his pocket and produced a small well-worn New Testament. "This little book contains power," he declared. "I read it daily during our hardship and one day I came to Philippians 4, verse 13." And he quoted: "I can do all things through Christ who strengthens me."

"Then," he continued, "I found another verse, Matthew 17:20: 'If you have faith . . . nothing shall be impossible to you.' As I pondered those two verses, I wondered. Is that really true? The words of an old friend came to me over the years: 'Only believe . . . have faith . . . trust God no matter the difficulty.' Well, I had plenty of difficulty. I sat thinking; then I found myself believing in this little book. I worked out a formula. Here it is, just the way I wrote it."

He took a piece of paper from his pocket. I read the words scribbled in pencil but still decipherable: "I believe + I can + I will = I did."

He repeated this formula several times daily. He said, "I just kept on believing and thinking and ideas began to come." He acted on them and, as a result, became a respected and successful businessman. "Believing works wonders," he said. How right he was. It does indeed.

I received the following letter while writing this book. It says so well what other letters have also said that I really want you to read it.

November 30, 1989

Dear Dr. Peale,

I became acquainted with your writing strictly by accident. If I had known you were a minister, I would not have touched your books with a ten-foot pole. I was searching for something; I wasn't sure what it was. I know now that I was searching for a relationship with our Lord.

During my search, I had gone to the psychology section of our public library and selected your book You Can If You Think You Can. *I was inspired by what you had written! Although I had picked up books by other authors, they left me cold. I returned to the library to find more of your books, and noticed that in the card file, your books were also listed under the "religion" section. This was not to my liking, but I was so inspired by the first selection I had read, that I checked out more.*

You see, I was brought up with a lot of religion which had left me very bitter; I wanted nothing more to do with it.

As I began reading your other books, I would skip over all of the Bible texts, feeling that the power of my own mind was enough. I typed pages of your tips from several books. After a while, I started to put "I can do all things through Christ who gives me the strength" at the bottom of my typed pages. This amazed me! I showed many of these pages to my teen-aged son, Todd. He was also inspired.

On a cold February day in 1988, the phone rang and I was told by one of my son's friends that there had been a terrible accident, that my son, Todd, had been killed.

I could not believe that this had happened. Here was a kid who was so positive! He had goals. He loved life. We had been so close.

The funeral home was packed. These teenagers and teachers had loved Todd. They all told me that he was always happy and a friend to everyone. One teacher said he had never known Todd to have a bad day. This was because of you, Dr. Peale. Each morning we had read your thought for the day from your Have a Great Day *book!*

Kids started coming to my home. They asked why Todd

*was always so happy, and I told them about positive think-
ing. I was even talking to them about the Lord.*

*I was seeing the Lord in a different way now. This didn't
happen overnight, however. I read* You Can If You Think
You Can *about 8 years ago. I know now that my strength
was coming from the Lord, but I was still holding on to my
own strong will.*

*One day, that all changed. I just couldn't muster up
enough "positive thinking" on my own to face the day. I felt
shaky and was afraid that I was going to fall apart. I knelt
down right where I was in the house and prayed. I finally
admitted to the Lord—and to myself—that He was the
power and I needed it right then. I felt such peace (what I
had always been looking for) and love. I felt as if He were
saying, "What took you so long, I've been by your side all
along." Nothing has been the same since.*

*I started this long letter by saying that I had become ac-
quainted with your writings by accident. We both know,
now, that it was no accident.*

> *Sincerely,*
> *Kay Heitsch*

▶ Belief gets results.

▶ Belief works even under the most difficult circumstances.

▶ The answer to difficulty is to be a believer. Believe in God. Believe in yourself.

Believe in the future. Believe that you *can.* Believe in people.

▶ Believe and keep on believing.

CHAPTER 15

GET THE FIRE OF ENTHUSIASM BURNING

■   ■   ■

LIFE IS NOT ALL FUN AND EASY GOING. FAR FROM it; there are many rough times. But, sadly, we too often let the hard times dull our enthusiasm. And that is dangerous, if not fatal, to our lives.

Enthusiasm is one vital element that the successful believer possesses in abundance. He or she uses it in meeting responsibilities, in succeeding on the job, and in solving daily problems.

We have been naturally endowed with enthusiasm. It is as native to us as laughing or smiling. The word "enthusiasm" derives from two Greek words, *en* and *theos*, which mean "in God" or "God within."

Enthusiasm . . . Entheo . . . God within.

When one gets enthusiastic, the entire personality lights up. The mind becomes sharper, more intuitive; the entire life force and creative ability are enhanced. Such a person is motivated, makes an impact.

As the philosopher A. B. Zu Tavern has written: "Before water will generate steam it has to boil. An engine won't move an inch until the steam gauge registers 212 degrees. The person without enthusiasm is trying to move the machinery of life with lukewarm water. Only one thing can happen; he will stall. Remember, enthusiasm is electricity in the battery. It's the vigor in the air, it's the warmth in the fire, it's the breath in all things alive.

"The successful man has enthusiasm: Good work is never done in cold blood, heat is needed to forge anything. Every great achievement is the story of a flaming heart." When I think back on all the new developments of past years, an enthusiastic man or woman was responsible in every case.

For example, take Bill Bowerman, who was the world-famous track coach at the University of Oregon. From 1948 to 1973 his teams won two NCAA titles, were runners-up twice, went undefeated ten seasons in dual meets, and for sixteen of those years were in the top ten in the nation. In 1971, he was named Coach of the Year by the U.S. Track Coaches Association.

And if you knew him, you saw that he was a man of enthusiasm. But there was a time in his life when he could have easily let that enthusiasm drain out of him like steam from a leaking boiler.

Back in the mid fifties he became concerned over the track shoes his team members had to wear. Back then track people didn't have much of a choice in footwear. And because of it, many suffered shin splints, foot sores, leg cramps, aching knees and backs.

In studying how people run, Bill could see that a new type of athletic shoe was needed, something with a heel wedge for better support, a lighter sole with more stability and traction.

In the evenings, while his wife was washing supper dishes and his three boys did their homework, he sat at the kitchen table designing a shoe he felt was right. When satisfied, he sent his design to leading sporting goods companies. All turned him down. Some felt the new design too risky; others claimed they were already making a fine product; one snappily told him since they weren't telling him how to coach, he shouldn't be telling them how to make track shoes.

That last turndown left him discouraged and his enthusiasm for developing a new track shoe flew out the window. However, some days later, while giving new team members a pep talk, he heard himself say, "So I want you to do your very best, not just for the prize, but also for what the very *trying* will do for you. Victory is doing the best you can."

When he finished, he realized he was also giving himself a pep talk on enthusiasm. "Somehow, in some way," he says, "I decided to get those shoes made. Even if I had to make them myself."

And that's just what he did.

With advice from his local shoe-repair man, he made patterns from brown-paper grocery bags. Then he cut out white kid leather for the uppers, reinforced them with nylon, set removable spikes in the soles, and glued everything together with a strong adhesive.

When the shoes were completed, he handed a pair to one of his track stars, who put them on, ran around the track, and didn't want to take them off because he was afraid he would not get them back again. Bill Bowerman enthusiastically continued to develop new designs, even using his wife's waffle iron once to come up with a waffle sole for a jogging shoe.

In the early sixties, Bill Bowerman, with a former student and track star Philip Knight, started his own company. And that was the beginning of the famous Nike track shoe.

In January 1988, Bill Bowerman told us at *Guideposts,* "At the age of seventy-six, I still feel the challenge of races to be run. I'm busy with Nike, I am developing a new breed of miniature beef cattle on my farm, and I'm also helping design shoes for handicapped people. It's exciting to think that the right shoes might help the lame walk and maybe, in some cases, even run!"

This is what I call real enthusiasm!

Now, in speaking of enthusiasm, I don't mean the flashy, overheated kind, shallow in depth. Rather I'm talking about a strong, positive, controlled motivation. Indeed, it may be present in the quietly restrained and thoughtful person quite as certainly as in the vigorously extroverted individual. As someone wisely said, "The world belongs to the enthusiast who can keep cool."

A former President of the United States was this type of personality. He had the kind of enthusiasm which is perhaps better defined as strong motivation. This President believed in something. It was a brand of Yankeeism that helped build our country: economy, thrift, hard work, honesty, and religious faith. His name was Calvin Coolidge.

Some folks may smile wryly when they hear his name, for down through the years this man has taken some unjust criticism. It came mostly because of his laid-back personality, for he was a brisk and decisive man, known for his New England simplicity and personal honesty. As Vice President under Warren Harding, he was untouched by charges of corruption leveled at the Harding administration. And when Harding died in August 1923, he took over as President. Elected in 1924, he had a strong popular backing and chose positive men for his Cabinet, who gave him a strong, businesslike administration.

True, "Silent Cal" was a quiet man. But he had a personality in which enthusiasm operated under cool control. He was one of the few politicians to use words sparingly. His speeches were short, succinct, and to the point. He said what he wanted to say and no more. He won the liking of a great many people simply by not talking too much.

Before his career as a public servant, Coolidge was a lawyer in Northampton, Massachusetts. He had a downtown office and his home was up the street. Coolidge never drove to his office; that would have been expensive and he was a frugal man. He walked from home to his office every morning at precisely the same time. This route took him past a house where a friend by the name of Hiram lived. Every morning when Coolidge came along, Hiram would be leaning over the fence. And for twenty years the daily conversation ran something like this:

"Hi, Cal," said Hiram.

"Hi, Hiram," said Cal.

"Nice morning," Hiram added.

"Nice morning," agreed Cal.

Then Coolidge was elected lieutenant governor, then governor, then Vice President of the United States. And then he became President. He was gone from Northampton for quite a few years. His presidency ended, Coolidge returned to Northampton and to law practice. He dusted off the furniture, got his office ready, and one morning, he walked once again from his house to his law office. And sure enough, there leaning on the fence was his old friend Hiram.

"Hi, Cal," said Hiram.

"Hi, Hiram," said Cal.

"Nice morning," Hiram added.

"Nice morning," agreed Cal.

Just as it had always been. But then the heavens fell. Hiram, this taciturn New Englander, added, "Ain't seen you around lately, Cal."

"Nope, been away a spell," Cal replied. All that business of being governor and President was over. Life was what it was now. Calvin Coolidge took it as it came. He had enthusiasm of the quiet kind, the kind that runs deep. He was enthusiastic about the United States and the American way. He stood for something. But as for himself, he did not take Cal Coolidge too seriously. He was a quiet, relaxed enthusiast. The drive was there, but it was controlled.

One purpose in writing this book is to point out the incalculable value of enthusiasm, especially to those who have the urge to accomplish something worthwhile in life. I agree with B. C. Forbes, who said, "Enthusiasm is the all-essential human jet propeller. It is the driving force which elevates men to miracle workers. It begets boldness, courage; kindles confidence; overcomes doubts. It creates endless energy, the source of all accomplishment."

It is utterly pathetic to go through life and never be moved, never excited, never enthusiastic, but always remaining listless. To be turned off and empty is surely to deny oneself the exquisite joy possible to a human being in the all too short span of years most of us have.

We all can come out of dull lethargy and really live with verve. This can happen when a person makes himself mentally available to change. Walt Whitman, an immortal in American letters, said of himself, "I was simmering, just simmering; Emerson brought me to a boil." What an apt description of a personality, gifted but in doldrums until the fire of enthusiasm crackled in his mind, motivating him to become what he could be!

This could be the solution to the turned-off and empty of this era. They admit they've got it made financially, but they feel empty and dissatisfied, looking for a sense of meaning. It is hard to understand how anyone with life and vitality can fail to be enthusiastic in this exciting time, when even the air seems full of dreams, plans, and terrific ideas. Thoreau's sad statement comes to mind regarding the listless: "None are so old as those who have outgrown enthusiasm."

To become an achiever, one must have the quality of a believer who is really enthusiastic. Sir Edward Appleton, whose scientific experiments and discoveries made possible worldwide broadcasting and won him the Nobel Prize, was asked for the secret of his amazing achievements. His ready answer was "It was enthusiasm." Then he added, "I rate enthusiasm even above professional skill." This appraisal is understandable, for a scientist would scarcely be able to endure the self-discipline, endless toil, and repeated discouragements which accompany scientific discovery without having boundless enthusiasm for the task. Enthusiasm is the force that keeps motivation going until a goal is reached.

I recall that Walter Chrysler, the noted industrial leader, once asserted, "A man can succeed at anything for which he has unlimited enthusiasm." And, of course, there is also that famous and often quoted statement of Ralph Waldo Emerson: "Nothing great was ever achieved without enthusiasm."

If the industrialist and Emerson were right about the importance of enthusiasm, the next logical question is, "OK, how does one get this enthusiasm when one just isn't enthusiastic? How about someone who has failed, perhaps more than once, and hasn't the heart to try a comeback? Or how does a man or woman who is fed up and has had it suddenly start working up enthusiasm?"

What would you say to people who come up with all the above negatives? Would you have any suggestions? Well, it's no iffy situation with me. In writing positive-thinking books I've been on the receiving end of all those cynical negative objections, and then some.

I have some answers and I am going to outline them clearly. They are practical and workable. I know, for they have worked for me more than once. And where disillusioned people gave these suggestions a real try, they were reactivated. They got over their depressed states of mind and became enthusiastic, motivated, excited. Our suggestions work, when worked. They have demonstrated their life-changing effect. If you go for them as others have done, they will produce the same good results.

One way to start is to take a big pad of paper. Be sure it is a large pad, for you are going to require a lot of space. Start listing your assets. Perhaps you will say, "Oh, now, Dr. Peale, come off it. You know I'm reading this book because I'm down. I've had one failure after another and what's the use of it all, anyway? And now you are telling me to list my assets. What assets?"

I know how you feel, but why do you think I spent time writing this book except that I thought it might help make you feel better and do better and live better?

So list your assets. And number them. See how they add up as you let yourself become excited.

1. *I am alive. If I was dead, I couldn't write this.*
2. *I can breathe.*
3. *I can walk.*
4. *I can eat.*
5. *I have a roof over my head.*
6. *I can read.*
7. *I've got a good brain. I know I have, for I can still think.*

Then go on and list everything that comes to your mind. Rack your brain until you think of some assets you never thought of before.

8. *The sun is shining.*
9. *It's raining—isn't that great? We need rain.*
10. *That trouble I have—it's going to make me stronger as I think my way over it and then out of it.*

You don't believe it will make you enthusiastic to make a list of your assets? Well, let me tell you of a man who came to see me once in great discouragement. He was really low—desperate, in fact. He telephoned from upstate and told me I was his last hope.

When he appeared, he paced up and down my office, then flopped into a chair and buried his face in his hands. "Oh, Dr. Peale, you are so kind to see me when all is lost, nothing left." I sat there reflecting.

Then I took a large yellow pad and drew a line down the middle, labeling one side "assets," the other "debits." "You'll have nothing to write in the asset side," he observed sadly.

"Well, let's see," I replied. "I'm sorry your wife has died."

He looked up in surprise. "No, thank God, she is alive and healthy. Where did you get that idea?"

I wrote in the asset column, "Wife not dead but alive and healthy." Then I said, as sadly as I could, "Sorry to hear that your house burned down."

"Who said my house burned down. My house is OK."

I wrote in my asset column, "House did not burn down."

"I'm sorry to know that your business is on the rocks."

"Where do you get all this foolish stuff," he bristled, "about my wife being dead, my house burning down, and my business being on the rocks?"

"Well, you told me that everything was lost."

It came out that a few investments had turned sour and certain "goals" had not yet worked out. He had turned fifty and gloomy thoughts had ganged up on him. He had been practicing negative thinking for a long time. Actually, he was a respected banker in a fair-sized town.

He sat thinking it over and his eyes brightened. "Give me that sheet of paper," he said. "I've been a fool. I can fill that asset column the way you're doing it." He began scribbling on it furiously, listing such assets as "Two healthy children," "Friends," and others.

Then I asked him, "Ever go to church?"

"Every Sunday," he answered.

"Hasn't taken yet, is that it?"

Contritely he agreed. "Maybe I had better concentrate on being more of a believer, really living and practicing my faith."

He must have achieved it, for I've never seen him again and he said that he would come back if he ever got so low again. Also, I've had good reports from him in enthusiastic letters.

So to really become enthusiastic, start on your list of assets. You can at least list "I'm alive," "I can read." And you must have some money, for you bought this book. And you must have some faith, at least in some people, at least in me, for you are reading this book. But be assured that I'm telling you a solid fact: You *can* be enthusiastic, you *can* be full of excitement, you *can* have a future, you *can*, you *can*, you *can*. Now affirm, "I can, I can, I can." Then say, "I will, I will, I will." And *do* it—do it *now*.

Still another way to be turned on to enthusiasm is by a process called the "as if" principle. This principle was first described by Professor William James, one of the early leaders in psychology.

He taught that a person wishing to cultivate a better way of thinking may "act as if" he did possess it; and if that individual continues persistently to act "as if," then he or she will, in fact, become as acted.

For example, if you are a fearful person and desire to be fearless, then act as if you are courageous. If you continue acting "as if" long enough, you will ultimately take on courage. Or if you find yourself to be a cold individual but want very much to be a caring person, then consistently *act* as if you are such. By continuing this practice until the caring attitude becomes habitual, you will ultimately become a truly loving individual.

So if you find yourself unenthusiastic, desultory, gripy, or the "I couldn't care less" type, you can, by persistently exercising the "as if" principle, actually turn yourself into an enthusiastic person. It's true; a self-image long held becomes a reality ultimately.

I know of a young farm boy from Illinois who found this out by accident. He traveled to Chicago to find a job and make a career. He clerked in various drugstores, but nothing seemed to work out. Finally, he landed a job with a druggist on Chicago's South Side. But still it didn't seem to promise much. He was bored and didn't care for his boss, who, he thought, was too hard on him. Finally he decided to quit. But then he thought this would only please his boss, who would be glad to see him go. A better revenge would be to do the very best job possible for a few weeks, and *then* quit. Wouldn't the boss be sorry to lose him?

So the young clerk threw himself into his work with enthusiasm. But he got a surprise. Before he could quit, the store owner, impressed by the sudden improvement, gave him a raise. The young man began to enjoy his work, studied pharmacy at night, and in 1901 purchased his own drugstore on Chicago's South Side. It was no different from the hundreds of other drugstores serving the city.

But by now his enthusiasm had become second nature to him. Shoppers noticed something extra that wasn't in the display window or on the shelves—a special spirit. Each customer felt as if he were the most important person in the store. And more and more people came to trade with him.

One of the young pharmacist's favorite gambits was used whenever a nearby customer phoned in for an order to be delivered.

While he talked with the customer, he would signal a helper and repeat the order out loud. Then while he engaged the customer in pleasantries, the helper would hustle out the door with the delivery. Soon the customer would interrupt the phone conversation to say, "Oh, excuse me, there's someone at my door." She would be astonished to find the delivery man waiting there with her order.

The pharmacist's enthusiasm inspired his staff. Soon he opened a second store, then a third. Eventually, they became one of the most successful chains of drugstores in the United States. The enthusiastic young founder? Charles R. Walgreen, Sr.

You may lift your eyebrows at the "as if" principle and put it down as an unrealistic and fanciful theory dreamed up by some far-out professor, or as something that was instrumental in the success of a company founded over seventy-five years ago. So the question is, will it work today?

Let's watch it in action.

Not long ago I went to see one of the heads of a major investment firm in the Wall Street area about a matter of mutual interest unrelated to investments.

I was received in the outer office by the president's assistant, a young man in his early thirties, nice-looking, an obviously intelligent fellow. While I waited, he engaged me in conversation. I asked how the market was that day and he replied it was a bit down but the economy was good, despite negative talk. He was positive the market was strong and would go up.

"You're optimistic, then, I judge?" I said.

"Oh yes, indeed I am," he answered. "This country is in for some great times and my boss shares the same view."

Just then the president came out and invited me into his office. "Nice talking to you," I said to the young man as I stepped into the executive's office. Then after the door was closed, I said to the president, "Quite a bright young fellow you have out there. Wall Street blues haven't got him. He's a real positive thinker."

The president faced me with a startled look. "Positive thinker?" he gasped. "Why he's actually one of the most negative fellows we have here, a real gloom artist." He smiled wryly. "He must have put on an act for the author of *The Power of Positive Thinking*. In fact, I told him last week if he didn't get some real enthusiasm going, I would have to let him go. But he has a family and I hate to turn him adrift."

On the way out of the office later I said to the young man, "I have an office in midtown. Why don't you stop in and see me; I'd like to talk to you."

A few days later he did just that, and I suggested he would do well to work on his optimism.

It came out that he was reared in a family who had it quite rough when he was growing up. His parents were very negative; pessimism filled the house, and the boy naturally absorbed it.

"Sure, I put on an act for your benefit when you came," he confessed. "I know my job is in jeopardy and I'm willing to try anything to save it."

I patted him on the back and told him about the "as if" principle. "Just keep on with that act you put on for me," I advised. "In a low-key but positive way, talk everything up, but," I smiled, "avoid overdoing it, or it will come off phony."

A few months later I was delighted to hear from my friend who was this young man's boss. "Hey, that young fellow is doing OK," he said. "I think he's becoming one of the best informed men on the market. He's all over that negative stuff; he must have taken my warning to heart."

"Smart fellow," I agreed. He had been turned on to enthusiasm.

A man as intelligent as Professor William James, who personified both the scientific and pragmatic viewpoint, certainly would not teach a method without verifying its workability. I have recommended the "as if" principle often and indeed used it personally with good effect, and I believe in its validity.

Recently I received a letter from a lady which shows that those same affirmative principles can apply to health problems or, for that matter, to most any human situation.

Dear Dr. Peale,

Several months after I had serious surgery, I still felt extremely weak and had no energy. I couldn't make myself eat, and just getting through each day at work was becoming more and more difficult.

I'd grown discouraged almost to the point of despair

when I read your booklet, Renew Your Energy.* !t suggested some positive affirmations and encouraged daily exercise. The plan sounded good, but I couldn't seem to get
started.

When anyone asked, "How are you feeling?" I'd reply, "I
have good days and bad." Or, "I'm not as strong as I'd like
to be."

One day I decided to reread your booklet. As I thought
about what you wrote concerning having a positive attitude
toward health, I remembered a friend who is legally blind
and severely diabetic.

When anyone asked, "How are you?" he always replied
with a big smile, "Why, I couldn't be better!" As I reflected
on my own situation, I decided to say—and mean it—something like, "I'm doing better," or, "I'm getting better by the
minute."

"But," I argued with myself, "If I do that, people won't
know how bad I really feel."

But then I said to myself, "Which do you want, sympathy
or healing?"

With my doctor's approval, I started to walk daily. I gradually increased the distance until I was walking at least 20
minutes a day, and I covered a mile in that time. As I
walked, I followed your plan. I breathed deeply and quoted
the Scriptures on health and strength that I'd memorized. I
declared aloud to the trees, the birds, and the sky that I
possessed vigorous health. Within a month, I had gained
ten pounds and was growing steadily stronger. Soon I had
no chest pain or shortness of breath, and was able to do a
normal day's work and not be tired.

I realize that I finally started to make real progress when I
became willing to talk about my health in a positive way
and to image myself as healthy instead of sick.

Thanks, Dr. Peale, for sharing some principles for good
health. They surely do work.

Sincerely,
Kathleen D. Wright

* A free copy of the 32-page booklet Renew Your Energy may be obtained by writing to Foundation for Christian Living, P.O. Box FCL, Pawling, N.Y. 12564.

Indeed, those principles sure do work, for I have seen many cases in which enthusiasm applied in the creative process of healing has resulted in improved well-being. As I've shown throughout this book, medical science is discovering the same fact. According to a report in *Newsweek*, November 7, 1988, ". . . positive mental states seem to bear favorably on health and longevity. One study headed by psychologist Sandra Levy at the Pittsburgh Cancer Institute this year found that a factor called 'joy'—meaning mental resilience and vigor—was the second strongest predictor of survival time for a group of patients with recurrent breast cancer. (First was the length of 'disease-free intervals.')

"The whole field of mind-body research has been percolating with excitement for a decade. University of Pennsylvania psychologist Martin Seligman calls the current era 'a golden age,' in which long-suspected mind-body interactions are being proved out scientifically."

The "mental resilience and vigor" described above is a result of enthusiasm. And it is a quality I continue to find rated exceptionally high in the business world. An executive with whom I was lunching one day commented on my book *Enthusiasm Makes the Difference.*

"As an employer I'm inclined to rank enthusiasm tops on the list of qualities I look for in a prospective employee," he said, adding, "Indeed, perhaps it is number one."

"Ahead of professional skill, or know-how?" I queried.

"Yes, ahead of everything really," he answered. "You see, a person can acquire professional skill by study and experience. But he or she either is naturally endowed with enthusiasm or not. Too bad it cannot be acquired like other skills," he concluded dolefully.

"But, if I may say so, that is where you are mistaken," I countered, thinking about the "as if" factor. "For I'm sure enthusiasm can be an acquired quality and it can be taught."

"Well, I doubt it," said Bill, and, in illustration, he went on to tell about one of his firm's middle management executives who "worries me a lot."

"This guy is a well-educated graduate of a fine engineering school. He had high marks and is a scholar in his field, not to mention having a wealth of knowledge and expertise.

"But, let's face it," he said, "his college didn't teach him anything about personal relations and he's a cold fish. You know," he continued with a puzzled look, "if he had *any* kind of enthusiasm he would already have advanced to a top post in our company. People with less training, but more enthusiasm, climb past this poor guy all the time. If it were not for his know-how I would fire him."

"Oh, never do that," I said. "Build a fire in him instead."

I happened to know that this executive attended church regularly, so I asked, "Does this man go to church anywhere, as you do?"

"Not that I know of," he answered.

"Well, then," I suggested, "let's try to build that fire in him, get him really fired up. I know that enthusiasm is acquirable, even by a 'cold fish.'" I told him about a minister in his city who was known for being "on fire," bursting with enthusiasm and the joy of living. I happened to personally know that this minister himself had suffered from a defeating weakness and failure. But he had been spiritually and mentally invigorated and he believed anyone else, no matter how badly off they were, could experience the same personality renewal.

"What do you say to exposing your man to this enthusiastic person?" I suggested. "At least, take him to hear such a terrific speaker."

Obviously surprised by my suggestion, my friend pondered it doubtfully. Then he said, "OK, it's worth a try."

Accordingly, he and his spouse invited the man and his wife to luncheon at their country club on a Sunday. But there was a catch to the invitation. The employee and his wife would accompany them to church beforehand.

The employee accepted his invitation and, later, my friend reported what happened. "Dour as usual, with customary lack of interest, he slumped in the pew. And when the pastor started to tell how anyone in the congregation could become a more happy, satisfying individual, he didn't seem impressed. But when the speaker confessed to once being dead from the neck up himself, I noticed my employee beginning to take interest. That preacher's face positively glowed," he continued, "as he described how a person could become enthusiastic and alive as never before. 'I'm not handing out theory, but dealing in facts!' he asserted. He spoke in such a down-to-earth, friendly style that my employee leaned forward seemingly enthralled.

"Later, while we lunched at the club, he said: 'You know, that man has something. He really does.'"

What eventually happened to that employee? He and his wife returned to that church the following week and successive Sundays afterward. The minister spotted him and they became friends. Finally, the same spiritual and mental renewal happened to him that had changed the minister from a weak, flabby personality into a man of dynamic influence. The listless, though scholarly employee developed into a vigorous, capable leader who, in addition to brain power, now had personality power as well. He advanced to higher positions in business and took others along with him.

A few years later his former boss (yes, another division in the firm had snapped up the changed employee) and I were talking about him and how he had changed.

"I wouldn't have believed it possible," said my friend, shaking his head. "He's the first guy I've ever seen acquire enthusiasm who wasn't born with it."

I couldn't let this pass. "*Everyone* is born with enthusiasm. Did you ever see an unenthusiastic baby, or little child? They're all born as positive, vigorous little people. But educators tell me that by the time they reach fourth or fifth grade many, perhaps 80 percent, become negative thinkers and their natural enthusiasm fades, in some cases forever."

He nodded his head and I knew he saw what I meant, for he had grandchildren, too.

The wonderful fact is every person can be changed into an enthusiastic thinker. Every one of us has the potential of being a released, joyful, vigorous, and successful human being. How? Remember those Greek words *en theos*, which mean "in God," or "God within"? Let the natural enthusiasm which has been placed within you come surging out.

Whatever you do, keep the fire of enthusiasm burning. And remember what Thoreau said so well: "None are so old as those who have outlived enthusiasm."

Act as if you have enthusiasm and soon the creative power of enthusiasm will manifest itself through your body, mind, and spirit to enhance your life.

So, dear reader, always think positively and

believe enthusiastically. That's living!

EPILOGUE

■   ■   ■

We have come to the end of this book. Thank you for staying with it.

The reader and the writer together have explored some questions important to a person's well-being and happiness. Perhaps at times you have differed with the writer's positions and conclusions. But I hope you have known at all times that the writer has your best interests in mind. He has worked all his life with the problem of himself and has found that for him positive mental attitudes bring much better results than negative thinking. And he has also discovered that the development of enthusiasm will greatly enhance life. This book has told you why. And further, it has told how to get genuine enthusiasm for yourself, how to have a good day every day, even the hard ones.

We call this experience *The Power of Positive Living*. And you will find that it does have power as you apply the principles described in this book.

They really work when worked. We do not deal in fantasy, nor are we dreamers. We are strictly practical. We have outlined a way of thinking and living that gave the writer, an average American, a sure way to Happiness and a good life. It will do exactly the same for you *if* you believe and go for it.

We are pleased that science in many fields has substantiated the claims made earlier for the effectiveness of the power of positive thinking.

To sum up what you have read, the book stresses these points:

1. *How to be turned on to a joy-packed lifestyle.*
2. *How to be a positive thinker.*
3. *How to really believe in yourself.*
4. *Ways to drop the "I can't" reaction.*
5. *Believe that happiness is always possible.*
6. *When things look bad, remember the word "but."*
7. *Affirm faith, the great enemy of fear.*
8. *Always remember the healing power in your mind.*
9. *Remember you have comeback power.*
10. *The secret of success is uncomplicated and possible.*
11. *Practice the positive power of believing.*
12. *No need to feel empty—get full of the power of faith.*
13. *Be an asset to yourself.*
14. *You have a censor. It pays to heed it.*
15. *Get the fire of enthusiasm burning and keep it going always.*

Warm personal regards and God bless you every day, all the way.

N.V.P.

Courage and Confidence
NORMAN VINCENT PEALE

Here is an anthology to quicken faith and
stimulate the mind to creative thinking.
Dr Peale has been painstakingly selective in
choosing the thoughts of great men and
women, believing that what we think
conditions our minds and ultimately our lives.

Selections range from short, pungent sayings to
anecdotes about remarkable people. Divided
into twelve sections, the chapter headings such
as 'How to Achieve Your Goals' and 'Finding
the Happiness You Want' are helpful when
using the book for any particular need.

This inspirational reader can bring tranquil
thinking at night and spiritual impetus for
each new day.

INDEX